START WITH STRATEGY

START WITH STRATEGY

Craft Your Personal Real Estate Portfolio for Lasting Financial Freedom

Dave Meyer

BiggerPockets®
PUBLISHING
Denver, Colorado

Start with Strategy: Craft Your Personal Real Estate Portfolio for Lasting Financial Freedom
Dave Meyer

Published by BiggerPockets Publishing LLC, Denver, CO
Copyright © 2024 by Dave Meyer
All rights reserved.

Publisher's Cataloging-in-Publication Data
Names: Meyer, David, author.
Title: Start with strategy : Craft your personal real estate portfolio for lasting financial freedom / David Meyer.
Description: Includes bibliographical references. | Denver, CO: BiggerPockets Publishing LLC, 2024.
Identifiers: LCCN: 2023936541 | ISBN: 9781960178060 (paperback) | 9781960178077 (ebook)
Subjects: LCSH Real estate investment--United States. | Investments. | Finance, Personal. | BISAC BUSINESS & ECONOMICS / Real Estate / General | BUSINESS & ECONOMICS / Investments & Securities / Real Estate | BUSINESS & ECONOMICS / Personal Finance / Investing
Classification: HD1382.5 .M49 2023 | DDC 332.63/240973--dc23

Printed in Canada
MBP 10 9 8 7 6 5 4 3 2 1

Dedication

To Jane,
How lucky we are to share this
beautiful life. I love you.

VISIT
www.biggerpockets.com/strategybook

to download the accompanying
STRATEGY TOOL KIT
to plan your portfolio, track your deals,
assess your finances, and more!

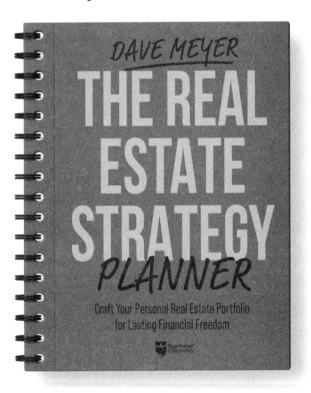

*Supercharge your portfolio planning
with the companion workbook!*

TABLE OF CONTENTS

Part 1
Financial Fundamentals

Part 2
Defining Your Vision

Part 3
Deal Design

Part 4
Portfolio Management

INTRODUCTION

I'm not the most prolific real estate investor in the world. I have spent more than a decade investing in real estate, and during that time I have built a business and net worth that I am proud of. But I don't count myself among the most active or the wealthiest real estate investors. I'm probably not even close. I've never flipped a house, I don't take on massive renovation projects, and although I invest passively in large multifamily deals, I don't sponsor them.

Don't get me wrong—I have loads of experience investing, and I can confidently say I know what I'm doing. But if my portfolio were compared to those of some of the most prominent names in the industry, I certainly wouldn't win any awards for total units acquired or cash flow earned. While this may seem like a confession of regret or an expression of jealousy, it's actually the opposite. My portfolio and investing career are precisely what I want them to be at this point in my life.

To me, real estate is a means to an end. I don't invest just for the sake of accumulating wealth. I invest because it supports the life I want—which entails travel, adventure, professional interests beyond real estate, and quality time with my friends and family. My metrics of success are my own quality of life and personal fulfillment, as well as financial stability. I've been very deliberate in only pursuing real estate investments that support these metrics.

There are many different deals and tactics available to real estate investors: flipping, rentals, multifamily, syndications, and many more. But not every approach works for every investor. What works for me and my goals may not work for you and your goals. I choose to equally prioritize financial stability and quality of life, and therefore pursue real estate strategies that are aligned with those priorities. Because your preferences are unique to you, you will likely pursue different real estate strategies than I do. Each one of us has our own expectations, resources, and preferences. Being a successful investor is not about picking the *right* strategy or finding the *perfect* deal. It's about finding the right strategies and the perfect deals for *you*.

My portfolio-building story started when I was about a year out of college. I was waiting tables in Denver and trying to figure out what I wanted to do with my life. I didn't know what I wanted my job to be, but I knew financial stability was a priority. Both of my parents are smart, hardworking people, but after their divorce our family faced a lot of financial stress. This experience impacted me a great deal and motivated me to earn money and achieve financial independence as an adult. But at the same time, I'm someone who craves adventure and meaningful relationships, and I didn't want to devote my entire life to work.

When I looked around, most people I knew were making trade-offs. Some of my friends were working crazy hours to get ahead financially. Others were focusing on fun and life experiences. Both paths felt valid and important to me, and I didn't want to choose between the two. I wanted both and was torn about which way to go.

After a lot of thinking and a late-night heart-to-heart with an old friend, I became determined not to settle for one or the other. The vision I had for my life was clear: I wanted to achieve financial independence without sacrificing my passions or relationships.

Around this time, a friend introduced me to real estate investing. I immediately saw it as a way to achieve my vision and I jumped in. At that point in my investing career, I had almost no money and knew even less about real estate investing. The "perfect deal" for me at that point was anything that would help me learn and get into the game. I wasn't all that concerned about my rates of return, tax plan, or anything else. Luckily, I found a deal, brought in several partners to buy a rental property with, and got my start.

Over the course of my investing career, the tactics I used to support my vision evolved as my life evolved. My personal definition of a "good deal" and a "good portfolio" shifted.

For the first few years, I was limited by a lack of money and experience. As such, I invested opportunistically and did as much of the day-to-day work as I could. A few years later, I temporarily moved to Boston and could no longer manage my entire portfolio myself. I adapted my portfolio accordingly by learning how to build a team and invest long-distance.

After earning my master's degree, I had more time and financial resources, and was ready to scale. My Portfolio Strategy changed again! I took on bigger projects in new locations and used new strategies. I learned a ton and my portfolio grew a lot. In 2019, my now-wife and I pursued our lifelong dream of living abroad. Again, I had to adapt my real estate investing to fit my lifestyle. I shifted my approach entirely to passive investments and away from direct ownership.

Throughout my investing career I have continuously adapted my investing strategy to adjust to my changing resources, circumstances, preferences, and goals. I have done this by taking a long-term, portfolio-level approach to real estate investing. Out of all the possible ways I could invest in real estate, I focus on only the deals that support the life I want to live and forget everything else.

As these few examples from my investing career demonstrate, real estate investing is incredibly flexible and can support almost any life you can envision for yourself. Hopefully my portfolio decisions resonate with at least a few of you reading this. But realistically, most of you would probably have made very different decisions than I did. Your values, risk tolerance, career satisfaction, current financial situation, and vision for your life are inherently different from mine. Perhaps you may have chosen to go full time into real estate following your first deal. Or maybe you would have forgone graduate school and spent that time flipping houses. Maybe living abroad sounds horrible to you. Luckily, you don't have to mimic my portfolio, or anyone else's. You can craft a personalized real estate strategy that supports your unique goals, whatever they may be.

Having a personalized real estate strategy has given me a rich and fulfilling life that I cherish. I wrote this book to provide you with the tools and knowledge to do the same for yourself. At the risk of sounding overly ambitious, I believe real estate investing offers you the best way to pursue your goals in life, regardless of what those goals may be. It's worked for me, and I am excited to help you achieve the same.

WHY REAL ESTATE INVESTING?

There are many ways you can invest your time and money. The vast majority of Americans who invest at all invest primarily in stocks and bonds. Cryptocurrency and digital assets have become increasingly popular over the last few years. You can invest in gold, commodities, fine art, fine wine, franchises, or start ups, or you can start a business. The list of ways to invest is long, so why should you invest in real estate?

Investing in real estate offers benefits that no other asset class does. It's highly customizable, predictable, and relatively low risk. It offers great returns, allows you to have full control of your finances, and perhaps most importantly, is by far the best way to achieve financial independence. Since you're reading this book, I'm guessing you're already somewhat sold on investing in real estate, but before we jump into Portfolio Strategy, let's quickly review a few reasons real estate is such a powerful asset class.

Financial Freedom

Anyone with an interest in investing is looking to improve their financial position. That's the whole point. But for most people, building wealth is about more than just the number in your bank account. Rather, it's about being able to live the life you want—on your own terms. Money doesn't buy happiness, but it can buy a liberating amount of choice, flexibility, and convenience.

This idea—obtaining enough wealth to unlock the life you want—is commonly known as "financial independence," or "financial freedom" (the terms are interchangeable). There's a misconception that financial independence is solely focused on retiring early or living super frugally, but it is broader than that. A better definition is having enough money to cover your living expenses without being dependent on a traditional income like a W-2 or 1099 job. Even if you want to retire at a traditional age or don't like the idea of slashing your expenses, you can still achieve and benefit from financial independence. Financial freedom means something different to each of us—which is why much of this book is focused on helping you figure out what your own financial goals are, and then building a real estate strategy to achieve those goals.

Perhaps the whole reason you're reading this book is because you're interested in financial independence, and if so, you're in the right place—and in good company! Many people are initially attracted to real estate investing because it is a proven way to achieve financial freedom. No other asset class that I know provides the same combination of cash flow, stability, control, and opportunity as real estate does. There are many great reasons to pursue a real estate investing portfolio, but for most people (including me!), financial independence is at the top of the list.

Great Returns

Investors generally want great returns, and real estate offers excellent return potential. There is a wide spectrum of potential outcomes in real estate, but as you'll see over the course of this book, even the lowest-risk real estate investments can achieve better returns than stocks or bonds. The outsized return potential of real estate is largely because there are multiple ways to generate wealth from a single real estate deal. It's not just cash flow and appreciation. As you'll learn throughout this book, there are multiple ways to drive profits from a real estate portfolio.

Predictability and Stability

If you read a lot of headlines, it may seem like real estate is a risky and volatile asset class. The reality is that for as far back as we have data, real estate prices and returns have been remarkably consistent and predictable. There is absolutely risk in real estate investing (we'll spend a great deal of time discussing how to identify and mitigate risk in this book), but experienced investors know that compared to other types of investments, real estate offers excellent risk-adjusted returns.

Anyone Can Do It

Although it may seem like you need a lot of time, money, or specialized skill to invest in real estate, that's not the case. Anyone can invest in real estate, regardless of their financial, personal, or professional background. As this book will show, there is a portfolio strategy for everyone, no matter where you're starting from. Real estate investing comes with challenges, but it's not rocket science. All of the tactics you'll use as an investor have been proven to work by hundreds of thousands of investors before you, from all walks of life.

Customizable

Real estate investing can conform to anything you want it to be. Want to be a tycoon? There's a portfolio strategy for that. Want a low-risk way to make some extra cash to support your family? There's a portfolio for that. Want to retire early and live off your passive income? There's a strategy for that too. There are infinite ways to make real estate work for you—and this book is designed to help you craft a Portfolio Strategy that meets your specific personal goals.

Empowerment and Control

Most investments are out of your control. If you buy a stock, you can vote at a shareholder meeting, but you don't really get a say in how the company is operated. You don't get to choose the strategy, pick the employees, or decide how much risk to take on. Real estate gives you a high degree of control over your investment and empowers you to directly impact the results of your portfolio. Other asset classes rarely offer this control.

Fun

One of the most overlooked aspects of real estate investing is how much fun it can be! To me, this is one of the greatest parts of investing in real estate. I love being an entrepreneur. I enjoy the problem-solving, providing a safe and high-quality place to live for my tenants, and the friends I've made as a real estate investor. There are difficult days being an investor, but overall, I think investing in real estate is rewarding far beyond the financial gains. Yes, it's mostly about achieving financial freedom and building wealth, but I think it's a huge bonus that the best way to achieve your financial goals is also rewarding and fun. I'm pretty sure no one has ever said bond investing is a joy.

With all these benefits, it's curious why more people don't invest in real estate. Given the list above, it should be pretty obvious that real estate is an excellent way to achieve your personal and financial goals. In fact, Americans believe, by a fairly large margin, that real estate is the best long-term investment.[1] So, why don't more people do it? For most people, the barrier is a lack of a coherent strategy.

YOU NEED A STRATEGY

Real estate investing is a unique asset class. In order to experience its many benefits, you have to put in some work. Real estate investing, although it can be relatively passive compared to your job, is a business. You cannot just open an app and buy a rental property or hand your money to a financial planner and expect to reach your goals.

To build a successful real estate investing business, you need a portfolio of multiple investments. I'm sorry to say this, but a single property will not make you wealthy. Hopefully each property you buy improves your financial position, but unless your first deal is unusually large and profitable, you will need to acquire a collection of investments to achieve your financial goals. This collection of deals is what we call your "portfolio."

In the literal sense, your real estate investing portfolio is just a collection of individual real estate investments that you have some stake in. If you take every deal that you have at least some ownership of, or involvement in, and put them all together, that's your portfolio. But a real

---

1   Lydia Saad, "Real Estate's Lead as Best Investment Shrinks; Gold Rises," Gallup.com, June 6, 2023, https://news.gallup.com/poll/505592/real-estate-lead-best-investment-shrinks-gold-rises.aspx.

estate portfolio can be much more than just a collection of individual deals. When properly constructed, a portfolio is far greater than the sum of its parts. It's your path to financial independence. But it needs to be built in a deliberate way. Your portfolio cannot just be a collection of *any* deals; it has to be the collection of the *right deals for you*.

As you will see throughout this book, there are countless deals you could do. There are many trade-offs to consider, risks to mitigate, and goals to achieve. But there are no "right" answers. The best path forward is entirely dependent on your unique goals, the resources you have at your disposal, your experience level, your risk tolerance, and so on. You need to understand the many varied and exciting ways you could invest in real estate and narrow them down to just the ones that will move you closer to your goals. In other words, you need a strategy.

Having a strategy from the outset will help you focus and move consistently toward your goals. It will make you efficient and confident. And best of all, it will put you in a strong position to succeed at whatever goals you set for yourself. Even if you're just getting started, you have to think about how the structure and contents of your portfolio will impact your long-term success. You need to *start with strategy*.

WHAT IS PORTFOLIO STRATEGY?

Developing a strategy for your real estate portfolio requires different processes and tools than other types of businesses and other forms of investments. When I began investing, I was eager to organize my plans into a coherent strategy and tried to use existing tools. First I tried a traditional business plan (because real estate investing is a business). Then I attempted financial planning tools (because they help investors plan for the future). Neither worked. Financial planning could help me understand my personal goals is geared towards stock and bond investors, not real estate investors. Business planning worked great for operational questions but failed to account for the financial and lifestyle motivations that fuel most real estate investors. I realized if I was going to create an effective Portfolio Strategy for real estate investing, I was going to need a new framework—one designed just for real estate investors. Over the next several years, I created it. The results of my efforts are the contents of this book.

> *It's important to note that the word "strategy" is used in many different ways in the real estate investing community. Some use it to describe what I call "deal types": rental properties, short-term rentals (STRs), flipping, wholesaling, etc. Others use it to describe the type of property you buy (what I call "asset classes"): single-family homes, multifamily, commercial, etc. Others use the word "strategy" to describe something else entirely. None of this is wrong per se because there is no universally accepted language in real estate investing.*
>
> *The dictionary definition of the word "strategy" is "a plan of action designed to achieve a long-term or overall goal." That is why, when I use the word "strategy" in this book, I'm talking about your long-term, portfolio-level strategy. I will be referring to any individual choices or actions that support your strategy (like buying a rental versus a commercial deal, or self-managing versus hiring a property manager) as "tactics."*

The new set of processes and tools I designed combines the best of financial planning, business planning, and real estate tactics into a simple framework that helps real estate investors craft their own completely personalized real estate investing strategy.

A good Portfolio Strategy consists of three parts: Vision, Deal Design, and Portfolio Management. Together they give you the tools to identify what you want out of your investing career, help you design deals tailor-made for your portfolio, and help you execute on your long-term objectives.

Vision

The first component of your Portfolio Strategy is Vision. This is where you examine your personal circumstances and preferences, and then set high-level goals. Vision helps you identify *where* you want to go and *why* you're investing in real estate in the first place.

Although I'm sure you're eager to start doing deals, this is a crucial first step. Strategies exist to achieve an objective. Your Vision is that objective. If you set out to build a house, you start with a blueprint. You need to know what the house is supposed to look like before you buy materials, procure tools, and hire contractors. You need to start with the end in mind when building a house, and the same is true of your Portfolio Strategy.

As an example, one of the most common questions I get is "Should I flip houses or invest in rental properties?" It's a logical question, but how can I possibly answer that if I don't know what the person's goal is? These are very different tactics that appeal to very different types of investors. Does this person want to run a time-intensive business like house flipping? Are they trying to work less, retire early, and spend more time with their family? Without knowing their Vision, I can't possibly give good advice. Likewise, if you don't know your own Vision, you can't make good real estate investing decisions for yourself.

Deal Design

The second element of Portfolio Strategy is Deal Design. This is where you consider the many possible ways to invest in real estate (like house hacking, flipping, etc.), and narrow them down to only the options that are aligned with your Vision. Deal Design is where you determine *how* you're going to use real estate investing to realize your Vision.

Your portfolio is comprised of many individual real estate deals, but to succeed you need them to be the *right deals for you.* There are dozens of real estate investing types, management styles, financing options, asset classes, and so on. While it's common to want to do them all, that's not a good idea. Instead, you should take advantage of the flexibility real estate investing offers and *design* deals that are best aligned with your Vision.

For example, investors wanting to retire in the next few years should probably be focused on cash-flow tactics like rental properties or commercial assets, and will probably want to outsource their management. Those who are looking to maximize their income today will likely want to look into flipping and will play an active role in their deals. Once you have your Vision set, you can design the right deals for you.

Deal Design, as we'll discuss in this book, has eight elements: deal type, ownership structure, financing, operational plan, management plan, asset class, market, and property class. We'll discuss each of these deal elements in detail in Part 3, but here's a quick overview. Having an understanding of these terms now will help you in the earlier parts of the book.

DEAL DESIGN

Deal Type	Rentals, flipping, short-term rentals, etc.
Financing	Conventional loans, hard money, equity, seller financing, etc.
Ownership Structure	Sole ownership, partnership, syndication
Operating Plan	BRRRR, house hacking, value-add, etc.
Management Plan	Active, passive, hybrid
Asset Class	Single-family, multifamily, retail, etc.
Market	State, city, neighborhood, zip code, block, parcel
Property Class	Class A, Class B, Class C, etc.

If you're unfamiliar with any of these terms, that's okay and expected. For now, just know that these are the components that make up the Deal Design portion of your strategy.

Portfolio Management

Once you have your Vision and Deal Design set, it's time to move on to the most granular phase of your strategy: Portfolio Management. Portfolio Management is where you get specific about what you're actually going to do in the coming months and years. In this phase, you will analyze your current portfolio and current market conditions and determine what next steps will benefit you most. You will use your Deal Designs to attain new deals and optimize your existing ones. Portfolio Management is the *what* and *when* of your Portfolio Strategy.

Portfolio Management does include buying new deals (the most exciting part), but also helps you plan and manage many of the behind-the-scenes elements of a successful portfolio. This includes decisions on whether to hold, sell, or refinance an existing deal, or perhaps reallocate the time you spend on one deal toward another. It will also help you decide how to continue your self-education, who you should be networking with, and more.

The Portfolio Management piece of your strategy will help you get over any indecision, and identify the specific next steps you should take to grow your portfolio.

Combined, your Vision, Deal Design, and Portfolio Management make up your Portfolio Strategy. You start broadly and get increasingly more specific with your strategy decisions. First, you set your Vision and determine where you're heading. Then you move to Deal Design, where you select how you'll use real estate to achieve your Vision. Last, you use your Portfolio Management skills to manage the day-to-day decisions about your portfolio. When used together, they enable any investor, regardless of experience level, resources, or ambition, to achieve their unique personal goals.

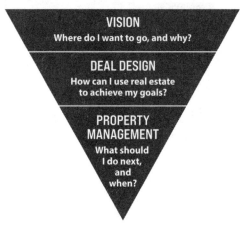

For many, the idea of crafting their own strategy is daunting. From rental properties to short-term rentals to flipping houses and everything in between, it can feel overwhelming to choose which approaches are right for you, and what to do first. It can even be tempting to simply follow the advice of an investor you know or someone you follow on social media. I strongly caution you against that approach. Remember, the whole point of investing is to achieve the vision of the future *you* want to create. How could you possibly get this from someone else? For real estate investors, strategy is personal. It has to come from you.

But don't worry, developing a personalized strategy is not hard, and is what this book is all about! I have spent years developing and refining the Portfolio Strategy frameworks you'll find in this book, and I am confident that when you're done reading it, you will have a personalized strategy that you are excited about, and ready to execute on. I hope this is what you signed up for!

ABOUT THE BOOK

The purpose of this book is to help you create your own unique strategy, as outlined above. The coming chapters will provide you with foundational knowledge, but they will also be interactive. You will learn everything you need to know about Portfolio Strategy, and simultaneously create one for yourself.

The book is organized into four parts. In Part 1 we will cover foundational knowledge. This part is not going to be unique to you, but will give you the basics of finance, investing, and real estate you'll need later for developing your own strategy

After you master the foundations of portfolio building, we'll start building your personalized portfolio by following the Portfolio Strategy framework: Vision, Deal Design, and Portfolio Management. In Part 2 we'll discuss every aspect of your Vision. In Part 3 we'll conduct a comprehensive review of Deal Design—from deal type to financing, management plans, asset classes, and more. In Part 4 we'll put your strategic decisions into action. By the end of this book you'll have a completely personalized strategy.

PERSONAL REAL ESTATE PORTFOLIO

To help you formalize and visualize your personalized strategy, I have created a tool to accompany this book called the Personal Real Estate Portfolio (PREP). The PREP is where you can write down the many decisions you'll make during your reading of this book, and throughout your investing career.

The PREP looks like a business plan and serves a similar function—but is purpose-built for real estate investors. It helps you think through all the key decisions needed to implement a successful strategy. It will ensure your strategy is fully formed. It will help you share and get feedback on your strategy. And it will help you move from planning to execution to results.

The PREP is broken down into the three main elements of Portfolio Strategy: Vision, Deal Design, and Portfolio Management. Within each element, you will be prompted to make key decisions about your strategy For example, in Chapter 14 you will read all about how to set good financial goals, and at the end of the chapter, you will find a section called "PREP Work" that provides (optional) exercises and questions to help you set your own financial goals, and you'll write them in your PREP. Each chapter in Parts 2, 3, and 4 will follow this format.

At the end of the book, you should have a completed PREP, which will spell out your personalized and actionable real estate strategy. It will be uniquely yours and ready for you to execute on.

SAMPLE PERSONAL REAL ESTATE PORTFOLIO

👁 VISION

Personal Values
What do you value most in life? What can you not live without?

Resource Audit
Money:
Time:
Current Skills:

Risk Profile
Time Horizon:
Risk Tolerance:
Risk Capacity:
Current Risk Profile:

Transactional Income Plan

Financial Goals
Reinvestment Rate:
Residual Income Goal:
Portfolio Value Goal:

🏠 DEAL DESIGN

Deal Type

Ownership Structure

Financing

Operational Plan

Management Plan

Asset Class

Location

Property Class

⚡ PORTFOLIO MANAGEMENT

Portfolio Performance
Total Equity:
Total Cash Flow:
Average ROE:
Average Risk:
Monthly Time Committed:

Market Conditions and Benchmarks

Scaling Plans	Resource Allocation

Investment Thesis

Action Plan	Buy Box

Of course, you don't have to fill out a PREP as you read. I have written this book in a way that it will be highly useful whether you complete a PREP or not. You can write your PREP as you go, or you can read the entire book and complete the PREP at a later date (or never at all, I suppose!). The concepts and strategic considerations discussed in the book will be helpful to anyone. That said, I included the PREP for a reason. This tool will help you enact your strategy, and I encourage you to use it!

BEFORE WE BEGIN

As you work through this book, there are a few important things to remember. I'll remind you about these things periodically, but I want to make them clear up front.

1. No matter where you're starting from, you can build a real estate portfolio. As we go through exercises to assess your current situation, you may not like what you see, or may wonder if you can actually succeed. That's okay and very common. The key to building a great portfolio is having a clear idea of where you are today and where you want to go—not where you're starting from.

2. Every portfolio is going to look different. The whole point of this book is to recognize that every investor has different goals, motivations, and resources—and to help you craft a strategy that fits your unique situation. So, if your plan doesn't look like your friend's or your uncle's or some influencer you see on Instagram, that's not only okay—it's the whole point! This is about you—what you want and what you're willing to do to get it.

3. This is a compass, not turn-by-turn directions. Your strategy is meant to point you in the right direction, but no amount of planning and strategizing can tell you the exact steps to take at any given point. Even with a clear idea of where you want to go, you are inevitably going to stray off course during your investing career. Every investor makes mistakes, gets sidetracked, and loses money from time to time. That's fine—it's part of the journey, and how you learn. Your strategy exists to keep you focused and pointed in the right direction, even when things go astray.

4. Your strategy is not set in stone. Your goals or life circumstance may change, new real estate tactics may arise, or you may decide you just don't like flipping houses. Your strategy is a guideline, not a binding contract. This is about you, and if you want to change your approach in the future, change it! This is a living plan, and you should be revisiting it regularly to make sure it still matches your situation. I recommend you review your strategy two to four times per year, but no more than that. You don't want to be constantly tinkering with your strategy—you need to be executing!

5. This book is meant to help you understand and develop a personalized real estate strategy. It's not meant to be a tactical guide for every part of your real estate investing journey. For example, we'll talk a lot about who should consider investing in short-term rentals and why—but I won't be getting into the details of how to successfully operate a short-term rental. Once you have your strategy, you'll want to continue your real estate investing education and learn more about how to succeed with the tactics you choose.

6. Real estate investing is work! Although many people consider it "passive income," you'll see over the course of this book that "passive" is a very relative term. Some tactics require a ton of time, while others require relatively less. But make no mistake about it: All real estate investing, regardless of approach, is entrepreneurship. Your portfolio is a business, and you need to put in the requisite time and effort to make your business a success.

7. This is not a scientific text. The frameworks, opinions, and advice in this book are a product of my personal investing experience and the conversations I've had with hundreds of other investors. As such, this book contains some subjective information. If you disagree with the way I name things, organize ideas, and assess different tactics, that's okay! I can't imagine anyone sees something as complex as real estate investing the exact same way I do—but that's not the point. My goal here is to provide you with the background information you need and some helpful frameworks for you to form your own strategy.

With that in mind, it's time to get started! The process of developing your Portfolio Strategy is self-reflective, exciting, and challenging. Most of all, it's an inspiring and rewarding endeavor. Having a personalized Portfolio Strategy has benefitted my life in more ways than I can count. It's helped me achieve the vision for my life to which I dedicated myself more than a decade ago, and I know it can do the same for you. I am thrilled you're taking the time to read this book and develop a Portfolio Strategy for yourself. It may just change your life.

PART 1
FINANCIAL FUNDAMENTALS

VISION

DEAL DESIGN

PORTFOLIO MANAGEMENT

The point of a real estate portfolio is to make money. I know I spent a good deal of the introduction talking about all of the lifestyle benefits of real estate, and it's all true. But the basic premise of financial freedom is that money, although it cannot buy happiness, can buy a great deal of time, flexibility, and convenience, and get you closer to your personal goals. This book—and your portfolio—exists to help you earn the money you need to feel comfortable pursuing the life you want. As such, to develop your personal Portfolio Strategy, you need to understand some finance and investing fundamentals. These concepts, although not complicated, will underpin every strategic decision you make about your portfolio. So, before we get into your personal portfolio, we need to start with the fundamentals. Part 1 of this book is devoted to teaching you the financial fundamentals that inform the composition and performance of your portfolio.

When I talk about your portfolio's "composition and performance," I am talking about what deals go into your portfolio, and how well your portfolio generates returns (profits). Although every portfolio's purpose is to generate returns, not all portfolios look and perform in the same way. Some are designed to grow quickly while taking on risk. Others will take a slow and steady approach. Some will focus on cash flow while others prioritize tax savings. Through your strategic decisions, you can compose your portfolio to deliver the exact performance you need from it.

For a moment, think about your portfolio like a vehicle. All vehicles are intended to get you from one place to another—but there are so many different types of vehicles. Some are designed to be fast and exciting. Others are designed to be reliable. Others are big and utilitarian. Which is best? It depends on your budget and what you're looking to do with your vehicle. The same is true of your portfolio. Do you want your portfolio to look and perform like a Ford F150, a Toyota Corolla, or a Ferrari?

Over the coming chapters you will learn about the most important strategic decisions that will impact your portfolio's composition and performance. In Chapter 1 we'll review the Resource Triangle—a simple framework that demonstrates how you can grow your portfolio with capital (money), time, or skill. You don't need all three, and you can choose what resources you'll use to get going. In Chapter 2 we'll discuss the difference between residual and transactional income, and how to balance the two to build a strong portfolio. In Chapter 3 we'll break down two of the most powerful concepts in all of investing: compounding and reinvestment. How you apply these ideas to your portfolio will make a huge difference in its performance. In Chapter 4 we'll discuss how real estate can generate returns in multiple ways, and which ones are most important for your portfolio. In Chapter 5 we'll address one of the least discussed but most important considerations: the trade-offs between risk and reward. In Chapter 6 we'll look at the various ways real estate investors can fund their deals. In Chapter 7 we'll dig into your timeline to demonstrate how time is a real estate investor's best friend. In Chapter 8 we'll get into hold periods and liquidity, which will help you optimize your portfolio's performance over the long run and help you mitigate risk.

The concepts you'll learn in Part 1 will lay the foundation for the rest of the book and will help guide your strategic decision-making throughout your investing career. By the end of Part 1, you'll understand the strategic trade-offs you'll need to consider for your portfolio, and you'll be ready to start developing your own personalized strategy in Part 2. Because Part 1 is focused on foundational knowledge, there is no PREP work or parts of the PREP to complete. That will start in Part 2.

Chapter 1
THE RESOURCE TRIANGLE

If you want to build something new, you need to contribute resources. It is literally a law of physics—you cannot create something out of nothing. You can't cook a recipe without ingredients, you can't open a store without products to sell, and you can't build a skyscraper without steel. The same is true for building a real estate portfolio. You need specific resources to create a profitable portfolio.

For real estate investors, there are three essential resources needed for every deal: **capital (money)**, **time**, and **skill**. Remember, a portfolio is simply a collection of deals, so if you need these resources for every deal, you need these resources for every portfolio. Capital helps you purchase property and pay for the operations of your business. Time is needed to find and operate the deals you do. Skill is required to make things run smoothly and to optimize your performance. You cannot invest in a deal, operate an investment, or build a portfolio without some mix of these three resources, but the amount of each resource needed will vary greatly from deal to deal, and from portfolio to portfolio.

For example, imagine you're investing in a single-family rental property that's great shape and in a great area, and you're hiring a professional property management company to oversee the day-to-day operations. For this type of deal, you'll need capital for the down payment and closing costs, but you won't have to commit a lot of time or skill to the deal long term. The deal still requires *some* time and skill (like every deal does), but since you're paying a property management company to oversee it, you are essentially using your capital resources to buy the time and knowledge of the property management company, rather than contributing those resources yourself.

Alternatively, imagine you're an experienced general contractor and want to get into flipping houses, but don't have a lot of capital. You could bring on a financial partner to fund the acquisition and material costs, and then contribute your skills as a contractor to manage costs, schedules, and subcontractors, as well as invest your time by actually doing some of the renovation work yourself. In this scenario you are contributing skill and time resources but are relying on someone else's capital to complete the flip.

As these examples show, every deal is going to require different resources at different levels, and you don't have to personally bring all three resources to every deal you participate in. You can partner, trade, or buy resources from other investors, banks, contractors, or anyone else who wants to participate in a deal. Each of the three essential resources can be exchanged for the other two. With capital, you can buy someone else's time or skill. With time, you can exchange your hustle for someone else's skill or capital. Last, you can contribute your skills to a deal in exchange for someone else's time or capital. How you acquire, trade, and utilize your resources is a vital part of your Portfolio Strategy.

THE REAL ESTATE RESOURCE TRIANGLE

For those getting started, I want to make it clear that you do not need an abundance of each of these three resources to get going. Most investors have a deficit in one, two, or even all three of these resources. If you're reading this and thinking, "I don't have a lot of money," "I'm already strapped for time," or "I don't know anything about real estate investing," don't be discouraged. The whole point of this book is to design a portfolio that works around your vision and your current situation—so wherever you are today, you'll be able to build a portfolio.

I'm a great case in point. When I first got into real estate, I had very few resources. I started back in 2010, and I had no capital. I was less than a year out of college and was waiting tables at a glorified Applebee's in Denver. The job actually paid pretty well, but I didn't have enough money saved up yet for a down payment on a property. I didn't even use a bank at the time. The restaurant paid me in cash every night, so I just stored it all in my bedside table. Back then, I also knew very little about real estate investing. I had an internship in college that taught me the basics of financial modeling, and I could put together a decent spreadsheet, but I didn't have the first idea how to manage a property or a portfolio.

Having no capital and no knowledge of real estate may sound like a bad place to start, but luckily, I had plenty of the third real estate resource—time. Working in the service industry is hard, but it comes with long stretches of uninterrupted time between shifts. I would typically use that downtime to go hiking or skiing, or just to hang out with friends. But once I started exploring the idea of real estate investing, I realized I could easily repurpose some of my free time toward my dream of financial freedom.

At first, I used my excess time to learn the basics of real estate investing by reading everything I could find. Then I took it upon myself to learn about my local market. I spent time driving and biking around Denver taking note of good areas in which to invest. I improved my knowledge of real estate finance and math and built out a credible business plan. I traded my time to acquire new skills.

After a few months of this, I had developed a sufficient skill set to attract partners. Now I had time AND skill to add to the party. I set up a deal where I would be the active partner and get paid 10 percent of the deal's income to manage the property. Four of us went in on my first deal, each contributing 25 percent of the down payment. It was a great deal, but there was just one problem—I didn't have enough capital, even for just 25 percent of the down payment. So, I borrowed my share, with interest, from one of the partners as a secondary loan and used my "salary" as the property manager to pay off that secondary loan. At this point my Resource Triangle worked out like this: I was trading my time and skill resources (managing the property) for someone else's capital (my share of the down payment, with interest).

This is just an example, but it's generally how most real estate deals are done. Investors are constantly exchanging resources they have for resources they don't. That's part of the fun! It's also why relationship building (aka networking) is so important for real estate investors .

Now that I am at a different stage of my investing career, it has flipped:

I regularly trade capital for the skills and time I don't have. When I invest in a large multifamily syndication, I am investing my capital (alongside other investors) with a sponsor who I believe has the appropriate amount of skill, and will commit the necessary time, to make the deal a success.

Of course, everyone's individual circumstances will be different. I was very fortunate to have people in my life with the financial means to partner on my first deal. Some of you won't have access to capital as easily, but that's okay and we'll talk more about financing later. Just remember you don't need to start with huge bags of money. With whatever resources you have (or lack), you can build a portfolio.

There's one catch, though. While it's true that you don't need an abundance of each resource, you need at least one. You have to contribute *something* to each deal you do, and to your portfolio as a whole. Imagine you're the general manager of a sports team trying to trade for a great player, but you don't have any draft picks, players, or cash to offer the other team. No one would even talk to you because you have nothing to contribute to the deal. (I grew up a Knicks fan, so I know this situation all too well.) The same is true in real estate—you need to bring at least one resource to each deal you do.

The good news is most people currently have at least one of these resources or can find a way to obtain one quickly. But bringing these resources to bear is not without sacrifice and prioritization: You may have some money saved up, but you have to decide how much, if any, you want to use for your portfolio versus, say, a vacation or a new car. If you have lots of time, you need to determine how much of it you want to use for real estate versus skiing, time with your family, etc. Your resources are your property, and you get to decide how to use them.

We'll talk a great deal more in Part 2 about your personal resources. We'll conduct a "Resource Audit" to identify the specific resources you have and how you want to allocate them toward real estate investing. But for now, there is one important principle you need to remember: The more resources you commit to your portfolio, the faster it can grow. How many resources you can commit, and how many resources you *want* to commit, will vary from person to person, but the principle holds true for everyone. The more of your resources you put toward your portfolio, the greater the potential. If you choose to use your capital, time, or skill for pursuits other than your portfolio, that is okay and completely normal. Everyone does that. Growing as fast as possible has never been my goal, and it's the goal of only a select few of the most ambitious investors I know. Nevertheless, it's important to understand that using your capital, time, and skill outside of your portfolio is accepting a trade-off. Your portfolio will have less potential for growth, but you'll hopefully be gaining something equally (or more) worthwhile elsewhere in your life.

RESOURCE #1: CAPITAL (MONEY)

Real estate is a capital-intensive pursuit. When it comes to investing, "capital" just means "money." You will need capital to purchase properties, make repairs, pay for labor, and many other things. Unlike investing in stocks, where you can get started with almost any amount, real estate has a relatively high barrier to entry. Even if you start with a fairly low-priced house hack for, say, $200,000, and put the minimum of 3.5 percent down, you still need $7,000 for the down payment, plus more for closing costs and reserves. We're talking about at least $10,000 needed even for a relatively inexpensive deal. That's a lot!

The more capital you have to invest, the faster your portfolio can grow, but don't be discouraged if you don't have a lot of money in the bank right now. Your portfolio does need capital to grow, but you don't necessarily need to have loads of capital yourself. As the Resource Triangle shows us, you can access other people's capital as long as you have time or skill to commit to a deal. If you're able to find great deals, manage properties, or offer something of value to a deal, you should be able to find financial partners who want to work with you.

I want to make clear how common it is to rely on partners for capital. I don't have any hard data to say how many people get started this way, but from my anecdotal experience, it's a lot—I think probably a majority of people. Many people partner on their first few deals, and in fact, many investors partner on *every* deal. It's extremely common to source your capital from multiple sources on a single deal, and even more common at a portfolio level. Very few people have sufficient capital to fund every deal in their portfolio on their own.

If money is the resource you *do* have, you will be able to easily secure the other resources in the triangle: time and skill. For example, if you have sufficient capital, you can buy a rental property and then pay someone to manage the property, which requires both time and skill. Like with everything in the Resource Triangle, if you have one resource in abundance, you will be able to exchange it for the other resources.

RESOURCE #2: TIME

Real estate investing is a business, and every business requires some investment of time. As we'll discuss later, there is a spectrum of how "active" your investments need to be, but even if you tend toward the more passive end of that spectrum, you'll need to invest some time. Despite all the hype about passive income, every individual deal you do, and your portfolio as a whole, will require time to operate successfully. Whether yours or that of someone you hire, time is a necessity in real estate investing.

It's common for investors to commit a lot of time to their deals and portfolio early in their investing career. At this stage, investors don't typically have a lot of capital or skill to contribute to their deals and rely heavily on their time resource. That's the beauty of the Resource Triangle. Even if you don't have money or skill, as long as you have time, you can get started.

As their portfolios grow, most investors tend to spend less time on individual deals and more time focusing on their portfolios as a whole. This can involve hiring property managers, hiring people to manage the books, or investing in more passive options like multifamily syndications. This trend exists for a few reasons. First, time is finite! As you grow your portfolio, the amount of time required to properly manage each of your individual deals will eventually exceed the hours you have in a day. You'll need to outsource something. Second, the vision that gets most people into real estate investing is to eventually work less. Once you have sufficient capital and skill, you can spend less time managing your deals and portfolio and more time doing whatever else you like!

RESOURCE #3: SKILL

Owning and operating real estate investments successfully requires a specialized set of skills. Even if you have all the money and time in the world, if you don't know how to run your business properly, your performance will suffer.

The skills needed for success will vary based on the tactics you pursue—which we'll talk about in detail in Part 3. For now, just know that the skills required are broad and diverse, and no one should reasonably expect to have every skill they need when first starting out. Some skills you might already have, or might be able to easily learn, but for everything else you're going to need to purchase or trade.

As a simple example, a relatively standard rental property invest-ment will require the following skills: deal finding, deal analysis, tenant management, repairs, operations, bookkeeping, and many more. Could you become an expert in all of those things? Maybe. Should you? I don't think so. The more efficient way to build your portfolio is to determine which skills you have currently or could easily learn and then trade either money or time for the skills you don't have.

I am good at deal analysis, market analysis, and partner management. I've learned to be proficient at tenant management. I tried my hand at doing repairs and bookkeeping, and I'm terrible at both. I could spend loads of time learning how to do those things better, but it's not an efficient use of my time resource. Instead, I pay people who are already experts in those fields to leverage their skill (trading my money resource for their skill resource, rather than trading my time resource to learn the skills).

If you're new to investing, it's unlikely you'll already be an expert in things like tenant management. That's okay! But you should pick a few new skills you want to learn and develop, such as deal analysis, location analysis, networking, or tenant management. Relying 100 percent on other people's skills for the success of your business is never a great idea. You'll want to have expertise in some areas of real estate investing to build your portfolio confidently. We'll walk through an exercise in Part 2 that will help you figure out which skills you can, and should, commit time to learning.

RESOURCE TRIANGLE: **RECAP**

Every portfolio—whether it's large, small, simple, or complex—requires the same basic resources. Whether you're working on your first deal or have hundreds of units in your portfolio, all portfolios need capital, time, and skill to operate. For you, some resources may be easy to come by, while others will be harder.

Some people choose to focus on acquiring tons of one resource and trading for the other two. For example, if you have a high-paying job, you may want to maximize your income to generate capital and then trade for others' time and skill to grow your portfolio. Other people may choose to dabble in each of the three resources—contributing some capital, some time, and some skill. This is a decision you get to make as part of your Portfolio Strategy. As you'll learn throughout this book, much of the art of Portfolio Strategy is how you allocate your resources.

You get to decide how to acquire, trade, and utilize resources in a way that best supports your Vision. But remember, you just need to have one resource to get started as a real estate investor.

As we move through the coming chapters, keep the Resource Triangle in mind, and start to think through some of these questions: Do you have capital you're willing to commit to your portfolio? Are you passionate about real estate investing to the point that you want to acquire new skills yourself? Are you willing to devote a lot of time to your portfolio, or would you rather only invest money? These are important questions and trade-offs you need to consider, particularly when we reach Chapter 10 on Personal Values. Building your portfolio requires personal contribution of some resources. Which ones are you willing to commit?

Chapter 2
UNDERSTANDING DIFFERENT TYPES OF INCOME

In the large and diverse American economy, there are many ways to earn income. I've been an investor, a cold-caller, a waiter, a data analyst, a caddie, a fund director, a dog walker, a tour guide, a consultant, an entrepreneur, and a whole lot of other things. I'm guessing you've earned money in quite a few different ways as well. Most of us have earned income through numerous sources because the variety of jobs, side hustles, and investments is pretty much endless. But regardless of the specifics, all money-making endeavors can be categorized into one of two types of income: **transactional** or **residual**.

The type and amount of income you generate is an important consideration in your Portfolio Strategy. The income you generate from your job impacts how much capital you have to invest in your portfolio. Over time, your portfolio will also be producing income for you as it grows—and it can produce either transactional or residual income, or a combination of the two. Understanding the strengths and drawbacks of both residual and transactional income will help you determine how to generate capital to invest with and how to construct your portfolio to deliver the types of income you want.

TRANSACTIONAL VS. RESIDUAL INCOME
Transactional Income

Transactional income is trading your time or knowledge for money. Pretty much everyone is familiar with this form of income, as almost all traditional jobs generate transactional income. Whether you are a salaried employee, get paid hourly, or are a gig worker and get paid per project, when you exchange your time and effort for money, that's transactional income. If your compensation is proportionate to your effort, it's transactional.

Some common roles that yield transactional income:

- W-2 job
- 1099 job
- Business owner
- Real estate agent
- Contractor

There's nothing wrong with transactional income—it's how most of us earn a living and is a very important component of your Portfolio Strategy. Most investors rely on their transactional income to generate capital to invest. However, transactional income has its limitations. First, it's not all that scalable. Hopefully your salary or hourly rate increases over the course of your career, or you start a business that earns strong transactional income, but ultimately there's only so much time and effort you can (or want to) commit to your work—and therefore there's only so much transactional income you can earn.

The second limitation of transactional income is that if you decide (or are forced) to stop working, your income stops. Since you're trading your time and effort for money, if the effort stops, so does the income. This is basically the opposite of financial independence and can be a frightening prospect. Who among us hasn't faced financial stress at the prospect of losing a job, having a health issue and not being able to work, or just wanting to take some time off? This is why so many people aspire to augment their transactional income with a more predictable and enduring form of income: residual income.

Residual Income

Residual income differs from transactional income in that it doesn't require continuous, or even consistent, inputs of time or skill. This type of income is generated while you're sleeping, watching a movie, or doing whatever else you please. Residual income comes in many forms, some that you're likely familiar with. When you purchase a stock that pays a dividend, that is residual income. You buy that dividend stock, and then you don't need to do anything. You sit around and wait for your dividend check to arrive. The same thing is true for bonds. You buy a bond, do nothing, and then receive interest payments.

When people talk about financial freedom, they are almost always talking about residual income. If you are able to generate enough residual income to cover your expenses, then you're financially free. That's all there is to it! Financial stability comes when you don't have to worry about losing your job and know that you can meet all of your obligations without actually "working" for any of your income.

There are many ways to generate residual income, but in my opinion, none are better than real estate investing. You can invest in stocks, bonds, or other asset classes, but there's a reason so many people who achieve financial freedom do it through real estate. Real estate offers proven and predictable ways to generate significant amounts of residual income. The most common real estate tactics that generate residual income are rental properties, house hacking, multifamily investing, commercial properties, and note investing, to name just a few. There are tons of ways to generate residual income from real estate!

Residual Income:
- Dividend stocks
- Bonds
- Rentals
- Lending
- Multifamily investing
- Commercial real estate

Using Transactional and Residual Income

While most people reading this book are here to unlock the power of residual income, transactional income shouldn't be ignored. Transactional income can be a very important piece of your Portfolio Strategy, especially when you're first getting started. Remember, your portfolio requires capital to fuel it, and transactional income is an excellent source of capital. The majority of people don't have sufficient residual income to fuel their portfolio when they're starting out, so they use transactional income from their job to generate the capital they need to build their portfolio. Most of you will likely start building your portfolio this way.

Real estate investments can generate either transactional or residual income, depending on the real estate strategies used. We'll get into this in detail in Part 3, but for now, just know that flipping houses and new construction yield transactional income, while rental properties, short-term rentals, and most commercial deals earn residual income. One of the key decisions you'll make when determining the composition of your portfolio is what type of income you want your portfolio to generate. You can focus entirely on one type of income or the other—or you can seek a balance of the two.

To help explain this idea, let's look at an example of an investor named Alicia. Alicia has saved $40,000 of transactional income earned from her full-time job and invested it into a single deal: a rental property that offers a 7 percent cash-on-cash return (cash-on-cash return is one of many rates of return used by real estate investors; I'll explain it in more detail soon). In this scenario, Alicia will earn $2,800 per year of residual income: $40,000 × 7 percent = $2,800.

In this simple example with just a single property, Alicia's portfolio is earning only residual income because she bought a rental property—a strategy that produces residual income. As Alicia scales, she can choose if she wants to keep earning only residual income or wants to seek balance. Let's presume that Alicia wants to achieve some sort of balance, and over the course of a few years, she is able to execute three deals, two rentals, and one flip. Alicia's rental properties build residual income while the flip property earns Alicia transactional income—all of which she funded using transactional income from her job.

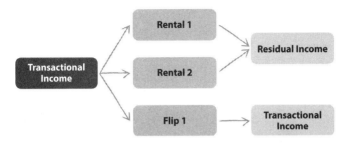

When you're first getting started, your income is likely to consist primarily of transactional income. Actually, most people start with 100 percent transactional income because their only income is their job before they start investing. Once you start investing, your portfolio will earn you new income streams—and you'll get to choose if you'll pursue deals that generate transactional or residual income. Generally speaking, most investors seek to earn a greater share of their income from residual income as their investing career progresses because it means they can spend less time working for money.

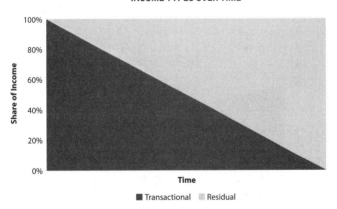

The progression of most portfolios looks something like the above graph. People start by having 100 percent of their income in the form of transactional income and end with 100 percent of their income coming from residual income (aka retirement). Of course, no portfolio actually works in a perfectly linear way like the graph, but hopefully you get the point—most people want to move from transactional to residual income over time. How quickly and in what way you do it is up to you.

Returning to Alicia, if she wants to retire early, she might prioritize getting to 100 percent residual income as soon as possible. The share of transactional versus residual income for an investor like Alicia would look something like this.

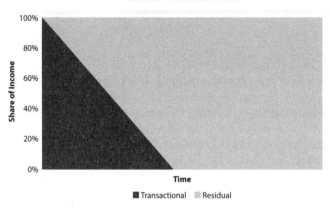

INCOME TYPES OVER TIME

If, instead of retiring early, Alicia wanted to retire at a traditional age, she would shift her income to residual more gradually until the point of her retirement.

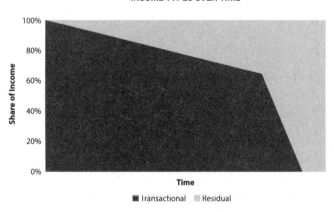

INCOME TYPES OVER TIME

There are no right or wrong answers in terms of how you structure your income distribution, but there are trade-offs. Shifting entirely to residual income early will make you truly retired and financially free, but could lead to a lower total income and net worth. Earning strong transactional income (from your job and/or real estate) while investing in residual income streams will result in excellent long-term wealth creation, but it requires more time and effort. Ultimately, whether you want to retire early or at a more traditional age, most people invest to eventually live entirely off residual income and aspire to end their career with a relatively simple portfolio.

PASSIVE VS. ACTIVE INCOME

A quick note about the term "passive income." You may have heard this term before, particularly when it comes to real estate investing tactics like rental properties. While residual income tends to be more "passive" than transactional income, I deliberately choose not to call residual income "passive income." To me, these are different concepts—both of which you need to consider for your Portfolio Strategy. Residual versus transactional income is a question of how the money is earned. Are you trading time for money? Or are you using your capital to earn more money? Active versus passive investing is a question of how involved you are in the operations of your deals. That's the central question of what I call your "management plan." You can have transactional income that is relatively passive and residual income that is time intensive. They are two different concepts.

Within real estate investment, there is a broad spectrum of how involved you need to be. On one end of the spectrum there is actively managed transactional income. For example, if you're personally over-seeing a house flip, you're going to have to be involved every single day. That's a lot of work. On the other end of the spectrum, there is passive investing in residual income, like buying a turnkey rental property or being a limited partner in a multifamily syndication. Those require some upfront work to source the deal and hire the right team but then become very passive.

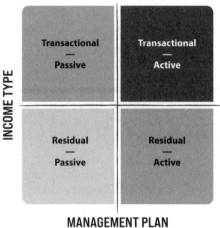

As you develop your Portfolio Strategy, make sure to consider these two concepts separately. Transactional versus residual is different than active versus passive.

UNDERSTANDING DIFFERENT TYPES OF INCOME: **RECAP**

While it can be tempting to focus on the financial independence that residual income provides, both types of income—transactional and residential—are important for building your portfolio. The more transactional income you generate, the more capital you can inject into your portfolio and the more residual income you can earn in the long run. Remember one of the key lessons from the previous chapter: The more resources you commit to your portfolio, the faster and larger it can grow.

Think carefully about how you want your income distribution to look over time. Do you want to focus on becoming financially free as soon as possible, at the expense of long-term upside and growth? Or do you want to focus on earning more transactional income to use as fuel for your portfolio, but give up time to do so? The choice is yours!

Chapter 3

EARNING YOUR RETURN

The objective of each deal you do, and your portfolio as a whole, is to earn a financial return (profit). You put resources in, you operate your business, and ideally the product of that effort is ending up with more money than you contributed to the deal. But how does that happen? And how do you maximize the financial gain from your deals and your portfolio as a whole? In this chapter we're going to discuss one of the most fundamental concepts in investing: compounding.

For some of you this might be a review, but I encourage you to read this chapter thoroughly nonetheless, as this chapter is designed to help real estate investors in particular make strategic decisions about compounding, and if and when they want to reinvest their profits.

Let's start at the top. As discussed already, every real estate deal requires capital, time, and skill. For now we're going to leave the time and skill resources aside and focus just on capital. The goal of your portfolio is to make money, after all, and we're going to talk here about how to turn your money into more money.

Every investment requires capital. Over the lifetime of your investment, you'll take money out as earnings, either upon the sale of the property or from cash flow. The difference between what you put into a deal and the total of what you take out is your profit.

Money Out – Money In = Profit

While there are many complex factors that impact the profitability of an investment, in the simplest (and the mathematical) sense, it comes down to just three things:

1. Principal (money)
2. Rate of return
3. Hold period

This is true whether you're investing in multifamily apartments, flipping a house, or even buying stocks or bonds. It's also true at a portfolio level, because a portfolio is just a collection of individual investments. To measure the profit of your portfolio, you just need to know the total money you've invested (known as your "principal"), the (average) rate of return, and the timeline (or "hold period") of your investments.

Let's define each of the inputs to figuring out profit.

DETERMINING PROFIT
Principal

This is the initial capital invested into an individual deal or your portfolio. For example, if you invest $80,000 as a down payment to purchase a $320,000 home and use a loan for the rest, the principal contribution would be $80,000. When capital is used to fund an investment, it's called "principal."

Rate of Return

This is the percentage of profit you earn on your principal. Typically, this is expressed as an annual percentage. For example, you might see that the stock market returns an average of 8 percent per year. That means, on average, you will earn an annual profit equal to 8 percent of the principal invested. For an individual property (like the $320,000 example above), an 8 percent annual rate of return on $80,000 of capital would be $6,400 per year. Note that in this instance the rate of return is calculated off of the investment's principal ($80,000), not the value of the property ($320,000).

> **NOTE:** *There are many different "rates of return" used by real estate investors:* **return on investment (ROI), cash-on-cash return (CoCR), compound annual growth rate (CAGR),** *and* **internal rate of return (IRR),** *just to name a few. We'll get into this more in depth later in the book, but for now we're going to use a very simple annualized return on investment for explanatory purposes.*

Hold Period

This is the period over which you hold an individual investment. If you owned the property in the above example for five years, you would earn $32,000 in total profit (assuming you don't reinvest your profits—which we'll talk about shortly).

Calculating Profit

If you know the following three things, you can calculate the profit for any individual deal:

(Principal × Rate of Return) × Hold Period = Profit
Example: ($80,000 × 8 percent) × 5 years = $32,000

Now we can calculate the overall return on investment (ROI). Earning $32,000 in profit on $80,000 of principal is equal to a 40 percent ROI ($32,000 ÷ $80,000) over five years. If you divide that 40 percent total ROI by the five-year hold period to get an "annualized ROI," you would get 8 percent—our rate of return!

This is a super-simplified example, but the point is to show you that to calculate the profit of a deal, all you need to know is the principal contributed, the rate of return, and the timeline of the investment. As I mentioned, this also applies to your entire portfolio.

If you're thinking, "But there are so many other variables in portfolio performance," you're right! There are many complex factors that influence how much principal you invest, your rate of return, and your timeline. For example, the level of time and skill resources you commit to the deal will greatly impact your rate of return. Or your personal goals will dictate how much capital you invest, and how long you hold your investments. But at a mathematical level, if you want to understand the performance of your deals, and how well your portfolio is tracking against your goals, you just need the principal, rate of return, and hold periods.

We'll cover ideal hold periods, and how to impact your rates of return, later in the book. For now, just focus on the mechanics of this equation and how principal, rate of return, and time interact to create profit. This concept will underpin may of the strategic decisions you make about individual deals and your portfolio.

SIMPLE VS. COMPOUND RETURNS

As your portfolio begins to generate profits, you will have a choice of what to do with them. Do you want to withdraw your profits from your portfolio for use elsewhere in your life? Or do you want to use your profits as new fuel for your portfolio by reinvesting them? Profits withdrawn from your investments are known as "simple returns," while reinvested profits are known as "compound returns"—and the distinction between them plays a huge role in your portfolio's performance.

Simple Returns

"**Simple returns**" are returns that are withdrawn from your investments rather than being reinvested. Simple returns didn't get their name because they're simple to earn, but because they are different from the more complex (and powerful) option of compound returns.

To explain the differences between simple and compound returns, we're going to follow an investor named Julio, who has $30,000 in principal to invest. Julio has many options for investing his principal: stocks, bonds, real estate, or just keeping his money in a savings account. Each of these options offers the potential to earn Julio a return on his investment.

We'll start simple—with Julio's savings account. Let's say that Julio's bank is offering him 2 percent interest per year on his investment. That 2 percent interest is Julio's rate of return. If Julio invested his $30,000 of **principal** into this savings account at a 2 percent **rate of return**, for a **time period** of one year, he would have $30,600. In other words, he would still have the $30,000 principal he invested, plus $600 he earned in profit. See how easy that is? If you know the principal, the rate of return, and the time period, you can easily calculate simple returns.

In this simple example, Julio has earned a 2 percent return on his investment (ROI) in one year. At any point Julio can decide to withdraw his principal or his profit, and do something else with that money. For the purposes of this example, let's imagine that every year, on the anniversary of his investment, Julio withdraws his $600 annual return and uses it to go on a trip with friends.

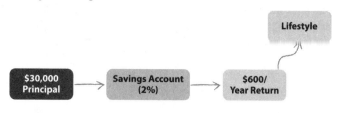

In this scenario, Julio would continue to earn $600 in profit, or a 2 percent ROI, every year.

YEAR	BEGINNING BALANCE	PROFIT	WITHDRAWN	ENDING BALANCE	ROI
0	$30,000.00	$600.00	($600.00)	$30,000.00	2%
1	$30,000.00	$600.00	($600.00)	$30,000.00	2%
2	$30,000.00	$600.00	($600.00)	$30,000.00	2%
3	$30,000.00	$600.00	($600.00)	$30,000.00	2%
4	$30,000.00	$600.00	($600.00)	$30,000.00	2%
5	$30,000.00	$600.00	($600.00)	$30,000.00	2%
6	$30,000.00	$600.00	($600.00)	$30,000.00	2%
7	$30,000.00	$600.00	($600.00)	$30,000.00	2%
8	$30,000.00	$600.00	($600.00)	$30,000.00	2%
9	$30,000.00	$600.00	($600.00)	$30,000.00	2%
Total		**$6,000.00**			

Each year, Julio starts with $30,000, earns a $600 return (2 percent ROI), withdraws his return, and then starts the next year with $30,000 again. At the end of ten years, Julio will have earned a cumulative total profit of $6,000 on his $30,000 investment. Because Julio withdraws his profit from his investment each year, he is earning simple returns. Had he reinvested his returns, they would be compound returns rather than simple returns (more on that shortly).

Simple returns are also applicable to real estate investments, like a rental property. Instead of a savings account, imagine Julio invests his $30,000 principal into a house hack (a rental property that the investor lives in) that earns him a 10 percent cash-on-cash return, for a total of $3,000 per year in cash flow.

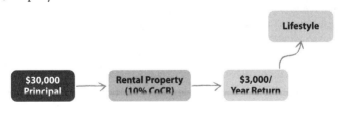

Just like with the savings account, if Julio followed this approach, he would earn the same amount each and every year, which he withdraws and uses to fund his lifestyle.

YEAR	BEGINNING BALANCE	PROFIT	WITHDRAWN	ENDING BALANCE	ROI
0	$30,000.00	$3,000.00	($3,000.00)	$30,000.00	10%
1	$30,000.00	$3,000.00	($3,000.00)	$30,000.00	10%
2	$30,000.00	$3,000.00	($3,000.00)	$30,000.00	10%
3	$30,000.00	$3,000.00	($3,000.00)	$30,000.00	10%
4	$30,000.00	$3,000.00	($3,000.00)	$30,000.00	10%
5	$30,000.00	$3,000.00	($3,000.00)	$30,000.00	10%
6	$30,000.00	$3,000.00	($3,000.00)	$30,000.00	10%
7	$30,000.00	$3,000.00	($3,000.00)	$30,000.00	10%
8	$30,000.00	$3,000.00	($3,000.00)	$30,000.00	10%
9	$30,000.00	$3,000.00	($3,000.00)	$30,000.00	10%
Total		$30,000.00			

If Julio withdraws his $3,000 per year in cash flow to support his lifestyle, he will earn $30,000 in total profit over the course of ten years. Pretty solid, but Julio could actually be earning significantly more if, instead of withdrawing his profits each year, he reinvested them. That's where compound returns come in.

Compound Returns

There's nothing wrong with withdrawing your profits. If you want to retire early, you'll need cash flow to live on, and profits from your investments is the way to get it. When you meet or read about people who are financially free, it's because they are able to withdraw enough profit from their investments to cover their living expenses. They're earning simple returns. Although they are called simple returns, don't write them off. Withdrawing profits is an important part of everyone's Portfolio Strategy at one point or another.

However, if you're focused on growth and you want to build wealth at the fastest rate possible, you will likely want to consider a different strategy for your portfolio: **compound returns** (also called **reinvesting**). The idea is that rather than withdrawing your profits and spending them, you're reinvesting your profits into another return-generating investment (aka putting it back in your portfolio).

In the first example above, Julio had contributed $30,000 in principal to a savings account that earned him a profit of $600 per year, which he withdrew annually. But what would happen if instead of taking the profits out, Julio simply kept all his money in the savings account? Rather than using the $600 to support his lifestyle, what if Julio reinvested?

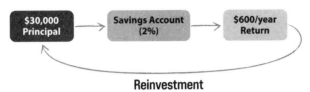

Reinvestment

The short answer is—Julio would make more money! After ten years, if Julio reinvested 100 percent of his profits, he would earn almost $6,570 and a 21.9 percent ROI as opposed to $6,000 and a 20 percent ROI when he withdrew his profits.

YEAR	BEGINNING BALANCE	PROFIT	WITHDRAWAL	ENDING BALANCE	ANNUAL INTEREST RATE
0	$30,000.00	$600.00	$0	$30,600.00	2%
1	$30,600.00	$612.00	$0	$31,212.00	2%
2	$31,212.00	$624.24	$0	$31,836.24	2%
3	$31,836.24	$636.72	$0	$32,472.96	2%
4	$32,472.96	$649.46	$0	$33,122.42	2%
5	$33,122.42	$662.45	$0	$33,784.87	2%
6	$33,784.87	$675.70	$0	$34,469.57	2%
7	$34,469.57	$689.21	$0	$35,149.78	2%
8	$35,149.78	$703.00	$0	$35,852.78	2%
9	$35,852.78	$717.06	$0	$36,569.83	2%
Total		**$6,569.83**			

Of course, $570 in additional profit over ten years is not going to make you financially free, but let's apply this concept to a real estate portfolio, where you often see 10 percent rates of return per year (or higher!). If Julio puts his $30,000 into a real estate investment that yields a 10 percent rate of return for thirty years, the outcomes are dramatically better if he reinvests his profits and allows them to compound rather than withdraw them.

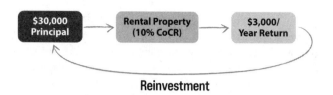

Reinvestment

If Julio withdraws his money every year (**simple returns**) for thirty years, he will make a total profit of $90,000—not too shabby. But if instead he reinvests his money (**compound returns**), he will make over $493,000. By reinvesting his profits, he would earn 548 percent more over the course of thirty years. Yes, you read that correctly. The difference is enormous. Compounding your returns is an incredibly powerful force! Remember in Chapter 1 when I said that the more resources you put into your portfolio, the faster and larger it will grow? Reinvestment is the perfect illustration of that idea. Instead of only using external capital from your job, you reinvest the profits from your portfolio and increase your invested capital. And more capital invested means more opportunity for profits.

By delaying withdrawing profits, you can grow your wealth exponentially. A lot of people use the term "exponential growth" to mean "really fast." But with compound returns, the growth is literally exponential. And the longer you wait, the more powerful the benefits of compounding become. This is why the time horizon of your portfolio is so important. The more time you give your portfolio, the more exponential growth you will see.

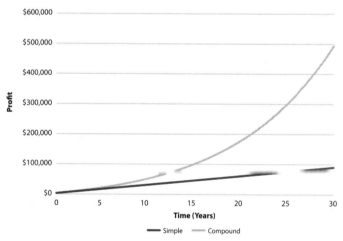

CUMULATIVE RETURNS OVER TIME

This chart shows the cumulative returns for the example earlier where Julio bought and held a rental property for thirty years. Notice that in the early years of the investment, the trade-off between simple and compound returns is not so impressive. But as time goes on, the benefits of compounding increase dramatically. In fact, the benefit of compounding *accelerates* over time.

Hopefully you can see the implication of this trade-off for your Portfolio Strategy. If you want to build wealth as quickly as possible, you should reinvest your profits as much as you possibly can and continue to compound your returns for as long as possible

Of course, not everyone wants to, or can, reinvest everything they earn for long periods of time. If you want to reduce your working hours or retire, you will likely need to withdraw some of your profits and lessen the compounding effects on your portfolio. That's perfectly fine, and very common. It's also important to note that in my examples, I assume Julio instantly reinvests his profits at a consistent rate of return, which is not realistic. You don't have to reinvest everything under perfect conditions—you simply need to understand the trade-offs between withdrawing and reinvesting your profits to inform your Portfolio Strategy.

ADDING MORE PRINCIPAL

The examples given so far show just a single investment of principal. This is useful for demonstration purposes and for anyone who is going to stop adding new principal to their portfolio in the near future. However, many investors choose to continue to add new principal to their portfolios over time, as this can really increase a portfolio's performance.

In our example above, Julio invested $30,000 of principal into his portfolio, and we compared simple versus compound returns. Now, let's look at what happens if Julio contributes an extra $5,000 of principal from his job to his portfolio each year in addition to reinvesting his profits.

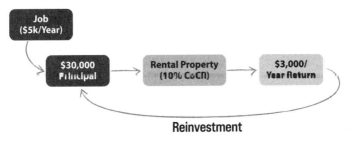

Reinvestment

In this scenario, Julio's total principal contributions over the course of his thirty-year investing career are as follows: a $30,000 principal contribution in year zero, plus $5,000 per year for the next twenty-nine years ($30,000 + ($5,000 × 29) = $175,000). If he invests all this principal at a 10 percent RoR and allows his returns to compound, he will earn a whopping $1,165,952 over thirty years—almost 7X his principal contributions.

Think about how that compares to the first scenario we discussed. If Julio had just stuck with his $30,000 initial investment and didn't add more principal annually, even if he allowed it to compound he would have walked away with just over $493,000. Pretty good, but adding $5,000 more principal per year for twenty-nine years led to an additional $673,000 in profits over the life of his portfolio. His portfolio value more than doubled by adding $5,000 in new principal annually.

	PRINCIPAL ADDED	BEGINNING BALANCE	RATE OF RETURN	ANNUAL RETURN	END OF YEAR BALANCE
0	$30,000	$30,000.00	10%	$3,000.00	$33,000.00
1	$5,000	$38,000.00	10%	$3,800.00	$41,800.00
2	$5,000	$46,800.00	10%	$4,680.00	$51,480.00
3	$5,000	$56,480.00	10%	$5,648.00	$62,128.00
4	$5,000	$67,128.00	10%	$6,712.80	$73,840.80
5	$5,000	$78,840.80	10%	$7,884.08	$86,724.88
6	$5,000	$91,724.88	10%	$9,172.49	$100,897.37
7	$5,000	$105,897.37	10%	$10,589.74	$116,487.10
8	$5,000	$121,487.10	10%	$12,148.71	$133,635.82
9	$5,000	$138,635.82	10%	$13,863.58	$152,499.40
10	$5,000	$157,499.40	10%	$15,749.94	$173,249.34
11	$5,000	$178,249.34	10%	$17,824.93	$196,074.27
12	$5,000	$201,074.27	10%	$20,107.43	$221,181.70
13	$5,000	$226,181.70	10%	$22,618.17	$248,799.87
14	$5,000	$253,799.87	10%	$25,379.99	$279,179.85
15	$5,000	$284,179.85	10%	$28,417.99	$312,597.84
16	$5,000	$317,597.84	10%	$31,759.78	$349,357.62
17	$5,000	$354,357.62	10%	$35,435.76	$389,793.39
18	$5,000	$394,793.39	10%	$39,479.34	$434,272.72
19	$5,000	$439,272.72	10%	$43,927.27	$483,200.00
20	$5,000	$488,200.00	10%	$48,820.00	$537,020.00
21	$5,000	$542,020.00	10%	$54,202.00	$596,222.00

22	$5,000	$601,222.00	10%	$60,122.20	$661,344.19
23	$5,000	$666,344.19	10%	$66,634.42	$732,978.61
24	$5,000	$737,978.61	10%	$73,797.86	$811,776.48
25	$5,000	$816,776.48	10%	$81,677.65	$898,454.12
26	$5,000	$903,454.12	10%	$90,345.41	$993,799.54
27	$5,000	$998,799.54	10%	$99,879.95	$1,098,679.49
28	$5,000	$1,103,679.49	10%	$110,367.95	$1,214,047.44
29	$5,000	$1,219,047.44	10%	$121,904.74	$1,340,952.18
Totals	$175,000.00			$1,165,952.18	$1,165,952.18

Remember in the previous chapter when I said that most investors (other than those who are truly retired) generate both transactional and residual income? This is one of the main reasons why! Even if you are generating great residual income, the best way to maximize your wealth creation is to keep adding more principal to your portfolio, and transactional income is a great way to do that.

I'll say it again because it's so important: If you want to build wealth as efficiently as possible, you should invest, and then reinvest as much as you can, at a high rate of return for the longest period of time possible. You'll make a lot of decisions over the course of your investing career, but this simple framework is the key to maximizing returns.

INCREASING THE RATE OF RETURN

At the beginning of this chapter, we discussed the three elements that dictate the performance of a deal: principal, rate of return, and hold period. At this point you know that adding principal and reinvesting your profits will grow your returns most efficiently. You also know that the benefits of compounding grow exponentially over time—the longer you let the machine run, the better. But what about the rate of return? Does it really matter if you earn 6 percent on your money versus 8 percent? In the short run, it won't really matter that much, but over the long run, the difference is remarkable.

Let's return to Julio and his $30,000 investment. At a 6 percent rate of return over thirty years, letting it compound, he'll wind up with just over $162,500. That's more than 5X his initial investment, which is solid! But what if he upped that return to 8 percent? His return would be over $279,500. By increasing his rate of return from 6 percent to 8 percent, he'd earn an additional $117,000 and turn his ROI from 542 percent to

932 percent. That relatively small change in the rate of return makes a big difference over time!

YEAR	6%	8%	10%	12%	14%
0	$30,000	$30,000	$30,000	$30,000	$30,000
1	$31,800	$32,400	$33,000	$33,600	$34,200
2	$33,708	$34,992	$36,300	$37,632	$38,988
3	$35,730	$37,791	$39,930	$42,148	$44,446
4	$37,874	$40,815	$43,923	$47,206	$50,669
5	$40,147	$44,080	$48,315	$52,870	$57,762
6	$42,556	$47,606	$53,147	$59,215	$65,849
7	$45,109	$51,415	$58,462	$66,320	$75,068
8	$47,815	$55,528	$64,308	$74,279	$85,578
9	$50,684	$59,970	$70,738	$83,192	$97,558
10	$53,725	$64,768	$77,812	$93,175	$111,217
11	$56,949	$69,949	$85,594	$104,356	$126,787
12	$60,366	$75,545	$94,153	$116,879	$144,537
13	$63,988	$81,589	$103,568	$130,905	$164,772
14	$67,827	$88,116	$113,925	$146,613	$187,840
15	$71,897	$95,165	$125,317	$164,207	$214,138
16	$76,211	$102,778	$137,849	$183,912	$244,117
17	$80,783	$111,001	$151,634	$205,981	$278,294
18	$85,630	$119,881	$166,798	$230,699	$317,255
19	$90,768	$129,471	$183,477	$258,383	$361,671
20	$96,214	$139,829	$201,825	$289,389	$412,305
21	$101,987	$151,015	$222,007	$324,115	$470,027
22	$108,106	$163,096	$244,208	$363,009	$535,831
23	$114,592	$176,144	$268,629	$406,570	$610,848
24	$121,468	$190,235	$295,492	$455,359	$696,366
25	$128,756	$205,454	$325,041	$510,002	$793,857
26	$136,481	$221,891	$357,545	$571,202	$904,998
27	$144,670	$239,642	$393,300	$639,746	$1,031,697
28	$153,351	$258,813	$432,630	$716,516	$1,176,135
29	$162,552	$279,518	$475,893	$802,498	$1,340,794

Of course, the benefits don't stop there. Every increase to your rate of return, no matter how small it is, will make a difference when you let your returns compound over a long period of time.

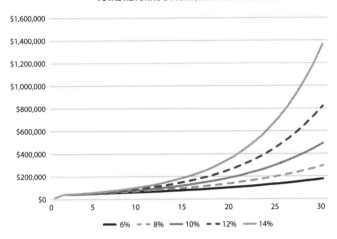

TOTAL RETURNS BY ANNUAL RATE OF RETURN

6% — 8% — 10% — 12% — 14%

As you can see, for the first ten years or so, the difference in total returns is not so dramatic. But over the lifetime of a portfolio, the difference is staggering. Over thirty years, a portfolio that averages a 14 percent return will earn $1,178,242 *more* dollars than a portfolio that averages a 6 percent return. And that's just on a $30,000 investment, without contributing any additional principal. If Julio invested $100,000 instead of $30,000, the difference between a 6 percent average return and a 14 percent average return over thirty years would be more than $3,927,000. Your rate of return is a big deal.

The above example is a bit extreme, as the difference between 6 percent and 14 percent returns is enormous. But even small increases in your rate of return will make huge differences over the lifetime of your portfolio. For an initial investment of $100,000, earning 7 percent instead of 6 percent will increase the value of your portfolio by more than $170,000 over thirty years. That's a considerable improvement in outcome by averaging just 1 percent better returns. Every bit makes a big difference over the long haul.

In this chapter we're talking a lot about the capital resource, but your time and skill resources really come into play in positively impacting your rate of return. Investing a lot of time or a high degree of skill in a deal can improve your rate of return considerably.

VARIOUS RATES OF RETURN FOR REAL ESTATE INVESTING

There is no single "rate of return" used by investors. There are many different ways to calculate your rate of return, and which one you use should depend on the type of investment and the question you're trying to answer. For the purposes of this book, I am going to use a few simple metrics, listed below. If you want to learn more about rates of return, the book I wrote with J Scott, *Real Estate by the Numbers*, goes deep into the topic.

- **Return on Investment (ROI):** Return on investment is the simplest rate of return. It is calculated by dividing your total return (profit) by your principal, then multiplying it by 100. If you invested $10,000 in principal, and earned a profit of $20,000 over time, your ROI would be 200 percent: ($20,000 ÷ $10,000) × 100 = 200 percent.

- **Annualized Return on Investment (AROI):** ROI is helpful but doesn't account for the timeline of the investment. You also need to know how much your average return is per year. To help understand the average return per year, simply divide your ROI by the number of years the investment is held. This is called annualized return on investment (AROI). Using the example above, if it took twenty years to earn $20,000, the AROI would be 10 percent: 200 percent ROI ÷ 20 years = 10 percent AROI.

- **Compound Annual Growth Rate (CAGR):** If you plan to reinvest the profits from your portfolio, a great metric to use is compound annual growth rate (CAGR). Like AROI, it provides an average annual return, but CAGR also considers the impact of compounding. CAGR isn't easy to calculate by hand, as the formula is (profit/principal) ÷ (1/n) − 1, where n = the number of years of the investment. However, if you know the number of years the investment is held, the principal, and the profit, you can use the RRI function in Microsoft Excel to calculate the CAGR. Using our example above where it took twenty years to earn $20,000 in profit on a $10,000 investment, our CAGR would be 5.6 percent.

- **Cash-on-Cash Return (CoCR):** Cash-on-cash is a metric that measures how efficiently your investment generates cash flow—which, as you'll see in the next chapter, is just one way to earn a return from real estate. CoCR is calculated by dividing annual cash flow by the principal investment. For example, if you invest $100,000 in principal into a rental property that generates $8,000 in cash flow each year, that property would have an 8 percent cash-on-cash return.

- **Return on Equity (ROE):** Return on equity is a metric similar to cash-on-cash return in that it evaluates how efficiently you generate cash flow. The difference is that ROE uses the equity value (the value of the property to the investor, should it be sold) of the investment as the denominator rather than the principal. This small difference makes ROE a more useful metric (in my opinion) for measuring cash flow efficiency over the lifetime of an investment than CoCR. The equation for ROE is annual cash flow divided by equity value. As an example, imagine you hold the property from the CoCR example above for seven years, over which time the annual cash flow grows to $9,000, and the equity value of the property grows to $150,000. The ROE for this property would be 6 percent ($9,000 ÷ $150,000).

Given what we've discussed above, it can be tempting to always pursue deals with the highest possible rate of return. But, as we'll learn in Chapter 5, deals with higher rates of return also tend to come with higher risk. So, you should be looking to maximize your rate of return within your risk tolerance and broader Portfolio Strategy. But the lesson remains true: A little difference in your rate of return makes a big difference over a long time period.

EARNING YOUR RETURN: **RECAP**

I've said it a few times already, but I'll say it one last time because I really want you to remember this: If you want to build wealth as quickly as possible, you should always be thinking how you can invest as much as possible, at the highest rate of return, for the longest period of time. This is a great mindset to have, but you have to recognize it won't always be achievable. Some years, you may not be able to add more principal. Other years, you may need to pull money out for an unforeseen expense, or maybe you want to enjoy the benefits of your portfolio's profit. Maybe in an uncertain economy you want to stow away some more cash in case of an emergency. Or perhaps the whole reason you're reading this book is because you want to live entirely off your investments. Life happens, and everyone's goals are different.

The lessons in this chapter do not propose that you always maintain a portfolio that builds maximum wealth as efficiently as possible. They are here to help you understand what a perfectly efficient portfolio would look like, so you can understand the trade-offs you'll face as an investor. If and how you reinvest and add more principal is a strategic decision for you to make about your portfolio. If you want to withdraw principal frequently, go for it! If you choose a strategy that is not perfectly efficient (as most of us do), that's great, as long as you understand why you're doing it and are comfortable with the trade-offs.

Chapter 4
PROFIT DRIVERS

Our discussion of Portfolio Strategy so far has remained fairly high level: transactional versus residual, active versus passive, and simple versus compound returns. These are concepts that apply to most investment types, not just real estate. But how does real estate investing in particular actually generate these returns? How does buying property actually earn you income, whether it's transactional or residual? Real estate investments are businesses, so how do these businesses make money?

Real estate investments make money and generate wealth in three different ways: **cash flow**, **equity growth**, and **tax benefits**. I call these three ways of earning returns "profit drivers." The fact that real estate has multiple profit drivers is one of the greatest advantages real estate has over other asset classes. Within each profit driver there are different ways to earn returns, but all real estate returns fall into one of these three categories. This chapter will introduce you to the three profit drivers and explain how each can be used in your Portfolio Strategy to help you build wealth and meet your financial goals.

PROFIT DRIVER #1: CASH FLOW

Cash flow is a return generated from an investment's operations, after subtracting expenses. In other words, it's your monthly profit. If you're doing things right, when you buy any long-term investment (rental properties, short-term rentals, commercial real estate, etc.), you should be generating more income than your expenses. The difference between this income and your expenses is your cash flow.

As a simple example, if an investor named Megan owns a rental property that collects $2,000 per month in rent, and her expenses are

$1,600 per month, her pre-tax cash flow will be $400 per month ($2,000 − $1,600 = $400).

Cash flow is not unique to real estate investing, but real estate earns cash flow very efficiently compared to many other asset classes. Dividend stocks and bonds offer cash flow, but they have, at best, returned somewhere between 2 percent and 6 percent since the Great Recession of 2008. Alternatively, real estate investors often see cash-on-cash returns that are much higher.

Cash flow is highly valued among investors because it creates residual income that mimics the consistency and stability of transactional income from a job. Put another way, cash flow is the one profit driver that provides monthly distributions of profit. You don't have to refinance or sell a property to recognize your profits with cash flow—most cash-flowing real estate investments allow you to collect profit every single month.

Getting returns on a regular schedule is highly valuable for two reasons: First, the time value of money tells us that the sooner we earn returns, the more valuable they are (because they can be invested sooner and have more time to compound!). So, getting cash flow from the outset of your investment makes it more valuable, on a dollar-to-dollar basis, than the same amount of money earned upon a sale.

Second, because cash flow is generated consistently like the income from a job, it can be used to cover everyday expenses, and potentially can even replace your transactional income. If you are aiming to be financially free, earning cash flow from real estate is the best way I know to achieve it. Of course, if you earn cash flow, you don't have to use it to support your lifestyle (simple return)—you can also reinvest it back into your portfolio (compound return)!

Because cash flow is so important to financial independence, and because real estate earns cash flow so efficiently, many investors are attracted to real estate for cash flow alone. Cash flow is a powerful tool for investors and a key component of most portfolios.

In the last chapter we discussed how many investors shift the balance of their portfolio toward residual income over time. The same is true for cash flow. If you work full-time in a job you love, you may not need to concentrate too heavily on cash flow early in your investing career. Instead, you may choose to use your resources to earn equity (which we'll talk about in the next section). But because cash flow is the best way to replace your regular income, many investors choose to shift the balance of their portfolio toward cash flow as they approach their retirement (whether that is an "early" retirement or at a more traditional retirement age).

Cash flow alone could be reason enough to build a real estate portfolio, but it's not the only way you can make money from real estate investing; you can also grow your equity.

PROFIT DRIVER #2: EQUITY GROWTH

Equity is the value of your ownership stake in a deal. Basically, if you sold a property, repaid all of your debts, and paid all the necessary expenses, how much would you walk away with? That's the equity you have in a deal. The same is true at a portfolio level. If you sold off all the properties in your portfolio, repaid all debts and expenses, and counted up what was left over—that's the equity value of your portfolio.

When you first buy a property, your equity in that property should be nearly equal to the down payment or the principal you invested. For example, if Megan purchased a property for $440,000 and put down 25 percent, her down payment would be $110,000, and she would get a mortgage for the remaining amount, $330,000. At the point of purchase, Megan's equity is worth $110,000. Although equity and principal are similar at the time of purchase, they will diverge over time. This is what you want! Equity growth is a significant source of returns for investors.

Returning to our example, let's imagine that Megan holds onto the property she purchased for $440,000 for ten years. Over that time, market appreciation increases the value of her property, and she pays down her mortgage, thereby reducing her liabilities. After ten years, Megan's property is worth $500,000 (up from $440,000), and her mortgage balance is $276,163 (down from $330,000). This leaves Megan with $223,837 worth of equity in the property—up from the $110,000 in principal Megan invested. In this example, Megan has more than doubled her money over ten years.

EQUITY GROWTH OVER TIME

The examples above were done at the property level but can easily be applied to an entire portfolio. For example, if the total worth of Megan's properties is $2,100,000, and her total liabilities are $1,300,000, the equity value of her portfolio would be about $800,000 ($2,100,000 − $1,300,000 = $800,000).

These examples are overly simplified but demonstrate the power of building equity through real estate. If you can increase the value of your properties or let market appreciation do its thing over time while maintaining or lowering your liabilities, you can generate great returns. This is known as "equity growth" or "building equity" and is the second profit driver investors use to generate wealth through real estate.

Unlike cash flow, equity returns are not easily accessible. You typically don't reap the benefit of equity gains on a monthly or quarterly basis. Instead, you realize these gains when a property is sold or refinanced. This doesn't make it any less important, though. Building equity can be a great way to build wealth and can provide you with large chunks of capital you can reinvest back into your portfolio. And as we'll discuss later, building equity early in your career can be transformed into cash flow later. Building equity is crucial to every Portfolio Strategy.

So how do you grow equity? There are three distinct ways: 1) market appreciation, 2) value-add, and 3) amortization.

1. Equity Growth Through Market Appreciation

Market appreciation is the value of an asset (like a property) going up over time due to market forces. When I say "market forces," I am talking about economic factors that are outside of our control. These are things like inflation, population growth, supply constraints in your market, strong wage growth, and so on. When you hear homeowners brag that they bought (or lament that they didn't buy) a property for $30,000 back in 1970, and now it's worth $300,000, they're mostly remarking on the power of market appreciation.

To demonstrate this, let's return to the previous example of Megan. She bought a property for $440,000, did nothing to improve it, and ten years later it was worth $500,000. Meaning, when Megan goes to sell, she will make $60,000 solely from market appreciation ($500,000 – $440,000 = $60,000).

Market appreciation can add value to an investment, but it's unpredictable, and the value it creates is often overestimated. Therefore, most experienced investors don't rely on market appreciation in their portfolio but instead view it as a bonus. Let me explain why.

First, the market doesn't always get better! The housing market works in cycles, and it's normal to see periods of declining property value. The risk of falling property values is an important factor to consider, as we'll discuss further in the next chapter.

Second, even when the national housing market is appreciating, it doesn't occur equally in every metro area, and where it does happen is notoriously difficult to predict. Even within a single metro area, different neighborhoods will see different amounts of market appreciation.

Third, it's not something we can control. As investors, we ideally want to generate returns in ways that are predictable to us and that we can directly influence. Market appreciation is not one of those things any one investor can really impact.

Last, despite the seemingly huge increases in home values over the last several decades, market appreciation doesn't always outpace inflation by a considerable amount. Over the last few years, home prices have outpaced inflation, but it's not a given. Since 1964, market appreciation has generated a real (inflation-adjusted) return of roughly 1.8 percent per year. Much of the increase in home values over time is just inflation.

Market appreciation is still really useful, though. As we just discussed, even if you earn money on a property in no other ways, owning property will provide value to your financial situation by serving as a very effective way to hedge the risk of inflation.

Market appreciation can also be an extremely powerful "bonus." It's not typically advised to buy a properly solely for its market appreciation potential—it's just too risky. However, if you buy a property that has strong fundamentals, and you happen to experience market appreciation, it can turn a good deal into a home run. This is particularly true if you have a loan on the property (known as leverage), which we'll discuss in the financing chapter later in the book. Just think about what happened from 2020–2022. No one could have predicted in 2018 or 2019 the huge increase in home values that occurred during the pandemic, but it was an enormous bonus to any investors who owned property.

2. Building Equity Through Value-Add

Value-add is one of the most popular and most powerful ways to build equity in real estate investing. The premise is pretty self-evident from the name: increase the value of a property by more than it costs you to add that value.

 NOTE: *You may hear value-add called "forced appreciation" in other real estate resources. That's correct too—I just chose to call it "value-add" investing in this book to provide a clear distinction from market appreciation.*

A good way to understand value-add is house flipping, because value-add is basically the only way you make money flipping houses. Let's say Megan buys a property for $200,000 and then spends $100,000 "adding value" to that property by adding a new kitchen and a small extension, in addition to a cosmetic makeover. Given the value of the improvements made, the market value of the property is now $350,000. In this example, Megan will have earned $50,000 in equity through value-add. Her expenses were $300,000 (purchase price + renovation costs), but she sold the property for $350,000, and she gets to keep the difference of $50,000. That's $50,000 of equity earned through value-add.

You can add value in types of deals other than house flipping (e.g., rental properties, short-term/medium-term rentals, multifamily investing, BRRRR). It's a very common and very profitable way to earn a return, when done properly. In some deal types, like flipping or ground-up construction, the whole point is to increase the value of the asset and then sell it for a higher price. But you can also use value-add to boost cash flow for properties you intend to hold on to. For example, if you buy a rental property and add value, you not only increase the value of the property, but you can also charge higher rent and earn more cash flow.

Value-add is popular because it tends to be a more predictable, controllable, and replicable way to build equity than market appreciation. Value-add is directly influenced by the investor. How much equity you gain through value-add is impacted by the decisions and skills of the investors and team involved. An experienced investor who knows how to underwrite deals, manage construction, control material and labor costs, and build strong systems can produce very high and relatively predictable returns. That said, value-add investing can be expensive and has a lot of operational risk—both of which we'll discuss in the next chapter.

3. Building Equity Through Amortization

Amortization is the return generated by paying down your mortgage. Or, more specifically, by having *someone else* pay down your mortgage. You may also hear amortization called "loan paydown." Both terms are correct, but I like the technical term.

The vast majority of people who own property buy it using debt (they take out a loan). There are many benefits to buying real estate using debt, which we'll discuss later, but amortization is one that directly contributes to your returns. Note that amortization is only present in investments that use debt—deals that are all cash do not benefit from amortization.

As the debt holder (borrower), you pay back your lender in installments, typically monthly. The money contained in that payment is not all the same, though (at least for a traditional mortgage—I'm not talking about interest-only loans here). Part of the monthly payment you make goes toward principal, and part goes toward interest. How much you pay of principal versus interest changes over time and is dictated by something called the "amortization schedule"—hence why this way of generating returns is called "amortization."

When you pay interest, you're simply paying the bank its profit. Paying interest has no benefit to the investor. When you pay off principal, you're reducing the amount you owe the lender (aka reducing your liabilities). So, when you pay down principal using someone else's money, you earn a profit.

Let's return to the example of Megan. She buys a home for $440,000, and because she is an investor, Megan puts 25 percent down ($110,000) with a fixed 6 percent interest rate. This means Megan is taking out a loan for $330,000, spread out over thirty years. Specifically, Megan is expected to pay back this $330,000 in monthly installments of $1,978.52 over the next thirty years.

When Megan makes her first payment of $1,978.52, $1,650 of it will go toward interest (the bank's profit), and $328.52 will go toward paying down principal and reducing her liabilities. This means after Megan's first payment, rather than owing the bank $330,000, she now owes the bank only $329,671.48 because she paid off $328.52 of principal.

Given that Megan is a landlord and she used her tenants' rent payment to pay off her mortgage, in essence Megan's tenants have just paid down her loan by $328.52 in just one month. That's $328.52 more Megan will get to keep when she sells or refinances this property—amazing! Over time, this can really add up. Using our example, if Megan used her rental income to pay down her mortgage for ten years, she would owe the bank just $276,162.89. Over that time, her tenants would have contributed $53,837.11 to paying down Megan's loan.

Considering that Megan put $110,000 down for this property, and her tenants contributed over $54,000 to her loan payments, Megan has earned a 49 percent ROI in ten years. In terms of a compound annual growth rate, that would be a 4.1 percent return. That's huge! A 4.1 percent compound annual growth rate isn't a home-run investment on its own, but remember this is just one of the (highly predictable and low-risk) ways a rental property makes money.

In terms of your portfolio, amortization is a very stable and predictable way to generate returns. As long as you pay your mortgage on time with rental income, you're earning a return. It doesn't matter if the housing market is up or down. Amortization alone is not going to make you fabulously wealthy, but I think of it as the "floor" of your investment. Even if your investment doesn't appreciate, and you just break even in terms of cash flow, you can still earn 4 percent (in this example)—that's a pretty good floor! More likely, if you buy a solid rental property deal, amortization will be just one element of your excellent return, on top of the market appreciation, value-add, and cash-flow returns you're earning as well.

The numbers above are just one simple example, and the amount you can earn from amortization will depend on the type, length, and interest rate of your loan. If you want to learn more about amortization and how it works on a mathematical level, you can google "amortization schedule" or learn more in my book *Real Estate by the Numbers*.

PROFIT DRIVER #3: TAX BENEFITS

Tax benefits don't earn a return on their own per se, but they play an important role in wealth creation and retention, as they help you hold onto more of your profits. The more of your returns you can keep and reinvest, the more capital you can keep in your portfolio, earning compound returns.

Real estate is one of the most tax-advantaged asset classes you can invest in. Before I explain a few of those advantages, let me just say that I am not a tax professional, and you should consult a CPA for formal tax advice. I am not an authority on the tax code, and therefore I'm not going to get into the gritty details of tax policy. For that, I recommend speaking with your own CPA or reading *The Book on Tax Strategies for the Savvy Real Estate Investor* by Amanda Han and Matthew MacFarland.

Caveats aside, I know enough to tell you that many forms of real estate investing offer ways to limit your tax liability. For some people, this is a major incentive for getting into real estate investing. For others, especially newer investors, taxes are an afterthought. But they shouldn't be! Learning to leverage the tax advantages available to real estate investors is a valuable element of your Portfolio Strategy.

I also want to say that these tax advantages are not illegal or cheating. They are deliberate tax policies enacted into law by Congress, most of which are aimed at stimulating economic growth and incentivizing behavior the government wants. The following is by no means a comprehensive list, just a few of the more common strategies used by real estate investors:

- Depreciation
- Capital gains
- 1031 exchange
- Deferring taxes

Depreciation

Depreciation is a tax deferral (a deferral means you still have to pay the tax, but you get to pay it at a future date) that accounts for the declining condition of a physical property. The basic premise is that properties deteriorate over time, and in order to help owners maintain their properties, they are able to delay paying some taxes. This in itself is a great benefit to property owners, but it can also help reduce your total tax liability.

Let's return to Megan, whose property value has appreciated to $500,000 over her ten-year hold period, and she generates $10,000 per year in cash flow on that property.

The depreciation law states that for residential properties like Megan's, the amount you can depreciate each year is calculated as your property value divided by 27.5. I know, 27.5 is an oddly specific number, but that's the law as of this writing! So, for Megan, she can depreciate $18,181.81. That's right, Megan can write off more than $18,000 of income, even though she profited $10,000 in cash flow. Meaning, not only will she not have to pay tax on that $10,000, but depending on her professional status and ownership structure, she may also be eligible to deduct $8,100 from income she earned from her job or any other income source. This is a very powerful thing!

Note that depreciation isn't the elimination of tax—it's a deferral. When Megan goes to sell her property, she will have to do "depreciation recapture" and pay the tax she owed.

Capital Gains

Most income is taxed as "regular income" according to tax laws. This includes a W-2 or 1099 job, as well as the money earned from flipping houses or wholesaling. Depending on your income level, your regular income is taxed somewhere between 10 percent and 37 percent on a federal level, as of this writing. However, investment income, known as capital gains, is taxed differently by the IRS.

Capital gains are defined roughly as the profit from the sale of a property or an investment and are taxed at either 15 percent or 20 percent, depending on your income (and provided that you own the investment for more than one year). Think about that. If you buy a rental property, not only are you making residual income, but when you sell your property, you'll likely also pay lower taxes on the equity gains than you do from your W-2 job or on that rental property's cash flow.

The growth in value of a property held for a long time can usually be taxed as capital gains, as long as it is held for longer than a year. But note that the cash flow from these properties is taxed as ordinary income. Additionally, note that short-term strategies like flipping are generally taxed as ordinary income, not as capital gains.

1031 Exchange

When you go to sell an investment property, you will likely have to pay 20 percent tax (capital gains) on your profits—that is, unless you use a 1031 exchange. Section 1031 of the IRS tax code states that you can "exchange" a piece of real property for a "like kind" piece of property and defer the tax you would have paid on the sale. This is a very common strategy used by real estate investors to scale their portfolios.

For example, let's say Megan sells her rental property for $500,000, and after she's paid commissions and repaid her lenders, she walks away with a profit of $100,000. If Megan wanted to, she could pay 20 percent capital gains tax ($20,000) and do whatever she wanted with the remaining $80,000. Or she could choose to roll that money into a new property without paying any tax. For example, Megan could use her $100,000 as part, or all, of a down payment on a new property. Note that, although a 1031 allows investors like Megan to purchase more and more valuable properties, the exchange doesn't eliminate your tax liability—it just defers it.

Deferring Taxes

You might be wondering at this point why delaying your taxes is beneficial if you're going to have to pay them down the road anyway. There are several reasons delaying tax payments can help grow your portfolio.

1. **Compounding:** As we discussed in the previous chapter, the more money you have invested, the more you can compound and earn. If you're able to delay paying taxes, you can keep that money invested and use it to generate more returns. You can see this in the example of Megan above. Because Megan deferred $20,000 of capital gains tax, she was able to buy another income-producing property. If she had paid the tax, she would have had $20,000 less capital compounding in her portfolio.
2. **Inflation:** Over time, the value of money goes down. So, if you can hold off on paying taxes, then you wind up paying your taxes in devalued dollars. You still pay the same amount in nominal dollars (not inflation adjusted), but less in real dollars (inflation adjusted). This means you pay less taxes in terms of actual spending power.
3. **Tax Rate:** Depending on your income level and tax policy, you may be able to get a lower effective tax rate by deferring your taxes.
4. **Death:** Yes, it's morbid, but if you die with delayed taxes and you structure your portfolio well, your heirs can pay reduced taxes.

Again, I want to stress that this is not a comprehensive list of tax advantages that real estate investors can use. There are also opportunity zones, self-directed IRAs, benefits for your personal residence, and more. To fully understand the tax benefits of real estate investing, consult a knowledgeable CPA.

That said, not all real estate tactics offer tax advantages, as we'll discuss in Part 3. But if limiting your tax burden is a priority for you, you'll want to focus on the tactics that offer the best tax advantages when we reach that part of the book.

PUTTING IT ALL TOGETHER

Each profit driver is powerful on its own, but putting them all together can hit it out of the park. Let's return to Megan's situation and see what it looks like when she puts it all together using a standard rental property as an example.

For this, we'll use a slightly more sophisticated scenario. Megan purchases a $300,000 home, putting 25 percent down ($75,000) at a 6 percent interest rate. She needs $5,000 for closing costs and $5,000 in cash reserves, bringing her invested capital to $85,000. Because Megan sees an opportunity to build equity through value-add, upon purchasing this property she invests another $10,000 in a bathroom renovation. This brings her total capital contribution to $95,000, and her property value to $340,000.

In this example (which is a relatively common type of deal), Megan is building residual income in several ways. She earns $6,650 per year ($554.17 per month) in cash flow. Megan will pay ordinary income tax on that cash flow and can then choose if she wants to use it to support her lifestyle or reinvest it back into her portfolio.

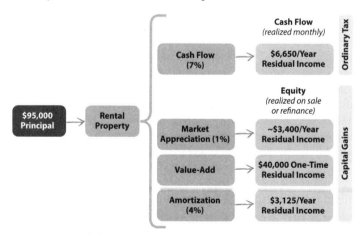

At the same time, Megan will build equity from market appreciation, has earned $40,000 in equity through value-add, and earns almost a 4 percent return from amortization. She won't be able to access the equity gained from these returns until she sells or refinances, but when she does access it, she will likely pay capital gains tax—which, for many people, is less expensive than their ordinary income tax.

Note that this is a very rough and oversimplified example. I am using estimations of returns, and this is absolutely not the proper way to analyze an actual deal. The point of the diagram is to show how a very simple rental property investment can build wealth in several ways. I hope you're starting to see how powerful just a single rental property can be for your financial position, but to further prove the point, let's extrapolate out this example over a five-year period.

If Megan holds this deal for five years, she will earn about $33,250 in total cash flow and $72,971 in equity—meaning she will earn over $106,200 on a $95,000 investment, which is over 110 percent ROI in five years. That's fantastic!

- $6,650 per year in cash flow × 5 years = $33,250
- $17,343 in market appreciation (1 percent property value growth per year)
- $40,000 in value-add
- $15,628 in amortization

In addition to these excellent returns, due to the tax advantages of rental property investing, if Megan were to sell after five years, she would get to keep a solid percentage of her profits. She could choose to pay capital gains tax on her $72,971 (roughly $14,594 in taxes), or she could choose to do a 1031 exchange, use her $72,971 to invest in another property, and defer up to 100 percent of her taxes.

As you now see, the combination of cash flow, equity, and tax benefits is extremely powerful in a single property. When these three wealth-creation tools are combined in a balanced real estate portfolio, they are even stronger. A portfolio with these three profit drivers is (at least in my opinion) the absolute best way to build long-term wealth.

PROFIT DRIVERS: **RECAP**

Real estate has the potential for above-average investing returns because it creates wealth in multiple ways: cash flow, market appreciation, value-add, amortization, and tax benefits. I know of no other asset class that offers such varied ways to make money. Stocks, for example, generate returns from market appreciation and a bit of cash flow from dividends, but offer no value-add opportunities or amortization. Bonds offer cash flow and a bit of market appreciation potential, and not much else. Crypto is all market appreciation. With real estate, you can earn multiple forms of return from a single investment! If you own a rental property with a loan, you'll earn cash flow, market appreciation, amortization, tax benefits, and (in some cases) value-add. That's incredible and gives you a ton of flexibility as you develop your own strategy.

As your portfolio grows, the relative importance of each profit driver will fluctuate. But pretty much every investor will utilize each of these profit drivers in their Portfolio Strategy at some point. You need all three because they work together to maximize your wealth. Growing your equity gives you capital to invest into deals. The more equity you invest, the more cash flow you can generate. Tax benefits help keep and utilize more of your equity to feed back into your portfolio. A well-balanced and high-performing portfolio builds equity, generates cash flow, and offers tax advantages.

Having multiple ways to earn returns isn't only great because it builds wealth—it also helps you mitigate risk. As you'll learn in the next chapter, diversification is one of the keys to managing risk in your portfolio, and real estate offers you diversification within a single investment! For example, if the housing market enters a downturn or correction, and market appreciation is flat or negative for a while, rental property investors still drive profit from cash flow, amortization, and tax benefits. Every real estate investment comes with risk, but this diversity of returns helps mitigate that risk.

Chapter 5
MANAGING RISK

Let's make something clear: Investing comes with risk. Whether you invest in real estate, stocks, bonds, crypto, gold, or anything else, there is a risk of loss or underperformance. Even holding your money in a savings account has some risk! Bank deposits are only insured up to $250,000, and by keeping your money in cash, you also risk losing spending power to inflation. You cannot avoid risk.

Over the years, I've noticed a lot of investor resources downplaying the risks of investing or avoiding the topic altogether. I hate that. Not only is it ethically irresponsible, but it also creates a false understanding of the role risk plays in investing. Failing to talk about risk suggests it's some evil force that dare not be mentioned.

In reality, risk is not your enemy; it's an important variable in your Portfolio Strategy. To be clear, I am not saying you should take on risk just for the sake of it. I'm saying that some level of risk is necessary to earn the rewards you seek. The job of a good investor is to craft a portfolio that properly balances risk and reward in a way that serves the investor's financial goals. To do this, you need to fully understand what risks exist in real estate investing and how those risks can be mitigated.

So, let's bring risk out of the shadows and embrace it for what it is—a critical component of investing that needs to be understood, discussed, mitigated, and used strategically to generate strong returns. In this chapter we'll review the basic trade-offs between risk and reward, and how real estate investors should think about managing risk at a high level. Of course, each of us will have a different approach to managing risk based on comfort level, which we will explore in detail in Chapter 13 when you construct a detailed, personalized Risk Profile.

RISK VS. REWARD

Every investment contains the potential for both risk (the possibility of loss) and reward (the possibility of generating a positive return). The unique makeup of risk and reward for a given investment is called the investment's **Risk/Reward Profile**. As investors, we want to find investments that offer the Risk/Reward Profiles that fit our personal risk preferences and overall Portfolio Strategy.

The amount of risk contained within each type of investment varies considerably from one investment to the next. The same is true of reward. There is a vast spectrum of Risk/Reward Profiles that goes from very low risk and modest reward to super-high risk with the potential for massive reward. Generally speaking, investments that offer the best returns carry the most risk. The inverse is also true—generally speaking, the safest investments offer the lowest return.

RISK VS. REWARD

On one end of the risk/reward spectrum are investments commonly referred to as "risk-free assets." These are investments like a certificate of deposit (CD) or U.S. Treasury bills. When you invest in a Treasury, you are essentially loaning the U.S. government money for a fixed period, which is paid back with interest over time. No investment is truly "risk free," but because the U.S. has the largest economy in the world, and to date has never defaulted on its debts, this is largely considered the safest investment there is.

As of this writing, the yield on a ten-year U.S. Treasury bill is about 4 percent per year. So, as an investor, you can earn 4 percent in annual returns by lending your money to the U.S. government. True, 4 percent isn't a huge return, but it's in high demand because it's so low risk.

Risk-free assets are important because they set the baseline expectations for investors. As you build your portfolio and consider new investments, you should be thinking about how the Risk/Reward Profile of the prospective investment compares to what you could be generating from a risk-free asset. For example, would you accept a high-risk investment, like an obscure cryptocurrency we'll call Risk Coin, that returns 6 percent? It's better than the 4 percent of the risk-free asset, but is it a good investment? Are you willing to go from no risk to high risk for a 2 percent increase in your return? Remember, you can get 4 percent for almost no risk, and since Risk Coin offers 6 percent, your decision hinges on whether to take on a lot of extra risk for an improved return of 2 percent.

The measurement I just used above, where I subtracted the return of a risk-free asset from the potential return of a deal, is called the investment's "risk premium." As you can see, it's super easy to calculate. All you do is take the potential return of an investment (6 percent in our example above) and subtract the current rate of return of a risk-free asset (4 percent in our example). The risk premium of Risk Coin is 2 percent.

Back to the question I posed earlier: Would you invest in Risk Coin? Would you go from risk free to high risk for a 2 percent risk premium? I wouldn't. The risk premium is just not high enough for the increased level of risk. A risky investment must provide the potential for much larger returns to compensate an investor for the much larger risk of losing some or all of their principal. As we've learned, you do want to maximize your rate of return, but there are probably lower-risk ways to get a 6 percent return than Risk Coin.

Think of a risk premium as hazard pay for investors. When a company is looking for an employee to take on a dangerous assignment, like handling toxic chemicals, they will often offer hazard pay—a financial incentive for taking on larger risk. Investing works in a similar way: Investors will only invest in risky projects if the potential for return is proportionally higher. With Risk Coin, the increase in risk is not proportionate to the increase in reward.

Obviously, Risk Coin is an extreme example. What about a medium-risk investment, like rental property investing, that returns 11 percent? Now that is pretty interesting. Generating an 11 percent return will yield exponentially better results than a Treasury bill over the long run and rental property investing is low to moderate risk.

What about a high-risk investment, like house flipping, that returns 22 percent? That could very well be worth it too! You may lose money on a couple of deals throughout your career, but if you generate returns above 20 percent the rest of the time, you'll probably become quite wealthy.

Each investor has a different tolerance and capacity for risk, so there isn't a right or wrong amount of risk to take. However, if you're going to take on risk, you have to make sure it's worth it. The risk premium has to be appropriate to justify the risk.

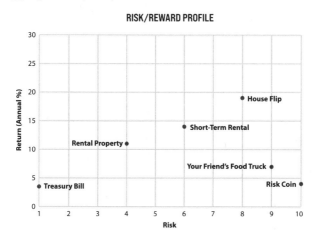

RISK/REWARD PROFILE

When you look at this chart, you can see I've plotted three different real estate investing strategies along a somewhat linear path. You can invest in a rental property and get solid returns at relatively low risk. You could invest in a short-term rental and get better returns, with moderate risk. Or you could seek excellent returns for relatively high risk by flipping houses. All of these strategies are good options because they offer proportionally increased returns alongside the increased risk.

The other examples on the chart, Risk Coin and Your Friend's Food Truck, are not good investments. I've got nothing against food trucks (I love eating from them), but they're notoriously prone to failure, and the upside just isn't very good. In my opinion, that's a lot of risk for minimal return. I'm not a huge cryptocurrency investor (I have some very small investments in the most common assets), but if you're going to invest in crypto, it had better have a great risk premium, because risk in crypto is super high. That may change in the future, but right now it's mostly speculation.

If you're wondering why there are no dots that offer exceptional returns with low risk, it's because investing markets are efficient. This means that most investments will fall into a relatively predictable distribution of Risk/Return Profiles. If you find something offering returns way above average with below-average risk, it's possibly too good to be true. You may encounter a few of these over the course of your investing career, but I would caution against seeking unusually high returns outside a normal distribution. Instead, focus on finding investments that land on the high end of the normal spectrum of risk versus return. Extreme outliers can be a red flag.

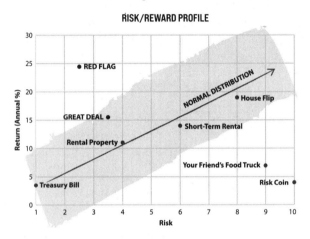

RISK/REWARD PROFILE

Unfortunately, there is no universally accepted measurement of risk. Risk is a measurement of the unknown, and how can you accurately measure something unknown? Not very easily. There are lots of complex methods for calculating "risk-adjusted" returns, particularly for stocks and bonds, but in this book, we're going to use a simple 1–5 scale, with 1 being low risk and 5 being maximum risk. Risk assessment is inherently subjective, so each of us will have to evaluate the risk level of an investment independently. For example, I've never flipped a house. So, for me, it's riskier for me to do my first flip than it is for someone who has done thirty flips to do their next flip.

I'll provide some guidance on risk for each investing strategy later in the book, but it will be inherently subjective because it's based on my personal perception of risk and my personal experience. Ultimately it will be up to you to determine how risky each potential deal you do, and your portfolio, should be.

Hopefully this discussion of risk has made you realize you cannot select investment strategies or investments solely based on the promised return. If you compare two investments, and Property A offers a return of 14 percent and Property B offers a return of 10 percent, you'd probably choose Property A if you had no other information, right? But what if I told you that Property A was built in 1921, is in an undesirable location, and has a history of high vacancy? Meanwhile, Property B was built in 2012, is in a high-demand location, and has minimal vacancies and high rates of lease renewals. Which one would you choose now?

There's no right answer; it's subjective. The point is you cannot evaluate potential returns without also evaluating the associated risks. You shouldn't *just* be looking for deals with the highest possible return. You should be looking for deals with the highest "risk-adjusted" returns. You need to consider both sides.

Which raises the question: What are the risks of real estate investing you should be considering?

RISK CATEGORIES

Not all risk is the same. There are actually three types of financial risk when it comes to investing.

1. **Principal loss**
2. **Underperformance**
3. **Inflation risk**

1. Principal Loss

As you know, principal is the money you invest into a deal. It's your starting amount. The premise of investing is that you contribute principal to an investment and hope to earn a return on your principal for the lifetime of the investment. Typically this happens, but returns are not guaranteed and you can lose some or all of your principal. Say you had $10,000 in principal and you invest it into the stock market, which averages about 8 percent annual returns. If you invest right before a stock market downturn, you could be left with less than $10,000 after the first year, or even five years down the line. If you sell your stock at less than $10,000, that is principal loss, and it is generally considered the most serious risk in investing. No one invests to wind up with less money than they started with.

Principal loss has degrees of severity, with the most extreme being a "total loss," where the entirety of your principal is lost. In the example above, that would mean after investing $10,000, you walk away with $0.

With most real estate investments, the risk of total loss is very low, but theoretically feasible.

On the other end of the spectrum are assets with almost no risk of principal loss. While no investment is completely immune, holding your money in cash or, as discussed earlier, investing in U.S. government bonds offers low risk of principal loss.

2. Underperformance

The potential that an investment generates returns lower than you are expecting, and lower than alternative investments you could have made, is the risk of underperformance.

Consider a short-term rental. If you buy a short-term rental with solid fundamentals, you should expect an annualized ROI of over 12 percent. But short-term rentals come with risks like market fluctuation, property damage, and lack of demand, to name a few. If something goes wrong or you have an unlucky year or two, it's possible that your short-term rental generates just a 2 percent total return, even while accounting for all profit drivers. Meanwhile, a bond would have yielded you 4 percent, or the stock market could have delivered 8 percent. With a 2 percent return, you're not losing principal, but you are underperforming.

The risk of underperformance is not generally as serious as principal loss because you're still making some money—just less than you could have. But, as an investor, you have to be thinking about the opportunity costs of your investments. If your short-term rental only returns 2 percent, but you could have earned 4 percent with a Treasury bill or 9 percent with a long-term rental property, your portfolio is underperforming. You could think of underperformance risk as "opportunity risk" too. Basically, you could have done something more profitable with your time and money. All real estate deals (as well as every investment in the world) have the risk of underperformance.

3. Inflation Risk

Inflation generally increases between 2 percent and 3 percent per year. We've obviously seen much larger numbers in recent years, but 2–3 percent is the historic average. Inflation has many definitions, but the one we'll use here is the devaluation of currency. In other words, inflation reduces the spending power of your money. If you have $100 in a checking account earning no interest, and inflation is at 3 percent, you're losing money. Sure, your bank account will still say $100 a year from now, but it will only be able to buy $97 worth of stuff. Put another way, in a normal year, you need to earn 2–3 percent returns on your money just to break even with inflation.

Inflation is risk! Don't think so? Consider the last few years, when inflation has been anywhere from about 2 percent all the way up to 9 percent, depending on the month. If you put $10,000 in a checking account in 2020, the value of that money would only be about $8,684 just two years later. By holding your money in cash, your bank account still says $10,000, but you lose over $1,300 in spending power. That is a financial risk.

While most investments carry inflation risk, tangible assets (like real estate) usually keep pace with inflation relatively well. There is still inflation risk in real estate, but it tends to be lower than in other types of investments—particularly bonds.

In terms of your real estate portfolio, inflation risk typically comes from holding too much cash (rather than investing it). I would never suggest you buy properties that don't align with your Portfolio Strategy just because you're sitting on cash, but cash management is important. Holding cash, especially during inflationary periods, comes with risk to your spending power.

SPECIFIC RISKS TO REAL ESTATE INVESTORS

Principal loss, underperformance, and inflation risk are broad categories of risk that every investor faces, regardless of asset class. In addition to these, there are specific risks that exist for real estate investors that can cause the principal loss and underperformance we just discussed. Although there are many unique risks for real estate investors, they are all manageable. If you understand the risks you're taking, you can proactively mitigate them.

Market Risk

When most people consider the risks of real estate investing, they primarily think of market risk. "Market risk" refers to broad macro-economic or local market-based forces causing the value of your investments to fluctuate. This is also known as "market volatility." For example, rising interest rates tend to put downward pressure on housing prices, increasing your market risk. We'll talk more about macroeconomics in Part 4, but for now, just know that although property values have always trended upward over time, the housing market is cyclical—meaning that over the long run housing prices go up, but there is short-term volatility in housing prices that can impact the performance of your investments. Market risk is just part of the game.

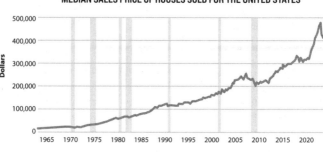

MEDIAN SALES PRICE OF HOUSES SOLD FOR THE UNITED STATES

Shaded areas indicate U.S. recessions   Source: fred.stlouisfed.org

Property Risk

There's a common saying in real estate that "you make money when you buy." Of course, you actually spend money when you buy, not make it, but the point is that you have to buy the right property to earn a good return. Properties come in all shapes, sizes, conditions, and locations. As an investor, you have to pick the right ones for your strategy. If you buy a property that doesn't align with your intended strategy, there is risk. Some examples of property risk are buying a house with a bad layout that fails to attract tenants, investing in a disaster-prone area, or buying in a location where regulations inhibit your operating plan, just to name a few.

Property risk varies depending on the tactics you use. For example, a red flag for a short-term rental may not be an issue for a traditional long-term rental property. The best way to mitigate property risk is to have a clear Buy Box that is aligned with your strategy—an exercise we'll complete in Part 4.

Operational Risk

Real estate investments are businesses, and just like any business, they need to be operated well. Depending on your chosen tactics, operations can include everything from hiring and managing employees to working with guests and tenants, keeping schedules, tracking finances, buying materials, sourcing deals, and everything else! If this sounds like a broad category of risk, that's because it is. "Operations" is a catchall term for "running your business," and if you don't run your business well, your returns can suffer.

You may "make money when you buy," but I think that's only half true. I'd argue that you create the *potential* to make money when you buy, but you can only *realize* that potential by operating your investment well. Poor operations can contribute to principal loss and are a common source of underperformance.

This book does not go into the operational details of every single tactic. But once you're done with this book and have selected the tactics you intend to employ, I recommend you find additional resources that cover the specifics of your plan (BiggerPockets books, forums, and resources are the best places to start). If you're going to flip houses, then read a book or listen to podcasts on flipping houses. If you're going to operate a short-term rental, then learn everything you can about how to manage that business well. Don't overlook operations!

Income Risk

Deals that are residual in nature and rely on rent (like long-term rentals, short-term rentals, commercial, lending, etc.) face risk when income is disrupted. This can happen from vacancy, nonpayment of rent , or a host of other unfortunate interruptions to income. Although tenants sign contracts, and the vast majority of them pay on time as agreed, rental income is not always a sure thing. There is a risk that, for one reason or another, your income may fall short of your expectations on a given month or year.

There are many good ways to mitigate income risk depending on the specifics of your deals. Generally speaking, you should focus on finding great tenants and maintaining appropriate cash reserves to ensure you can cover any unforeseen income shortfalls. The last thing you want is to have to sell or change your operating plan because you lack the cash reserves to weather short-term income disruptions.

Labor Risk

Hiring the wrong team is a common risk that real estate investors face. As an investor, you are inevitably going to delegate some of the work you need done. Working with a bad contractor, property manager, or anyone else you hire can add significant risk to your deals. You need to surround yourself with experienced, honest, and accountable professionals.

Every single experienced investor I know has fallen victim to labor risk at one point or another—it's just part of the journey. Get a bunch of experienced investors in a room, and I guarantee the conversation will eventually turn to complaining about contractors who have not performed. In some sense, it's just part of the business—but it's something you should obviously try to mitigate as much as possible. Seek recommendations from your network, call references, and develop a strong working relationship with the people you hire.

Material Risk

Value-add investing strategies (basically anything that requires renovation or construction, like flipping, BRRRR, development, etc.) require materials. This can include everything from lumber to roofing shingles, appliances, paint, and everything in between. If the cost of these materials goes up, or these materials become unavailable due to supply chain issues, your returns face risk. This risk became particularly acute during the COVID-19 pandemic. Supply chains were disrupted, creating surges in lumber prices, shortages of everything from appliances to garage doors, and price inflation across the board. But material risk exists even during more "normal" times.

The best way to mitigate material risk is to check with your suppliers, or even purchase your supplies before starting any major value-add project so you know your costs and availability up front. Delaying a project due to material costs/shortages is no fun, but finding out your materials are unavailable or increasingly expensive *during* a value-add project is much worse.

Regulatory Risk

Real estate is subject to regulation from the government, usually on the state or local level. This can occur in the form of zoning changes, rent control, restrictions on short-term rentals or accessory dwelling units (ADUs), or anything else a local government passes into law. As an investor, the prospect of changing regulation carries risk. For example, if you buy a property intending to use it as a short-term rental and then the city bans short-term rentals, your business will be in trouble!

While there's no way to truly control regulatory risk, you can mitigate it. The best way to mitigate regulatory risk is to understand it and stay ahead of it. Educate yourself on local laws and make sure they are aligned with your plans. Stay informed, go to local government meetings, and understand what's happening in your area. This will help you plan and adjust your strategy.

The second way to mitigate regulatory risk is to purchase properties that have strategic flexibility. For example, when buying a short-term rental, find a property that works both as an STR and a traditional rental.

This way, the property can still earn a great return even if a short-term rental ban is enacted.

Partner Risk

Many investors choose to take on partners over the course of their investing career. This can be a capital partner who contributes money, or an operating partner who runs the business with you. One of the beautiful things about a partnership is that it can be structured however works best. But taking on partners carries risk. If partners argue, disagree on strategy, or don't have a good framework for resolving differences, your investments can suffer. A partnership gone awry is a surefire way to add risk to your deals.

Mitigating partner risk is simple on paper, but harder in practice. The first rule is to only partner with people you really know and trust—specifically, people you trust to do the work the partnership requires. You may know and trust your uncle, but can you trust your uncle to keep detailed financial records, develop great relationships with your tenants, or whatever else is expected of him in the partnership? Don't just pick people you know as partners. Pick people you know can do the job.

Second, set very clear expectations about who does what and how the partnership will work. Create an operating agreement and set up frameworks for resolving conflict *before* you partner up. It might seem overly formal, but trust me, it's not. Write everything down on paper and hash out the worst-case scenarios (i.e., what happens if someone is forced to sell, goes bankrupt, or dies?) with any potential partner before you go into business together.

Debt Risk

As we'll discuss in coming chapters, most real estate transactions are financed, at least in part, by debt (taking out a loan). Although debt can help you scale your portfolio quickly and can even help you boost your returns through positive leverage, all debt comes with risk.

When you take out a loan, you are obliged to pay the bank back, regardless of the performance of your deal. This can compound other risks like market risk and income risk. Even if the value of your asset declines or you have an income shortfall, you still need to make your debt payments. This can put you at risk of default, foreclosure, and, in a worst-case scenario, bankruptcy.

Certain types of loans carry more risk than others. Adjustable-rate loans, for example, are particularly risky during rising-interest-rate environments. If you have an adjustable rate and rates go up, your monthly payments will go up too, decreasing your cash flow and increasing your chances of loss or default. Partially amortized (balloon) loans require a large lump sum payment, typically seven to ten years after the loan origination, and if the investor can't pay the lump sum or refinance the property, they risk default and foreclosure as well.

The best way to mitigate debt risk is to only use debt you're absolutely sure you can repay using the income from your deals. Cutting it close on your debt service is a big risk.

Liquidity Risk

The "liquidity" of an investment is a subjective evaluation of how easily an investment or other type of asset can be converted into cash. Investments like stocks and bonds are relatively liquid because they operate on massive public exchanges where there tend to be ample buying and selling opportunities. If you want to sell a stock, you can usually do it within one or two business days. Real estate, on the other hand, is generally considered an "illiquid" investment. Even during a hot market, real estate sells on a time frame of weeks, at best. During cooler markets, it can easily take months, or even years, for a house to sell and the investor to get their money out.

Investing in assets with relatively low liquidity comes with risk. When your money is tied up, it can be difficult to reallocate your capital to adjust to changing conditions. If the macroeconomic environment changes, you can't "get out quick," meaning you may be forced to hold on to your real estate investments longer than you would choose to. Alternatively, if your personal circumstances change, you may not be able to rely on real estate investments to provide cash in a pinch. For example, if you need money next week to cover an emergency expense, it's unlikely you'll be able to get that from your real estate portfolio.

As a real estate investor, this means you need to carefully manage your capital and your liquidity on a portfolio scale. You need to maintain significant reserves in highly liquid assets (like cash) to compensate for the fact that so much of your money is tied up in your real estate portfolio and cannot be relied on for short-term liquidity. We'll talk about liquidity more in Chapter 0.

Forced Selling

One situation every real estate investor wants to avoid is being forced to sell an asset at an inopportune time. Of course, you want to be able to sell your properties at a time that is profitable and beneficial to you. Being forced to sell when you don't want to usually leads to lower profits, or even principal loss. Imagine being forced to sell at the bottom of a market cycle rather than waiting for the market to rebound. It's not ideal.

Forced selling can happen due to any one of the risks we've outlined: a shortage of income, unforeseen expenses, labor problems, partnership problems, or almost anything else. Most of those risks can be mitigated and handled as long as they don't reach the point of forced selling. You can work to repair a troubled partnership, help a tenant get on a payment plan, or replace a bad contractor. Most risks are annoyances, some can be expensive and stressful, but they can usually be overcome. Once you sell an asset, there's no way to rescue a deal. Whatever challenges you encounter as an investor, selling at an inopportune time should be a very last resort. Your portfolio will benefit greatly if you can dictate the timing of asset sales.

TIPS FOR MITIGATING RISK

I've provided some quick tips above for how to mitigate risk, but there are some big-picture mitigation strategies that you need to consider as you formulate your Portfolio Strategy. Below are some of the most common risk-mitigation techniques you can use.

Mitigate Risk with Time

The longer you hold onto an asset, the less risky it becomes. It may sound overly simplistic, but time is perhaps the best way to mitigate risk—especially market risk.

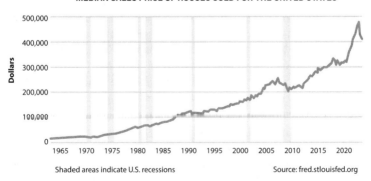

MEDIAN SALES PRICE OF HOUSES SOLD FOR THE UNITED STATES

Shaded areas indicate U.S. recessions   Source: fred.stlouisfed.org

Property values fluctuate in the short term, but over the long run they have always gone up. Time is your friend. By holding onto an asset, you increase the probability that the value of your asset will be above your purchase price by the time of sale. Looking at the chart above, you can see that if you buy real estate and hold onto it, the value of that real estate will increase.

Let's look at an extreme example to prove this point. If you purchased a property in Q1 of 2007, it was pretty much the worst possible time to buy a property in American history (or at least as far back as I have reliable data for). According to the U.S. Department of Housing and Urban Development (HUD), the median home price back then was $257,500, but fell over the course of two years before bottoming out in Q1 of 2009 at $208,400. If you bought the median-price home and sold it at the bottom, your property would have declined in value by roughly 19 percent. Ouch.

However, if instead of selling, you used time to your advantage and waited it out to Q1 2013, you would have broken even in nominal (not inflation-adjusted) terms. If you just kept holding on until Q1 of 2022, your property would have appreciated 76 percent. The longer you can hold onto a property, the less risky it is. As an investor, you should focus your risk mitigation around preventing forced selling because it gives you the benefit of time.

To help demonstrate this point, I did an analysis to find out exactly how much time helps real estate investors. What I found is that over the last fifty years, when factoring in inflation, if you hold onto a rental property for one year, you have about a 19 percent chance of principal loss (when factoring in market appreciation, cash flow, and amortization). After five years, the probability drops to 15 percent, and by Year 11, it drops to zero percent. Said another way, if you bought and operated a rental property in the United States at any point in the last fifty years (including at the peak of the 2000s housing bubble) and held onto it for eleven years or longer, there would be a near-zero percent chance you would lose money, even when adjusting for inflation.

I did the same calculation for the stock market (using the S&P 500—the gray line), and you would have to hold onto your stocks for twenty years in order to get to a zero percent probability of loss. While the stock market takes longer than real estate (hooray, real estate!) to reach near-zero risk, the point here remains the same: If you hold onto assets that appreciate over a long time horizon, your probability of loss is drastically reduced.

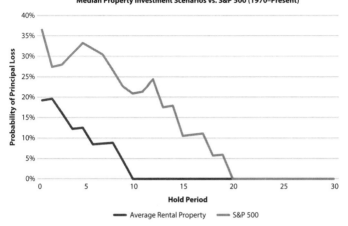

PROBABILITY OF INVESTING LOSS BY HOLD PERIOD

Median Property Investment Scenarios vs. S&P 500 (1970–Present)

Time really heals all, and this is one reason flipping houses is so risky. For a flip to be successful, it needs to be purchased, renovated, and resold as quickly as possible. But what happens if property values in your area drop 6 percent during your six-month hold period? You might be forced to sell at a lower-than-expected valuation, leading to underperformance or principal loss. When your hold period is short, you are vulnerable to short-term market volatility.

Holding onto a property allows you to wait out any short-term fluctuations in the market. If you can bide your time and pick the optimal conditions in which to sell your property, you could see some underperformance, but you greatly reduce your risk of principal loss.

Mitigate Risk with Cash Flow

Investments that cash-flow are less risky than ones that don't.

First, cash flow allows you to bide your time! As we just discussed, time is your friend when it comes to property values. As we learned earlier, the longer we allow our portfolio to compound returns, the stronger it gets. If your properties are cash-flowing, it removes much of the pressure to sell an asset, allows you to compound your returns, and lets you decide the optimal time to sell.

Think back to the example above of buying at the height of the market in 2007. Remember, if you were forced to sell in 2009, you would have lost 19 percent on your property value. If you waited until 2013, you would have broken even, and any time after 2013 you would have earned a profit. If this property were cash-flow positive, you could have simply waited for your property value to recover, collecting rent checks all the while and earning a return. This is just one reason cash flow is so powerful—it allows you to comfortably hold on to your properties as long as you need or want to. Even if the value of a cash-flowing rental property goes down on paper, you're still building wealth through cash flow, amortization, and tax benefits. Because no one is actually losing any money out of their pocket during these years, this makes the decline in property value a "paper loss." The "loss" in property value is theoretical unless you sell.

However, if the property is not producing cash flow, it could be difficult for the investor to hold on long enough to see the property value recover. The investor would have been coming out of pocket to cover expenses during a difficult economic period, which makes it more likely the investor would have had to cut bait and sell at a loss.

Second, cash flow adds a way to make money beyond just the value of the home. To build on the research I showed before, I tested the probability of principal loss for a rental property by the property's cash-on-cash return (CoCR, which is annual cash flow divided by the principal investment).

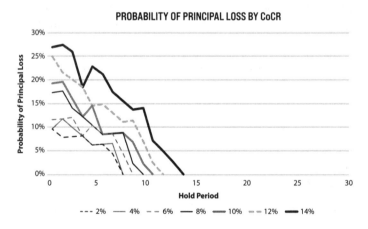

PROBABILITY OF PRINCIPAL LOSS BY CoCR

This is probably obvious, but the higher the cash on cash return, the lower the probability of principal loss. If you have a modest 2 percent CoCR, you need to hold a property for fourteen years to get your probability of principal loss to zero. However, if you have a CoCR of 8 percent, it takes just ten years.

This research can be extrapolated out to a portfolio level as well. The higher your portfolio cash flow and CoCR, the less risk you have overall. Cash flow allows you to earn a return even during periods of down markets and, as I mentioned, it lets you pick the optimal time to sell a property.

Third, we just talked about how there is income risk inherent in any type of long-term investing strategy. The higher your cash flow, the better you'll be able to absorb any short-term disruptions to your income and avoid forced selling.

Mitigate Risk with Cash Reserves

Don't invest 100 percent of your cash! I know I said earlier that if you want to maximize your wealth building you should invest as much principal as possible, but your reserves are not principal! Your portfolio is a business, and as a business, you need to keep some money stowed away for emergencies or large expenses. Depending on the condition of your property, and the strategy, you'll generally want to keep somewhere between three and six months of operating capital in reserve.

Owning real estate comes with some large expenses, like roofs, boilers, renovations, vacancies, and, unfortunately, periodic evictions. You need to be prepared to cover those costs when they inevitably arrive. Failure to maintain reserves means you could be forced to sell a property at a suboptimal time or take on unneeded or high-interest debt. Maintaining appropriate cash reserves will help you mitigate income risk, labor risk, material risk, and forced selling.

Mitigate Risk with Strategic Flexibility

When you buy an individual property, you should have a plan in mind for how you'll operate it. You don't want to buy a single-family home and then, once you own it, decide if it will work best as a rental, short-term rental, or a flip. When you make an offer on a property, you should have an operating plan.

Unfortunately, not everything goes according to plan. As Morgan Housel, author of *The Psychology of Money*, puts it, "the most important part of a plan is to plan for the plan to not go according to plan." You need a plan, otherwise you'll be lost. But you also need to be able to adapt in case your plan goes awry, because life happens.

In real estate investing, my preferred way to mitigate the risk from plans going off track is what I call "strategic flexibility." Strategic flexibility is the idea that you should buy properties that can work with several different operating plans. If you buy a property that works equally well as a long-term rental or a short-term rental or a house hack, it offers you flexibility. If one plan stops working, you can pivot to one of the other options you've lined up.

You may have heard the advice to "have different exit strategies," which basically means that your properties should ideally appeal to many different buyers. Having multiple exit strategies is an important part of strategic flexibility, but to me, strategic flexibility is about more than just whom you sell to. If you're a buy and hold investor, you want to have flexibility while you're holding the property, not just when you go to sell. Strategic flexibility helps you mitigate income risk, regulatory risk, and forced selling.

Mitigate Risk with Experience

This isn't exactly a groundbreaking concept, but experience reduces risk. This is true for you as an individual investor and for the team you have around you.

When you first get started, there is more inherent risk. This isn't a real estate investing thing, it's just a life thing. If you're new to something, it's less likely to go perfectly. The first time you go skiing, you're probably going to fall a lot and the risk of breaking your arm is decently high. But over time, you get better, fall less, and your risk of a broken arm goes down.

Luckily in real estate investing, you don't need to have all the experience yourself (and there is little risk of breaking a limb!). Instead, you can surround yourself with people who can help you succeed on your very first deal. There are loads of experienced people who can help you with deal analysis, managing tenants, maintenance, etc. Building out your team to complement your skills can be time-consuming and can eat into your profit a bit, but most of the time it's worth it—especially when you're new. Sacrificing a little profit to avoid big losses is a good trade in my book!

Using experience to mitigate risk isn't just for newbies, though. As you progress through your investing career, you're inevitably going to have to take on new challenges you're unfamiliar with. For example, maybe you spend the first few years of your investing career focusing on short-term rentals and consider yourself an expert in that tactic. But then STR markets dry up or you want to diversify, and you decide to get into multifamily syndications. You may know everything there is to know about short-term rentals, but you are a newbie when it comes to multifamily. This adds risk because you lack the experience in your new tactic.

I'm not saying you should avoid branching out into new types of investments. On the contrary, diversification helps you build a balanced portfolio, and it's fun! Most investors try out new things. Just don't go it alone. Be humble, admit what you don't know, and enlist the help of someone more experienced than you to help offset your risk. Experience helps you mitigate every type of risk.

Mitigate Risk with Diversification

While we often talk about "the economy" like it's one thing, it's not. Instead, the economy is really an aggregate of many individual industries, and not all industries perform at the same level at the same time. For example, when the overall economy is booming, certain industries like luxury goods and travel do very well. During economic downturns, other industries, like low-cost retail and healthcare, do the best, while the travel industry suffers.

As an investor, exposing yourself to multiple types of investments, commonly known as "diversification," will help reduce risk in your portfolio. If you spread your investments out across different sectors of the economy, it's less likely you'll suffer a catastrophic loss due to a major downturn in a single industry.

Diversification is key, no matter where you invest: stocks, real estate, crypto, precious metals, etc. Although I am primarily a real estate investor, I do keep about 30 percent of my net worth in other asset classes. I genuinely believe that real estate offers the best returns of any asset class, but I don't want to have all my eggs in one basket. Even though investing outside of real estate might reduce my overall returns, it aligns better with my risk preferences. I do know plenty of real estate investors who invest 100 percent of their capital into real estate, though.

Within real estate itself, there are plenty of ways to diversify your portfolio. Even if you intend to invest 100 percent of your capital into your real estate portfolio, you'll still want to consider diversifying within real estate. The key to good diversification is to spread your investments in a way that provides ample opportunity for growth while reducing overall risk.

Here are a few of the most common ways to diversify your real estate portfolio.

- **Deal Type Diversification:** Investing solely in short-term rentals, for example, carries high regulatory, labor, and cost risks, and is vulnerable to market cycles. If you invest some of your portfolio into short-term rentals while also investing in note funds, buy and hold rentals, or commercial properties, you will have less overall risk on the balance.

- **Asset Class Diversification:** Within a single strategy, you can also diversify your portfolio with different types of properties. For example, if you are a buy and hold investor, you can buy single-family residences, small multifamily properties, and condos to diversify your holdings. You can also diversify across property classes by buying Class A, Class B, and Class C properties (we'll discuss this more later). This allows you take advantage of a boom or a bust in any one property type.
- **Geographic Diversification:** Real estate markets behave differently across the country. Just like the economy is really just a collection of individual industries, the "housing market" is really just an aggregation of many regional housing markets. Investing in multiple regions is an excellent way to diversify.

But remember: *everything in moderation.* After reading the above section, you wouldn't be blamed for thinking you should try to maximize diversification at all costs. But remember that experience is also key to mitigating risk. Diversifying to the point where you're taking on investments that you (and your team) have little or no experience with can outweigh any diversification advantage.

I recommend diversifying patiently. I wouldn't change up my strategy, asset class, and geography from deal to deal. Instead, I'd try to hold two of those variables constant and just change one. For example, if my first deal is a single-family rental property in Nashville, Tennessee, I wouldn't make my second deal a short-term rental duplex in Boise, Idaho. Instead, I'd pick one thing to change. I'd either do a single-family rental in Boise or a short-term rental in Nashville to ensure I leverage some of my experience while I diversify.

MANAGING RISK: RECAP

Risk is a fact of life, not your enemy. Taking on an appropriate level of risk is what gives you the potential to earn investing returns. However, risks that you don't understand, or that you don't plan for, can be disastrous. The key to managing risk as a real estate investor is not to ignore or dismiss the existence of risk—it's to embrace and plan for it!

As you build out and execute your Portfolio Strategy, think carefully about the risks that exist in each and every deal you do. In Chapter 13, you will assess your own risk tolerance and risk capacity, which will help you understand what deals you should pursue. While it's tempting to want to take big swings on high-risk/high-reward deals, you have to be able to sleep at night. High-risk deals are not for everyone. By understanding what risks are acceptable to you, and what risks you're taking, you can determine if the potential reward of any given deal is worth the risk. I cannot stress this enough: You need to be selecting investments and building your portfolio while considering the risk-adjusted return.

No matter how much mitigation you do, the reality is that you still might incur principal loss during your career, and I can guarantee you will experience underperformance—because every single investor does. It's just part of the game. But let me also tell you from experience that underperforming, or even taking a principal loss, is a lot easier to stomach if you went into the deal understanding the risks and having done your best to avoid them in the first place. What you really want to avoid is experiencing principal loss or underperformance due to ignorance or blind optimism.

Note that not every deal you pursue has to perfectly meet your risk preferences, as long as your overall portfolio is aligned. The goal should be for your portfolio as a whole to be aligned with your risk profile. For example, I consider my personal risk tolerances to be moderate. However, I don't only pursue moderate-risk deals. I pursue low-risk deals, medium-risk deals, and high-risk deals. I just make sure that, on the whole, the average risk across my deals is moderate.

Helping investors get over their fear of risk is something I am really passionate about. I hope this chapter has helped you understand the importance of risk in investing and have a better relationship with risk. Don't fear risk! Understand it, account for it in your deal designs, and mitigate it as best you can.

Chapter 6
FUNDING YOUR PORTFOLIO

Buying properties, building a strong portfolio, and taking advantage of the many profit drivers of real estate investing is exciting, but also expensive! As of this writing, the median home price in the United States is about $390,000—and that's just for a single-family home. If you're looking to buy a multifamily or commercial building, the price can be many times that, costing many millions of dollars. Even if you're in a strong financial position, it can be hard to buy properties and scale just using your personal capital. Luckily, there are many options that real estate investors can use to help them pay for their deals and support long-term portfolio growth.

How you pay for an individual real estate deal is known as "financing." If you ever hear someone talk about "financing strategies" or "creative financing" they are simply talking about how they plan to pay for their deal. There are literally dozens (if not hundreds) of different ways to finance real estate deals, which is amazing but can also be daunting. How do you know which financing options best support your Portfolio Strategy? Luckily, they all boil down to one of two options: equity or debt. Yes, there are many different debt structures to consider, and equity options, but at the end of the day they are all either debt or equity.

The word "equity" is used to describe a few different concepts in real estate, so let's just take a minute to clarify how we're going to use it. First of all, "equity" in the context of real estate always refers to "ownership" in one way or another. In the previous chapter, when we talked about how appreciation, value-add, and amortization "build equity," we were essentially saying that these profit drivers increase the value of your ownership stake in a property, thus earning a return. When we talk about using equity to finance a deal—which we are going to call "equity financing" for clarity—we're talking about using your principal to secure an ownership stake in a deal.

"Debt" is just another word for a loan. Using debt to finance a real estate investment means you borrow money from a bank, credit union, or other lender to pay for some portion of your investment. I'm sure you're familiar with mortgages, which are the most common form of debt financing found in real estate, but there are plenty of other types of loans available. Debt allows you to purchase properties that are worth far more than the money you have and, when used correctly, can lead to something called "positive leverage"—one of the most powerful tools available to real estate investors.

As I've said, of all the many ways to finance real estate deals, everything falls into one of these categories: debt or equity. Some deals can be financed entirely with equity (known as an "all-cash deal"), and on some rare occasions there can be deals financed 100 percent using debt, but the vast majority of deals use some combination of debt and equity. As an investor, it is your job to figure out the right combination of debt and equity for your Portfolio Strategy.

For many investors, figuring out how to finance a deal feels like a major hurdle, but in this chapter I will show you that financing can, and should, be seen as a strategic opportunity to maximize the value and performance of your portfolio. We're going to discuss the considerations and trade-offs related to financing your portfolio with equity versus debt and how strategically using debt to achieve positive leverage can supercharge your returns.

FINANCING TRADE-OFFS

As with almost all decisions in this book, there is no "right" or "best" way to finance a real estate deal or portfolio. Instead, there are strategic trade-offs to consider and match to your vision. Equity financing has some big advantages and some drawbacks. The same is true of debt— there are good elements and some negative elements. For each deal you do, and for your portfolio as a whole, it's up to you to structure how you're going to pay for it.

In this chapter we're going to follow an investor named Paul, who is looking to purchase a short-term rental property as the next deal in his portfolio. The property Paul intends to buy costs $300,000 and will require $25,000 in additional costs to get up and running (closing costs, furnishings, and cash reserves). All-in, Paul will need $325,000 to finance his deal.

PURCHASE COST	AMOUNT
Purchase Price	$300,000
Closing Costs	$5,000
Furnishing	$10,000
Reserves	$10,000
Total Costs	$325,000

For the purposes of this example, we're going to make the following assumptions, including that Paul holds the property for five years before selling.

	VALUE	ANNUAL GROWTH RATE
Property Value	$300,000	2%
Rental Income	$32,400	2%
Expenses	$9,600	2%

The simplest option Paul has for financing is to buy the property himself, for cash. I know buying a property entirely in cash is not a realistic option for most people, but it's important that we discuss this option to help everything else make sense. So, let's conveniently imagine Paul just sold his start-up and got a big payout of $500,000. Nice job, Paul.

If Paul wants to buy the property himself with cash, that would also be referred to as financing his deal with 100 percent equity. Remember, equity financing is capital that comes directly from the owner(s) of a deal. All cash = all equity. In this scenario, Paul is personally contributing 100 percent of the capital needed to finance his deal, and therefore retains 100 percent ownership of the deal.

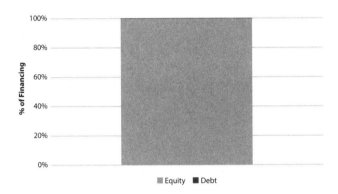

FINANCING BY SOURCE

■ Equity ■ Debt

I've put together an (oversimplified) analysis of what this deal might look like for Paul if he held it for five years. Take note of a few things.

FINANCING: 100% PAUL'S EQUITY

	YEAR 1	YEAR 5
Property Value	$300,000	$324,730
Rental Income	$32,400	$35,071
Operating Expenses	$9,600	$10,391
Debt Service	$0	$0
Cash Flow	$22,800	$24,679
Cumulative Cash Flow	$22,800	$118,652
Cash-on-Cash Return	7.0%	7.6%
Paul's Profit at Sale		$95,651
Paul's ROI		29.4%

1. Paul contributed 100 percent of the equity for this deal and used no outside financing. Meaning, Paul retained 100 percent of the ownership of the property and was able to make 100 percent of the decisions about the deal. And when the property sold five years later, Paul kept 100 percent of the profits.
2. Paul has $0 in debt service. "Debt service" is a term used to describe the expense of paying back a lender, like a mortgage. Because Paul financed this deal with 100 percent of his own equity, he has no debt service, which improves his cash flow immensely.

This structure is simple but relatively uncommon. Who has all that cash sitting around? Instead, most investors turn to one of two options: a) raising equity from other investors or b) taking on debt. If Paul decides he doesn't want to put $325,000 of his own money into this one deal alone, he can explore either of these two options.

Paul's first choice is to bring in other equity investors. Because equity means ownership, this essentially means Paul would be selling ownership in his deal to another investor in exchange for capital. As a simple example, Paul could sell 25 percent of his ownership in a deal to his investor friend Anna in exchange for 25 percent of the needed funds. In other words, Anna would contribute $81,250 ($325,000 × 0.25) to Paul's deal and would receive a 25 percent ownership stake in return. This would still be an all-cash, all-equity deal, but the capital would come from two separate investors.

FINANCING: TWO EQUITY INVESTORS, NO DEBT

At this point the deal is no longer Paul's alone—in terms of property ownership, the deal would be 75 percent Paul's and 25 percent Anna's because they have both contributed equity. Of course, this is just an oversimplified example. In practice, Paul might retain 80 percent of the deal, even if Anna contributes 25 percent of the capital/principal, as his compensation for finding and structuring the deal. Alternatively, Paul could raise money from five different investors, or ten, and the relative ownership can be whatever the equity partners agree upon. One of the great advantages of equity financing is how flexible the structures can be. If it's legal, and two or more investors can agree on it, it can be done.

If Anna and Paul held their deal for five years, it would play out as follows.

FINANCING: 75% PAUL'S EQUITY, 25% ANNA'S EQUITY

	YEAR 1	YEAR 5
Property Value	$300,000	$324,730
Rental Income	$32,400	$35,071
Operating Expenses	$9,600	$10,391
Debt Service	$0	$0
Cash Flow	$22,800	$24,679
Cumulative Cash Flow	$22,800	$118,652
Cash-on-Cash Return	7.0%	7.6%
Total Profit at Sale		$95,651
Pauls Ownership		75%
Paul's Profit at Sale		$71,738
Paul's ROI		29.4%
Anna's Ownership		25%
Anna's Profit at Sale		$23,913
Anna's ROI		29.4%

Again, notice:
1. There is no debt service because the two investors have financed this deal with 100 percent equity, which helps Anna and Paul earn more cash flow.
2. Anna contributed 25 percent of the equity for the deal and receives 25 percent of the profit. Her ROI is equal to Paul's because they have the same ratio of equity to profit.

Although some investors prefer all-equity deals like the examples above, equity financing is most commonly used as just a portion of the financing—as a means of securing debt. As a reminder, debt is just a loan. There are tons of different types of debt available to real estate investors (as we'll discuss in Chapter 18), but they all have the same basic premise. The borrower (who can be an individual investor, a group of investors, or an investing company) borrows some amount of money from a lender (a bank, lending company, or private lender) and agrees to pay that money back over time, with interest. One of the primary benefits of debt financing is that it allows investors to finance their deals without giving away ownership.

No matter the type of debt, most lenders require the owners of a deal to put in some equity in order to have some skin in the game. Lenders don't want to lend you 100 percent of the funds needed to complete a deal, because it's too risky for them. Instead, lenders require that investors bring some equity to each deal, in the form of a down payment. For an owner-occupied home, the required down payment is most commonly 20 percent, but can be as low as 3.5 percent for some loan products. For investment properties, lenders typically require at least 25 percent equity to secure a loan, and for commercial properties the minimum equity can be even higher. The ratio of debt to equity in a deal is known as the loan-to-value ratio (LTV) of a deal. If a lender gives you 70 percent of the funds needed to finance a deal, the LTV would be 70 percent. As we'll discuss later, the LTV of a deal plays a central role in the overall Risk/Reward Profile of a deal.

To explore this idea further, let's imagine that rather than partnering with Anna, Paul wants to use some debt to finance his deal. Paul's lender is requiring he put 25 percent down in exchange for a thirty-year fixed-rate mortgage, with a 6 percent interest rate, for 75 percent of the purchase price of the property. In other words, Paul will need to contribute $75,000 in equity as a down payment (25 percent of $300,000) and $25,000 in equity to cover his closing costs, furnishings, and cash reserves (same as before), and will use debt to finance the rest.

FINANCING BY SOURCE

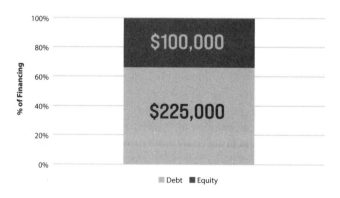

The benefit of this scenario is that Paul can put in $100,000 of equity ($75,000 for his down payment and $25,000 for his closing costs, furnishings, and reserves) to buy a property worth $300,000, and he still retains 100 percent ownership of the deal. The lender in this scenario does have some rights to the property should Paul default on his loan (not pay back his loan as agreed) but does not actually own any of Paul's deal. This is a key distinction between debt financing and equity financing. Debt does not require giving up ownership of the property. As long as Paul pays back his loan as agreed, he owns his deal and gets to retain all of the profits. As investors, we like this!

FINANCING: $100,000 EQUITY, $225,000 DEBT AT 6% INTEREST RATE

	YEAR 1	YEAR 5
Property Value	$300,000	$324,730
Rental Income	$32,400	$35,071
Operating Expenses	$9,600	$10,391
Debt Service	$16,188	$16,188
Cash Flow	$6,612	$8,492
Cumulative Cash Flow	$6,612	$37,713
Cash-on-Cash Return	6.6%	8.5%
Paul's Profit at Sale		$30,038
Paul's ROI		30.0%

This deal requires Paul to bring $100,000 of equity, which is considerably less than either of the equity scenarios we discussed. This is one of the major benefits of using debt to finance a deal. Paul can use less of his own capital to purchase an investment.

But there are trade-offs. Paul now has less cash flow ($37,713 in cumulative five-year cash flow versus $118,652 for the all-equity deal) because he has considerable debt service of $16,188 per year. This is one of the major drawbacks of using debt financing—you need to use some of your income to make debt payments each month.

Despite lower cumulative cash flow, Paul is actually earning cash flow more efficiently when using debt. After five years, his CoCR with debt is 8.5 percent, versus 6.6 percent for the all-equity deal. This happens because even though Paul is earning less total cash flow, he is putting way less capital into the deal. When all is said and done, using debt earns Paul more cash flow for every dollar of principal invested than he does when using all equity. Additionally, Paul's ROI is higher (30 percent) when using debt over the course of five years than when using all equity (29 percent).

As you can see from this example, using debt doesn't just allow Paul to pay less and keep ownership; it significantly changes the return profile of the deal. When using all equity, Paul earns more in absolute terms. This means the total amount of dollars he collects from cash flow and from the sale of the property after five years is higher than when using debt. However, using debt makes Paul's investment more *efficient*, as seen by the higher ROI and CoCR.

By borrowing money, not only did Paul get to use less of his own money, but he was also able to increase his CoCR and his ROI. If you choose to use debt for your purchases, this is what you should be aiming for! Debt isn't just a way to afford a property you couldn't otherwise buy (although that is a great benefit); it should also be used to boost your returns.

This example is a good demonstration of the concept of how debt, when used well, can boost returns. It's important to know that it doesn't always work this way, though. There are also scenarios where using debt hurts your deal's performance. Given the nature of debt, it can be either beneficial or detrimental to a deal.

When you take out debt, you are making a legally binding agreement with the lender to pay back the money you borrow, at a certain interest rate, over a certain amount of time. This agreement stands whether the deal goes well or poorly. The repayment of your loan isn't tied to the performance of the deal. No matter what, you have to pay back the money. When a deal goes well, this can work out very well for the investor. If you have a deal that turns out to be a home run, the bank doesn't get any more than you agreed to, and you keep the upside. Lenders have a right to their regular payments, but they have no claim on the additional profits of a successful deal .

When a deal underperforms, debt can be very detrimental to the investor. Even if the investor makes less than expected (or even loses money) on a deal, the lender is still entitled to repayment. Unfortunately, you don't get out of paying back a loan just because your profits were low or negative. This dynamic can make a bad deal a terrible one.

Because the repayment of a loan is not tied to the performance of the loan, whether or not debt is beneficial depends on equity growth. When property values go up through appreciation or value-add, debt can be extremely powerful. But the inverse is also true. Using debt on a deal where property values decline can make a poor deal even worse. So far in our example of Paul we've only factored in modest market appreciation of 2 percent per year. But what happens if Paul's property value changes more dramatically over the course of his five-year hold period due to market fluctuations?

ROI BY FINANCING STRATEGY

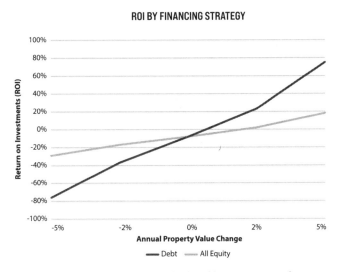

When things go well with Paul's deal and his property value increases over his hold period, his ROI is positively impacted by using debt. In this scenario, if Paul's property value grows by 5 percent a year for five years, his ROI would be 75 percent with debt, but just 18 percent with equity. That's a huge difference! But notice the opposite is also true. If Paul's deal averages a decline in value of 5 percent a year for five years (a very unlikely scenario, but I'm trying to make a point), Paul's ROI would be -76 percent when using debt versus -29 percent when using all equity. In both scenarios Paul loses money, but the use of debt makes Paul's ROI worse than if he used equity (even though he'd lose more in absolute terms using equity). Debt comes with both risk and reward.

Debt can be really beneficial when used on a deal with great appreciation. But don't assume just because property values increase on a deal that debt is always the right answer. There are other scenarios in which, even when the deal goes relatively well, debt reduces returns.

The example we've been discussing where Paul borrows $225,000 at 6 percent interest rate over thirty years is an example of debt enhancing Paul's returns. By using debt in that specific example, Paul has increased his rates of return. But what would happen if the terms of Paul's debt were slightly different? Would he still be adding value to his deal and portfolio by using debt? To explore this question, let's imagine that Paul is investing in a high-interest-rate environment and his lender's best offer is a thirty-year fixed-rate mortgage with a 7.5 percent interest rate (rather than the 6 percent loan we used in the previous example).

FINANCING: $100,000 EQUITY, $225,000 DEBT AT 7.5% INTEREST RATE

	YEAR 1	YEAR 5
Property Value	$300,000	$324,730
Rental Income	$32,400	$35,071
Operating Expenses	$9,600	$10,391
Debt Service	$18,879	$18,879
Cash Flow	$3,921	$5,801
Cumulative Cash Flow	$3,921	$24,258
Cash-on-Cash Return	3.9%	5.8%
Paul's Profit at Sale		$13,126
Paul's ROI		13.1%

Even though every other assumption about Paul's deal stays the same, Paul's returns have declined. Note that Paul's returns are still positive (5.8 percent CoCR in Year 5 and a 13.1 percent ROI), but they are lower than what Paul would get using all equity (7.6 percent and 29 percent, respectively). In this case, taking on debt has made Paul's outcome worse instead of better even though the deal is performing as expected in terms of cash flow and building equity.

Interest rates are a big factor in how beneficial or detrimental debt is to a deal, but not the only factor. Another important component is the loan-to-value ratio of the loan. (Remember, this is the proportion of the deal that is financed by debt. A deal with a 20 percent down payment would have an 80 percent LTV because 80 percent of the purchase is funded by debt.) The higher the LTV, the higher the debt payments—so you need to be careful with high LTV (low down payment) loans. So far in our two examples, Paul has put 25 percent down, but let's go through one more example, where Paul is going to owner-occupy his deal and put just 10 percent down. For a means of better comparison, we're also going to give Paul a 6 percent interest rate again.

FINANCING: $55,000 EQUITY, $270,000 DEBT AT 6% INTEREST RATE

	YEAR 1	YEAR 5
Property Value	$300,000	$324,730
Rental Income	$32,400	$35,071
Operating Expenses	$9,600	$10,391
Debt Service	$19,425	$19,425
Cash Flow	$3,375	$5,254
Cumulative Cash Flow	$3,375	$21,525
Cash-on-Cash Return	6.1%	9.6%
Paul's Profit at Sale		$16,916
Paul's ROI		7.5%

In this final scenario, even though Paul is putting only $55,000 of equity into the deal and getting a 6 percent interest rate, his debt is reducing his returns. Notice that his ROI in this deal is just 7.5 percent after five years—by far the lowest of any of our examples.

EQUITY	NO DEBT	25% DOWN @ 6%	25% DOWN @ 7.5%	10% DOWN @ 6%
Down Payment (%)	100%	25%	25%	10%
Equity (Purchase)	$300,000	$75,000	$75,000	$30,000
Equity (Closing Costs/Furnishing Reserves)	$25,000	$25,000	$25,000	$25,000
Total Equity	**$325,000**	**$100,000**	**$100,000**	**$55,000**
DEBT				
Loan (%)	0%	75%	75%	90%
Loan Amount	$0	$225,000	$225,000	$270,000
Interest Rate	N/A	6%	7.50%	6%
RETURNS				
Year 5 Cumulative Cash Flow	$118,652	$37,713	$24,258	$21,525
Year 5 CoCR	7.6%	8.5%	5.8%	9.6%
Year 5 Profit at Sale	$95,651	$30,038	$13,126	$16,916
Year 5 Simple ROI	29.4%	30.0%	13.1%	7.5%

As you can see from the table, the type of financing used has big implications on deal and portfolio performance. Of course, sometimes you may want to use debt, even if it reduces your returns, because you're not able to finance a deal entirely with equity. My point in showing you this is to understand the strategic trade-offs of using debt. I hope you now see financing is not just a hurdle you need to overcome when identifying a deal. You need to think strategically about how you want to finance your portfolio to maximize deal performance, analyze multiple financing scenarios, and maintain an appropriate level of risk.

FINANCING: **RECAP**

Thinking through the types of financing you want to use is critical to a strong Portfolio Strategy. Of course, you'll need to pick the most advantageous financing option for each individual deal you do (which we'll talk more about in Chapter 18), but it's also important at a portfolio level for several reasons.

First and foremost, you need to think about who you want involved in your portfolio. Using equity and partners means you'll divide your profits, but it also gives you access to the knowledge, resources, and capital of other investors. Second, although debt allows you to get bigger faster, it comes with additional risk. Ensuring your debt levels are appropriate for your personal risk tolerance and risk capacity is crucial.

Last, financing will play a big role in your overall capital allocation. For most investors, the amount of capital (money) we have to invest is the largest limiting factor to scaling a portfolio. As such, making the best possible use of your financial resources is key. For example, if you have $150,000 of investable assets, how will you use it? Would you put 50 percent down on a $300,000 house so you can maximize your total cash flow and have a deal with relatively low risk? Or would you put $50,000 on three $200,000 houses when this would help you scale faster but expose you to more risk?

As you craft your Portfolio Strategy, think about how you intend to use financing over the course of your portfolio. Too often I see investors who will accept any financing terms presented to them just to get a deal done. I like the hustler spirit in this, but it can be very risky and lead to very poor outcomes. As you build your portfolio, you should draft a financing strategy based on your personal resources, goals, and risk tolerances and then stick to that plan, even if it means missing out on a few deals. Remember to think long term!

Chapter 7
TIME HORIZON

How long do you intend to operate your portfolio? Are you looking to get into real estate for a few years, make some money, and get out? Or are you trying to invest and build a portfolio over a long period of time? While it may seem odd to set a time frame for your portfolio, having at least a general idea of how long you intend to invest has big implications for which deals you pursue and your overall Portfolio Strategy. It's time to talk about time.

Within the context of your real estate portfolio, there are actually two different time-based topics you need to consider: **time horizon** and **hold period**. These terms are used somewhat interchangeably by investors, but for clarity's sake, we're going to use the following definitions in this book.

Your **time horizon** is the period of time over which you intend to operate your portfolio. For example, if you want to be financially free in fifteen years, that would be a time horizon because it's long term and is the objective of your entire portfolio, not just a single deal. Your time horizon is your big-picture time frame for investing. For many people, their time horizon is the length of time until the day they can feasibly live off their portfolio's profits (i.e., financial freedom).

A **hold period** is the length of time you intend to own a specific investment. If you're flipping a house, the hold period might be around six months. If you own a rental property, the hold period could be years, or even decades. Hold periods vary for each individual deal you do.

Time horizons and hold periods both play a large role in the makeup and performance of your portfolio and should work together to achieve your portfolio objectives. In this chapter we're going to focus on the concept of a time horizon. We'll talk more about hold periods in the following chapter.

In Part 2 you'll need to decide on your specific time horizon, but for now we're going to focus on its strategic, portfolio-level implications—how long to let your returns compound and determining the right amount of risk to take.

In Chapter 3 we discussed how time and compounding go hand in hand, but here's a brief reminder: The longer you allow your returns to compound, the more impactful they become.

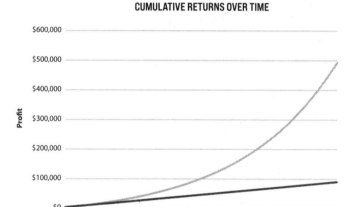

CUMULATIVE RETURNS OVER TIME

Remember this chart? I hope so because it very simply illustrates how the benefits of compound returns are exponential. When you compound, your returns don't grow linearly; they grow by more and more each passing day, month, and year.

Need more convincing? Consider a $100,000 investment with a 10 percent rate of return. If you allowed this investment to compound for twenty years, you'd walk away with $672,750. If instead, you allow the investment to compound for thirty years (just a 50 percent increase in your time horizon), you'd walk away with $1,744,940—a 159 percent increase in your portfolio value. Put another way, it would take you twenty years to earn the first $672,750, but just ten years to earn an additional $1,072,190. Compounding works! From a Portfolio Strategy perspective, the lesson here is clear: The longer you allow your returns to compound, the more wealth you can generate.

In the previous chapter, we briefly talked about how time is one of the best risk mitigation strategies. Time helps mitigate risk because it allows you to wait out short-term market volatility. Because property values trend upward over time, the longer your time horizon, the better chance you have of avoiding the regular but relatively infrequent (about once every seven years) periods of declining asset values in real estate.

Once again taking a Portfolio Strategy perspective, the longer your portfolio's time horizon, the less risk you face. The inverse of this statement is also true: The shorter your time horizon, the more risk there is. Put another way, the longer your time horizon, the more risk you can take. If your time horizon is long, you should feel comfortable exploring riskier real estate investing tactics. If your time horizon is short, you may want to consider sticking to more stable investments to mitigate the possibility of short-term volatility.

As an example, let's consider a new investor named Charles, who has $50,000 to invest and is eager to flip houses. Since Charles didn't read this book and doesn't know his time horizon, he jumps right into flipping, and on average he does really well! Flippers can earn huge returns, but even the best flippers lose money on some projects—that's the nature of the business. Charles makes great returns on most deals, but once in a while he takes a loss. Since Charles is a good flipper, when he averages out the wins and losses over the long run, he has a solid rate of return.

If it turns out that Charles has a long time horizon—say, twenty years—this would work out great for him!

Starting Value $50,000

YEAR	ANNUAL RETURN	PORTFOLIO VALUE
1	28%	$64,000
2	5%	$67,200
3	-31%	$46,368
4	-6%	$43,586
5	22%	$53,175
6	25%	$66,469
7	33%	$88,403
8	-4%	$84,867
9	-4%	$81,472
10	19%	$96,952
11	28%	$124,099
12	17%	$145,195
13	24%	$180,042
14	0%	$180,042

15	22%	$219,652
16	35%	$296,530
17	26%	$373,627
18	-24%	$283,957
19	28%	$363,465
20	25%	$454,331
ROI	**809%**	
CAGR	**12%**	

Even though Charles's rate of return fluctuates a good deal from year to year, over time he accomplishes a strong compound annual growth rate of about 12 percent. A long time horizon allows Charles to smooth out his short-term losses and concentrate on the long-term average return.

But what if Charles's time horizon is not twenty years? What if he needs to withdraw his capital to help his daughter with college tuition four years from now?

SAMPLE NET WORTH OVER TIME

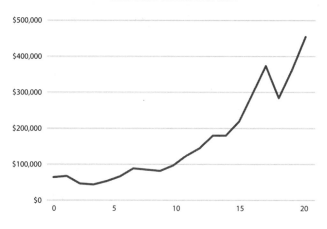

In that case, Charles—who averages great returns—would be unlucky and have to withdraw money from his portfolio during one of his very few bad years, and would actually take a principal loss. This isn't because Charles is a bad flipper per se—it's just because flipping is inherently volatile, and four years isn't a long enough time horizon for Charles's averages to smooth out the volatility.

As this example shows, taking on riskier investments with a short time horizon can be dangerous. We've all heard stories about a person who works hard their entire life, invests diligently in their 401k, and six months before retirement, the stock market crashes and they have to work several more years because of short-term market conditions. People with short time horizons should generally take less risk.

On the other hand, people with a long time horizon, who don't need to live off their investments anytime soon, don't need to be as worried about short-term volatility and are free to pursue the higher return potential of riskier investments.

For these reasons, for most investors who have at least a medium-term time horizon (seven years or more), the relationship between risk and their time horizon looks something like this:

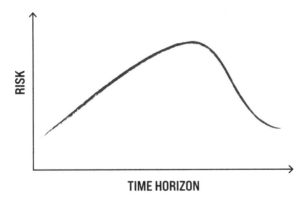

At first you don't want to take on too much risk, because you're new. When you have a limited amount of experience and principal in your portfolio, it's best to choose safer deal types like rental property investing. Learning should be your priority at the outset of your investing career, not maximizing your returns. As you gain experience and build capital, you can take on more risk to maximize your return potential if your time horizon remains relatively long. Finally, as you approach the end of your time horizon, you de-risk your portfolio to ensure that no short-term volatility throws your plan off track right before the finish line.

This trajectory is a solid and common approach, but is, of course, a broad generalization. There are infinite ways to configure your risk profile around your time horizon.

TIME HORIZON: **RECAP**

As an investor, time is your friend. The more time you give your portfolio to compound, the greater returns you'll enjoy. The more time you have until your retirement date, the more risk you can take in pursuit of strong returns. These truths have considerable implications for your Portfolio Strategy. Investing for a long time minimizes risk and can help maximize returns, but of course, it takes more effort. A short time horizon can minimize the amount of work done, but it comes with more risk and less time to compound.

In Part 2 you'll determine your personal time horizon as a crucial part of your broader Vision and Portfolio Strategy. As with everything related to Portfolio Strategy, there is no right or wrong time horizon for you to adopt—what's important is that you understand the implications of your decisions.

Chapter 8
LIQUIDITY

Your time horizon gives you a target end date for your portfolio. Due to the power of compounding, the longer your time horizon, the higher your growth potential. But investing over a long time horizon does come with some additional risks and considerations. Namely, how do you balance investing your money *and* using your money? How do you ensure that you have enough money on hand to cover your expenses *and* take advantage of future opportunities? The answer is liquidity.

"Liquidity" is a term used by investors to describe the relative ease of turning an asset into cash. In other words, if you have an asset, like a car, a share of stock, or a property, how easily could you sell that asset for cash? Note that in terms of liquidity, "cash" means money you actually have. It doesn't need to be in physical bills; money in your savings or checking account is also considered "cash." If your capital is spread across many different assets, how easily can you access and use that money? As you'll learn over the course of this chapter, liquidity is a crucial consideration for investors of all types but is of particular importance to real estate investors.

Liquidity is expressed as a spectrum, with some assets being highly liquid (easily converted to cash) and others being illiquid (taking time and effort to convert to cash). This likely can go without saying, but cash is the most liquid of all assets. You don't need to do anything to convert cash to cash!

Stocks and bonds aren't as liquid as cash, but they are still fairly liquid. You can reasonably expect to sell your stocks and bonds quickly on any day when the markets are open and turn those assets into cash.

Real estate, on the other hand, is not a very liquid asset, but there are assets that are even less liquid than real estate. When trying to sell assets with a limited pool of buyers, like a small business or an art collection, liquidity can take a long time.

| Cash | Bonds | Stocks | Crypto | Real Estate | Businesses | Collectables |

High   **LIQUIDITY**   Low

It's important to recognize that real estate is relatively low on the liquidity spectrum. Even when things go perfectly well, real estate takes a minimum of a few weeks to sell. When selling conditions are poor, it can take months or even years to sell a property. The fact that real estate is not very liquid doesn't mean it's a bad thing to invest in, but it does mean real estate investors have to be more diligent about their capital management to ensure they maintain an appropriate amount of liquidity.

Before we get into how to manage your capital and liquidity, I want to address why liquidity is important in the first place. At a high level, liquidity is important because it provides flexibility. When you have cash, or an asset that can be quickly converted to cash, it gives you maximum control of your assets. For example, if you need to buy a new roof for a rental property, you'll almost certainly have to pay in cash (or with your credit card, which you'll then need to pay off in cash). I've yet to meet a roofer who will accept your shares in an index fund or a valuable handbag as payment. When at the closing table for a property, I haven't yet been able to use my bond holdings or the equity value of my car. You need cash to transact on pretty much everything in the economy, and as such, being able to convert your investments to cash is crucial. Cash gives you the flexibility you need to mitigate risk, cover unforeseen expenses, and take advantage of new opportunities.

Within your portfolio, liquidity might be required to pay for big-ticket items, but it can also help carry you during times of vacancies or other forms of income loss. It's also important that you maintain sufficient liquidity to cover non-investing expenses. If you have a big expense like a wedding, a college tuition payment, or an unforeseen emergency expense, you'll need cash or other liquid assets to help you pay for it. If you have all of your money tied up in rental properties (which are not very liquid), you may find yourself short of capital when you need it most. This is a bad situation to be in, as it can lead to forced selling, taking on high-interest loans, or any number of other undesirable, nonstrategic options. Having $100,000 of equity in properties will be little consolation if you need $10,000 in cash today to assist with an emergency and don't have it. Liquidity helps you navigate the inevitable challenges and expenses that come up in life and in your portfolio.

In our discussion of liquidity so far, we've identified two key points: Liquidity is important to your portfolio, but real estate is a relatively illiquid asset. So, the question becomes, how do you get and maintain liquidity as a real estate investor? If we want to invest over a long time horizon, and we want to invest as much principal as possible, how can that be done while maintaining adequate liquidity? There are three ways: cash reserves, cash flow, and "liquidity events."

CASH RESERVES

The simplest way to ensure liquidity in your portfolio is to maintain a reasonable balance of cash in "reserve." This means that rather than investing or spending all of your available cash, you keep a balance of capital in the bank that is available for immediate use. Remember, cash is the most liquid of all assets, so keeping cash is a surefire way to have at least some liquidity. Cash reserves shouldn't be used to cover normal operating expenses for your business like paying a mortgage or utilities. Instead, cash reserves exist to cover large unforeseen expenses. It is a cushion to protect you against big expenses and risks. Having sufficient cash reserves will ensure you can pay almost all expenses and take advantage of new opportunities. No matter the Portfolio Strategy, everyone needs some cash reserves.

How much capital to keep in cash reserves is a decision each investor has to make for themselves based on the types of deals in their portfolio. For example, if you are buying new-build construction in a high-demand area, you probably don't need as much cash in reserve as if you are buying a thirty-year-old building in an area with low demand. As we'll discuss at length in Part 3, each deal you do is going to have its own Risk Profile, and you need to plan your cash reserves accordingly. That said, there are some common approaches to estimating cash reserves.

- **Flat Number:** Some investors choose a number based on what they believe would cover most major expenses. For example, for a rental property in good shape, $10,000 would probably suffice. A large multifamily property could need $100,000. This method works well if you have a good feel for what repairs and maintenance costs are in your area.

- **X Months of Expenses:** For each property you buy, you can multiply your monthly expenses to figure out a reasonable cash reserve. For a property in good shape, three months of reserves can be enough, but if you want to be conservative or have a property that's in frequent need of repair, you should shoot for six to nine months.
- **Share of Rental Income:** Some investors calculate their reserves as a percentage of annual rental income. For example, if your annual income is $24,000, you could keep 20 percent of your income in reserve ($4,800).

Regardless of the method you use, you need to maintain cash reserves sufficient to cover the expenses you could feasibly incur across your portfolio. If you're uncertain how much cash reserves you should maintain in your portfolio, err on the side of caution and keep high reserves.

Here are a few more tips for maintaining liquidity through cash reserves.

- The examples above use an individual deal to calculate the necessary reserves. This is a good approach for those just getting started. As you scale, you can start to plan your cash reserves on a portfolio level. This makes sense if you think about the statistical probability of unlikely events. It's unlikely that you will face large unforeseen expenses for all of your properties at one time. Therefore, you can keep relatively fewer reserves per property, as long as your portfolio as a whole has adequate liquidity.
- The more transactional income you make, the less reserves you need on a portfolio level. If you have a high-paying job where you make more than you spend, you have some built-in liquidity that you can use to cover expenses. This doesn't mean you shouldn't set aside some capital for reserves—you still need those—but it means you can rely on your transactional income as well as your reserves should an emergency arise.
- Cash reserves are not principal! In our discussion of compounding interest, I said that to maximize growth potential you want to invest as much principal as possible, and that's true. Both principal and cash reserves are ways to use your capital, but they serve very different purposes in your portfolio. Do not confuse them. Principal is for investing and earning a return. Cash reserves are

for covering unforeseen expenses. Keep your cash reserves and your funds for investing in different bank accounts so as not to muddle them.

- Cash reserves are the first way to maintain liquidity as a real estate investor. When you determine your "investable assets" in Part 2, and plan your resource allocation in Part 4, make sure to plan for adequate cash reserves.

CASH FLOW

Properties that cash-flow have built-in liquidity. Remember, liquidity is about maintaining access to cash, and cash flow gives you cash each and every month. Even if your properties cash-flow, you'll still want to maintain cash reserves, but having cash flow allows you to increase liquidity, even while your capital is invested elsewhere.

For example, consider a rental property purchased by an investor named Sarah for $400,000, which earns $1,000 per month in cash flow and has monthly expenses of $1,500. Sarah is a relatively conservative investor, so she sets aside six months of expenses as her cash reserves ($9,000) when she purchases the property.

As long as no major expenses come up that force Sarah to tap into her reserves (remember, normal expenses shouldn't be coming out of reserves), she will gain $1,000 of liquidity per month from her cash flow. That's great! Sarah can choose to reinvest that $1,000, add it to her cash reserves, set it aside for future opportunities, or do something else with it entirely. The point is that by earning cash flow, Sarah enjoys the flexibility of liquid assets.

Another benefit of cash flow is that it can be used to refill your cash reserves, should you need to tap into them. For example, if Sarah's property needs a new furnace, which costs her $3,000, her cash reserves would dip down to $6,000. If Sarah feels good about the condition of her property after the repairs, she can apply three months of future cash flow to refill her cash reserves rather than refilling from out-of-pocket sources.

Cash flow should not be considered a substitute for cash reserves, but it is a stable, predictable way to add liquidity to your portfolio. It can be used to refill reserves, to supplement your lifestyle, or as principal for a future investment. It is the only profit driver that allows you to earn profits in the form of a liquid asset.

LIQUIDITY EVENTS

The last way to gain liquidity in your portfolio is through a "liquidity event." This is when an investor deliberately takes steps to liquidate (turn an asset into cash) some piece of their portfolio. Investors do this when they want to tap into some of the equity they have sitting in a deal, either to take advantage of a new opportunity, diversify, or to take some profit off the table. There are two common liquidity events that real estate investors utilize: **selling** and completing a **cash-out refinance**.

Selling a property is a pretty straightforward proposition and generates a lot of liquidity. When you sell a property, you turn an asset into cash—liquidity! Upon sale (assuming the deal goes well), you should get 100 percent of your principal back, plus any equity you have built up in that deal, minus any expenses. Selling provides you with the maximum possible liquidity. Everything you have in that deal turns to cash. Selling provides liquidity, but selling is not always desirable.

Determining when to sell depends on a lot of variables, which we will discuss in Part 4. But there is one key variable we need to touch on here: hold periods. A **hold period** is exactly what it sounds like. It's the amount of time you hold (own) a given investment. It's the time frame for each deal you do. Note that a hold period is different than your time horizon; a time horizon is the time frame of your entire portfolio, while a hold period is the time frame for an individual deal within your portfolio.

The ideal hold period for a deal will look very different depending on the deal type you select. For deal types that earn transactional income, like flipping, new construction, or development, the ideal hold period is simple—the faster the better! If you hold onto these types of deals too long, your holding costs (like mortgage payments, insurance, taxes, etc.) will increase, and your profit will fall. Because these types of deals are predicated on speed, they have the additional advantage of frequent, preplanned liquidity events.

For traditionally long-hold deal types like rental properties, short-term rentals, or commercial real estate, determining the ideal hold period is more complex. Holding too briefly for these types of deal designs can lead to severe underperformance and unnecessary market risk. Due to the slow and steady nature of most real estate deals, and the high transaction costs (it can cost about 8 percent of the purchase price to sell a house), selling too soon can turn a great deal into a bad one.

Look at this example of a rental property, held for ten years.

HOLD PERIOD (YEARS)	PROPERTY VALUE	CASH FLOW	CoCR	ROI	ANNUALIZED ROI
1	$250,000	$5,000	8.0%	-30.3%	-30.3%
2	$255,000	$5,100	8.2%	-13.7%	-6.9%
3	$260,100	$5,202	8.3%	3.3%	1.1%
4	$265,302	$5,306	8.5%	20.8%	5.2%
5	$270,608	$5,412	8.7%	38.7%	7.7%
6	$276,020	$5,520	8.8%	52.8%	8.8%
7	$281,541	$5,631	9.0%	67.2%	9.6%
8	$287,171	$5,743	9.2%	81.8%	10.2%
9	$292,915	$5,858	9.4%	96.7%	10.7%
10	$298,773	$5,975	9.6%	112.0%	11.2%

By all accounts this is a good deal. The property value is increasing, and it has strong cash flow. But look at the ROI. If you were to sell this deal in the first or second year, it would have principal loss! This is due to high transaction costs both on the purchase and the sale of a property. Many deals don't build equity quickly enough to allow for a short hold period (unlike flips). This makes liquidity a challenge for rental property, commercial deals, and short-term rentals.

On top of the need to hold most real estate deals for a few years to optimize returns, many investors find themselves in a situation where they want or need liquidity yet don't want to sell property to get it. That's where the other liquidity event option comes in: the cash-out refinance. "Refinancing" is when you take out a new loan to finance your property that replaces your first loan (hence the prefix "re"). A **cash-out refi** is a form of refinancing that allows you to pull out a portion of the equity you've built in a deal in the form of cash. I am not going to go too deep into the math of a cash-out refi here (definitely check out my book *Real Estate by the Numbers,* where I go into detail on this), but let's look at a super-simple example.

Recall that Sarah bought a property for $400,000. Let's assume she put $100,000 down to buy that property (25 percent down payment) and borrowed the remaining $300,000. If her property grows in value over time to $500,000, she could pull out a good chunk of equity in a cash-out refi. When Sarah applies for a new loan to replace her previous one, she will need to keep 25 percent down ($125,000) and will be borrowing the other 75 percent ($375,000). Sarah will need to use the funds from her new loan to first pay back her first loan, which has a balance of $290,000 now due to amortization, and then she'll get to keep the rest.

$$\$500,000 - \underset{\text{(equity in new deal)}}{\$125,000} - \underset{\text{(repay old loan)}}{\$290,000} = \$85,000$$

This is an oversimplified example, of course, but hopefully you can see how this works and the benefits. By completing a cash-out refinance, Sarah is able to gain liquidity in the form of $85,000 in cash while keeping her property. It's worth noting that cash-out refinances have trade-offs like higher debt service costs (because you're borrowing more on your new loan than on your original loan) and work best in interest-rate environments that are stable or declining, but we'll get to that later in the book.

Selling and **cash-out refinances** are both ways to achieve liquidity for real estate investors, but it's important to note that these are slow processes. These still take weeks, typically months, and sometimes don't happen at all! Liquidity events need to be planned well in advance. As a result, liquidity events like these should be used to take advantage of new opportunities, or to take profit, and not used to cover unforeseen expenses.

LIQUIDITY: RECAP

Investing as much principal as possible for as long as possible is the key to maximizing your portfolio's growth potential. But allocating all of your capital into long-term investments comes with risks. You need to strike a balance between long-term investing and maintaining liquidity. Liquidity provides your portfolio with flexibility. It ensures you'll be able to meet any expenses and therefore helps to prevent forced selling. It means you'll be able to take advantage of opportunities as they arise. Everyone needs some level of liquidity in their portfolio.

While real estate is a relatively illiquid asset, there are ways to maintain appropriate levels of liquidity: cash reserves, cash flow, and liquidity events. You don't need liquidity from all three, but you definitely need cash reserves. For example, if you have proper cash reserves, you don't need a ton of cash flow or to complete liquidity events. But even if you have great cash flow, or plan to sell a property in the future, you still need cash reserves. Cash reserves are crucial.

Once you have cash reserves properly planned for, you can use your other forms of liquidity strategically. You can use your cash flow or proceeds from a liquidity event to fund or replenish cash reserves, to fund your lifestyle, or as principal for a future investment. Liquidity is flexibility, and it gives you plenty of nice options to choose from.

As we move through the rest of the book, we're going to return to the idea of liquidity time and again. In Part 2 we'll conduct exercises to help you identify your current liquid and investable assets. In Part 3 you'll consider which deal types you're interested in, and liquidity should be a key consideration. And finally, in Part 4 we'll do a deep dive into the idea of resource allocation, which is heavily dependent on liquidity . As you read, consider what liquidity you'll need and how you plan to get it.

Chapter 9

THOUGHTS ON PART 1

There are many excellent and exciting ways that a real estate portfolio can earn you money and help you achieve your financial goals. Over the course of your investing career, the deals you pursue and decisions you make will change based on your shifting goals and circumstances. The concepts you've learned in Part 1 of this book will give you the foundational knowledge to continuously evaluate and update your Portfolio Strategy.

When I first started investing, I had limited resources: no capital, few skills, but a decent amount of time. I needed income to support my lifestyle, and I couldn't afford to take a loss. As such, my strategy involved simple, low-risk deals that earned cash flow I used to support my lifestyle. Was this the ideal, perfectly tuned portfolio? No! I wasn't reinvesting, I was afraid to do value-add projects, my property management skills were awful, and I took on little risk. But it worked anyway! My strategy when I first got started was not to maximize returns but to get into the industry and learn as much as possible. I understood the trade-offs and made a conscious decision about was best for me at the time.

Today, my strategy is much different. I am fortunate to have capital to invest, but now have more commitments that take up my time. I have built up a solid skill set, but by no means am I a master of all things real estate. Given these realities, my Portfolio Strategy has changed. The trade-offs I choose to make are different. I take on more risk now because I have strong income from a variety of sources. I invest primarily in passive deals in markets across the country. Given my current income and my still-long time horizon, I am able to reinvest 100 percent of the profits from my portfolio.

Is this strategy perfect? Of course not. If I had more time, I could probably run my portfolio more efficiently, but that would come at the cost of working a job I love and pursuing nonfinancial goals. Right now, my strategy is working great for me!

If you check back with me five or ten years from now, I'll probably have a different-looking strategy. Maybe I'll be living back in the U.S. and buying deals in my local market. Perhaps I'll have more time on my hands and be looking to learn a new skill. We'll just have to wait and see!

As my vision and circumstances change, I will adapt my Portfolio Strategy accordingly. I can do that because I have a strong understanding of the fundamentals of investing and can thoughtfully consider the strategic implications of each decision I make. Having read Part 1 of this book, you're now in a great position to do the same.

If you're not yet sure what you want your portfolio to look like, that's okay. At this point in the book, that is to be expected! Part 1 is meant to provide background information to help you understand the opportunities, risks, and trade-offs inherent in building a real estate investing portfolio. These are the tools you'll need to continuously evaluate and adjust your portfolio going forward. Now that you've learned the fundamentals, it's time to move on to Part 2, which is where we get more hands on and apply what you've learned over the last several chapters to your personal situation and goals. As you create your Vision in Part 2, remember that there are no "right" and "wrong" answers. Let the concepts you've learned in Part 1 help you decide what strategic choices are right for you.

PART 2
DEFINING YOUR VISION

VISION

DEAL DESIGN

PORTFOLIO MANAGEMENT

When you decided to read this book, you probably had a desired outcome in mind. Are you looking to achieve financial freedom? Free up some time? Maximize your wealth? People don't generally pick up investing books for the sheer pleasure of them, so there must be some reason you are interested in investing in real estate. Why are you reading this book right now?

As we shift from foundational concepts to creating your personalized strategy, you need to start with an idea of where you want to go and what you'll commit to get there. I'm sure you're eager to pick and execute on deals, but having a clearly defined Vision comes first. Good strategy starts with a specific objective. Your Vision, which you'll define in Part 2, is that objective.

When I was close to completing my bachelor's degree, I was deeply conflicted about what to do post-graduation. I wanted to travel the world, be a ski bum, go into finance, start a company, and everything else in between. I couldn't decide. One day I went out to breakfast with my grandfather. I told him some of my big ideas and asked him which path he thought was right for me.

He thought for a moment and asked, "Where do you want to end up?"

I had never even considered the question. I was frantically trying to decide what to do right after college. How could I possibly know what I wanted further down the road?

"I have no idea," I replied, followed by a jaded, "I just need to know what to do next."

He laughed and then replied with a famous Lewis Carroll quote: "If you don't know where you're going, any road will get you there."

That quote, and my grandfather's reaction, really stuck with me. Of course I couldn't decide what path was "right" when I didn't even have a general idea of where I wanted to go in my life! I needed a vision to help me frame my decisions and narrow my focus.

When companies build out their business plan, they start with their mission and vision. When a financial planner helps a client plan for retirement, they first ask what the client wants from their post-work years before recommending an investing approach. Portfolio Strategy is no different. You start with a Vision, and then develop your tactics. Without a clear idea of what you're trying to accomplish, how will you choose which real estate deals to pursue? How will you decide how much risk to take? Who to partner with? Which resources you'll commit? Good strategy starts with the objective.

Perhaps you have a general idea of what you want to accomplish through real estate investing. That's a great start. A specific Vision is even better. Your Vision, in the context of Portfolio Strategy, is a set of decisions you need to make about what you want out of your portfolio, the type of business you want to run, and what you're willing to commit to achieve your goals. Developing your Vision entails five components: Personal Values, Transactional Income Plan, Resource Audit, Risk Assessment, and Goal Setting. Each chapter in Part 2 covers one of these components and will correspond to the Vision section of your PREP.

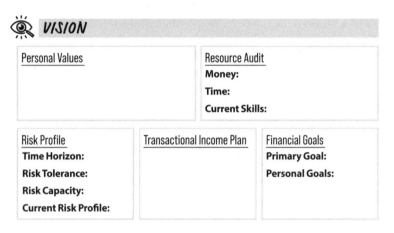

The first step in your Vision is defining your personal values. Some people call this "defining your why" or "your core values," but whatever you call it, it means the same thing—clearly stating what you care about most in life. If this seems like an odd place to start crafting an investing strategy, it will all make sense soon. If you know what you care about most, every other decision in this book will become easier.

Next, we'll work through your Transactional Income Plan. As we learned in Part 1, there are two types of income: transactional and residual. Because transactional income is closely associated with a "job" and can consume a lot of your time, it's important to get clear on if and how you want to earn your transactional income.

In Chapter 12 we'll conduct the Resource Audit. Every successful portfolio needs capital, time, and skills to succeed, and in this section you'll complete exercises that will measure your current resource levels and determine what resources you have (and want!) to commit to your portfolio.

Once you know the resources you'll put in, you need to decide what you're willing to risk. In Chapter 13 you'll set your time horizon, assess your risk tolerance, and evaluate your risk capacity to create your own Risk Profile.

In Chapter 14 we'll finalize your Vision by setting specific goals that your portfolio will be designed to hit.

By the end of Part 2 you will have a personalized Vision that will help guide all your future portfolio decisions. Keep in mind that your Vision is not a step-by-step guide for getting from where you are today to where you want to go. The point of your Vision is to aim you in the right direction over the long run. It's a compass, not a roadmap. We'll work on the specifics like what deals to pursue and in what order in Parts 3 and 4. For now, the focus should be on where you want to go.

Before we get started on your Vision, here are two quick pointers on how to approach Part 2 and the rest of this book.

First, for the remainder of the book, we'll be talking about concepts while you actively build your strategy. As such, I will start each chapter by explaining concepts and providing examples, and I'll end each chapter with a section called PREP Work. In this section you'll find specific instructions for how you can fill out your PREP. As a reminder, your PREP stands for Personal Real Estate Portfolio and is the framework that accompanies this book. The purpose of the PREP is to walk you through the most important strategic decisions impacting your portfolio and to help you visualize your strategy in one concise and actionable way. The exercises contained within each PREP Work section are designed to help you complete your PREP. These exercises are not required, but if you want to develop a PREP as you read this book, I recommend you complete them.

Second, I wrote this book as if you're completing your Portfolio Strategy and your PREP as an individual. If you're reading and completing the exercises with a significant other, that's no problem! The PREP works great for couples too. Most of the PREP work is the same, but I will call out any modifications couples should make.

Enough with the caveats—it's time to start creating your Vision. This process is introspective, exciting, and essential. The more time and thought you put into your Vision, the more you'll get out of this book. Having a clear Vision is the first step in developing a clear path to your financial goals. Let's get to it!

Chapter 10
PERSONAL VALUES

The first step in defining your Vision is to take a look at your own personal values. This may surprise you, as it has seemingly little to do with real estate investing. But I assure you, the reason we start with personal values will make perfect sense as you create your Vision. You're about to start the process of personalizing a real estate investment portfolio to your specific needs and goals—so doesn't it make sense to start by defining what is important to you as an individual?

Even if you haven't heard the term "personal values" before, you may have come across this concept, just called by a different name. In the real estate investing community, you often hear people talk about defining "your why." In the corporate world, almost all businesses have "core values" that govern how that business conducts itself. Whether you call it personal values, core values, or your why, they're all the same idea: core principles that guide the way a person or a business operates and behaves. While these terms are somewhat interchangeable, I will use the term "Personal Values" in this book.

So, what are Personal Values? In the literal sense, they're nothing special. Just a few words that describe the things you care about most in life. But in practice, they are much more than that. They provide focus, motivation, purposes, and fulfillment—things I think we can all agree are exciting and important!

There is a reason almost all successful businesses, investors, and individuals take the time to identify their Personal Values—they drive progress. They motivate and inspire. They help us frame decisions and prioritize our time. They ensure we move toward our ultimate goals.

Hopefully you're starting to see why Personal Values are important for your Portfolio Strategy.

I know this concept is a little abstract, and don't worry if you don't get it just yet. When I was first introduced to this idea by my coach, Lauran Alredge, I was deeply skeptical and confused. But over time, I realized how having a clear set of Personal Values makes every decision in your life (not just professionally or with investing) easier. Since I set my own Personal Values a few years ago, I make decisions more confidently, feel more fulfilled in my work, and am generally a happier person. I know that may sound like a stretch, but it's true!

To give you a concrete example of how Personal Values are helpful for decision-making and for your Portfolio Strategy, let's look at an example of two very different investors who are each independently seeking their first deal: Mark and Tamara. Let's imagine both have come to me looking for advice on how to get started, and to best help them, I ask each of them to provide some personal information: a brief introduction, what their goals are, and what their Personal Values are.

Mark, thirty-eight years old, is the father of two young children and works full-time as a teacher. He is passionate about his job, but money is tight, and to make extra cash he does private tutoring on nights and weekends. This helps Mark save for the future, but it means he spends less time with his family and with his mountain biking buddies than he'd like. He is interested in real estate investing primarily to give his family some extra spending money, work less, and hopefully to move up his retirement date by a couple of years. Mark's personal values are:

- Family
- Work/life balance
- Security
- Community
- Passion

Tamara is a twenty-two-year-old recent college graduate who took a job in marketing right out of school. Unfortunately, she hates her job and the entire concept of working for other people. She has been reading about financial freedom for about a year and is ready to jump into real estate headfirst. She wants to be financially free within ten years so she can spend her time traveling, volunteering, and doing anything else she feels inspired to do. Tamara's Personal Values are:

- Financial freedom
- Wealth
- Learning
- Joy
- Generosity

Mark and Tamara are both beginner investors looking to land their first deal—but they're coming from very different places and have very different values. Now that I know their respective values, I can start offering advice.

Given what I know about Mark, I could recommend that he continue to work at his full-time job, because he enjoys it, and use his income to purchase rental properties every two years or so. Rental properties are relatively low risk and provide enough residual income to allow Mark to stop tutoring and regain some time. If he were to combine this residual income with his transactional income, he would be in a great place to retire from teaching when he's ready. For Mark, this seems like a great path forward as the strategy is well aligned with his values of family, work/life balance, and security.

If I recommended this strategy to Tamara, she'd probably be disappointed! My recommendations to Mark are not aligned with Tamara's values of wealth, financial freedom, and joy. Remember, Tamara hates her job and is looking to achieve financial freedom and wealth as soon as possible. Mark's strategy wouldn't be aligned with her values and wouldn't work for her.

For Tamara, I need to suggest an entirely different approach. First, I would tell her to immediately purchase a house hack to get into the game. Then, I'd recommend she transition the time she spends at the job she hates into a full-time real estate job—perhaps becoming an agent, a property manager, or a loan officer. This would allow her to learn the industry and build her network while she accumulates cash with which she can flip houses or pursue other active investments. This strategy could work for Tamara because it's aligned with her values of wealth, financial freedom, joy, and learning.

Can you see how Portfolio Strategy stems from these investors' personal values? Two aspiring investors, two sets of values, two totally different strategies. You, too, need to start forming your strategy from what you value and why you're investing in the first place. Defining your Personal Values will make all other strategic questions you face in this book, and over the course of your investing career, easier to answer. Your values are the lens through which you'll view all other decisions. And if you're anything like me, it may just help you find clarity in other aspects of your life as well.

STRATEGIC DECISION: To complete the Personal Values section of your PREP, create a list of your Personal Values. You should have no more than five personal values, and they should be written simply. See below for exercises and an explanation of how to define your own Personal Values.

In the literal sense, your Personal Values are simple things: just a few words on your PREP. Yet, for most people, narrowing down what they actually value most in life is a challenging—but very rewarding—process. Your Personal Values are the things you care about most in life, and getting really clear about your values takes self-reflection.

The objective of the following exercises is for you to write down no more than five Personal Values, each of which is only a few words. Each Personal Value should represent something you care about deeply. It should be something you cannot live without. Since I'm sure you care about many things, it can be tempting to write down a lot of values, but that defeats the purpose. The benefit of your Personal Values is to narrow focus and provide clarity. Having too many values will create complexity, not clarity. Strive for as few and as simple Personal Values as possible. For reference, my personal values are a total of ten words.

- Personal growth
- Meaningful relationships
- Mental and physical health
- Adventure
- Freedom

If you happen to be someone who can very easily write down your Personal Values, go ahead and write them in your PREP! I was definitely not one of those people, and if you're like me, you'll need a process to follow. Below, you'll find a process I learned from my coach, Lauran, which I have adapted slightly for this book.

The process is three steps:
1. Start with a big list of words for inspiration and select words that resonate with you.
2. Narrow down your list of values until you have five or fewer.
3. Personalize the words to make them feel like your own.

> *For people completing their PREP as a couple, you'll want to focus on your "shared values," i.e., the values that you two as a couple can agree on. You will likely have some values that don't overlap as a couple, but for the purposes of your PREP, just focus on the values you both share.*

Let's work on the process step by step.

The Big List

Start with a big list of common values and circle any words that resonate with you. You can find these lists online or in the Workbook,[2] or see the one just below this paragraph. As you review your list, circle any words that you feel describe something you value. You can start broad, but remember you're going to be narrowing down your list of values to five or fewer, so don't circle just anything. You want to be selective, but at this point in the process you can comfortably select ten to twenty words.

Core Values

Abundance	Communication	Excitement	Independence	Patriotism	Speed
Acceptance	Community	Experience	Individuality	Peace	Spirituality
Accomplishment	Compassion	Expertise	Inner Harmony	Playfulness	Stability
Accountability	Competence	Exploration	Innovation	Poise	Status
Accuracy	Confidence	Fairness	Insightful	Positivity	Stewardship
Achievement	Consistency	Faith	Inspiring	Power	Strength
Adaptability	Contentment	Fame	Integrity	Productivity	Structure
Adventure	Contribution	Family	Intelligence	Professionalism	Success
Affection	Control	Fearless	Intuitive	Prosperity	Support
Alertness	Cooperation	Fidelity	Joy	Purpose	Surprise
Ambition	Courage	Fitness	Justice	Quality	Sustainability
Assertiveness	Courtesy	Focus	Kindness	Recognition	Teamwork
Attentive	Creativity	Foresight	Knowledge	Respect	Temperance
Authenticity	Credibility	Forgiveness	Lawful	Responsibility	Thankful
Awareness	Curiosity	Freedom	Leadership	Restraint	Thorough
Balance	Decisiveness	Friendship	Learning	Results-oriented	Thoughtful
Beauty	Dedication	Fun	Logic	Rigor	Timeliness
Boldness	Dependability	Generosity	Love	Security	Tolerance
Bravery	Determination	Giving	Loyalty	Self-actualization	Toughness
Brilliance	Devotion	Goodness	Mastery	Self-development	Traditional
Calmness	Dignity	Grace	Maturity	Self-reliance	Tranquility
Capable	Discipline	Gratitude	Meaning	Self-respect	Transparency
Careful	Diversity	Growth	Moderation	Selfless	Trustworthy
Caring	Efficiency	Happiness	Motivation	Sensitivity	Understanding
Certainty	Empathy	Hard Work	Obedience	Serenity	Uniqueness
Challenge	Endurance	Harmony	Openness	Service	Unity
Charity	Energy	Health	Optimism	Sharing	Vision
Cleanliness	Enjoyment	Honesty	Order	Silence	Vitality
Clear	Enthusiasm	Honor	Organization	Simplicity	Wealth
Clever	Equality	Humility	Originality	Sincerity	Welcoming
Comfort	Ethical	Humor	Passion	Skillfulness	Winning
Commitment	Excellence	Imagination	Patience	Solitude	Wisdom

Here's what mine looked like.

- Relationships
- Accountability
- Growth
- Freedom
- Financial independence
- Travel
- Adventure
- Health
- Achievement
- Success
- Community
- Fun
- Friendships
- Exploration

Narrow Your List

Next, it's time to make some difficult decisions. You need to prune your list down from the ten to twenty you started with to five or fewer. I find this part to be the most difficult, so feel free to do it in stages. For example, try to get down to ten, then to seven, and then to five. If you feel stuck or are having difficulty eliminating potential values, here are a couple of tips.

- Look for any overlapping or redundant values and home in on the most important one. For me, I noticed a theme among three of my potential values: travel, adventure, and exploration. This is a good sign, as it demonstrates that I value something related to these words, but I only need one. I love to travel. When I daydream, that's usually what it's about. But travel didn't wind up making my list. Why? Because when I sat down and thought very deeply about *why* I love to travel, I realized it was the adventure that I crave. I like the feeling of doing something new and taking calculated risks. I love to travel, but what I really value in my life is adventure.
- For each value, think about whether you can envision scenarios where you wouldn't value that word. For me, I did this with the word "success." I genuinely want to be successful in everything I do, but when I asked myself, "Is there any scenario where I wouldn't value success?" the answer was yes. Success would be meaningless to me if I did it unethically, or sacrificed my health or personal relationships to achieve it. So, success was out. Growth, on the other hand, I found no exceptions for. I will always value growth.

If you're tempted to have more than five values, I highly discourage it. The point of this exercise is to identify the things that matter most to you. These are the things you cannot live without. If you have nine values, it will be exceedingly difficult to make decisions that are aligned with nine different ideas at the same time. If you keep it to five or fewer, it will be a lot easier to make decisions that align with all of your values.

Remember, omitting something from your Personal Values list doesn't mean you can no longer experience it. I eliminated "fun," but it's not like I don't have fun anymore—I have fun pretty much every day. This list is about your most important priorities, but it doesn't eliminate anything not selected from your life.

Take your time with this exercise. You want your values to feel right to you. If you have to revisit the list several times, that is entirely normal. I changed my fifth value about eight times before it felt right. Which brings us to the last step: making it personal.

Making It Personal

Once you've narrowed your list down to five or fewer values, it's time to make this list feel unique to you. Your Personal Values shouldn't just be a list of words on a piece of paper—they should be something you feel attached to and motivated to pursue every day.

To ingrain your values in your head, take some time to tweak the wording of each of your values to make sure they reflect your priorities perfectly. Some values may be fine the way they are, while others might take a bit of thought and iteration before you nail it.

When I arrived at this stage of the process, my list of values looked like this.

- Relationships
- Health
- Adventure
- Freedom
- Growth

I was happy with this list, but it felt a little sterile. To make it mine, I played with the wording a bit to make sure it was all in my own words. After all, this list is personal! You want it to be in your own words and something that you can quickly and confidently recall.

As an example, "relationships" was always going to be on my list. I love spending time with my friends and family and would never take a job or make an investing decision that would compromise that. But "relationships" as a single word just sounded too generic. After all, I'm not really interested in accumulating as many relationships as possible. To me, it's all about having deep connections with the people I care about most. After trying out a few iterations of the word, I settled on "meaningful relationships." That small distinction gave me a strong connection to the value.

At the end of the personalization process, my values list was done! It came out like this.

- Meaningful relationships
- Mental and physical health
- Adventure
- Freedom
- Personal growth

Having this list has made a huge difference in my life, and I think it will make a big difference in yours. It has helped me make important decisions about investing, my personal life, and my time management every single day.

Take some time to personalize your list of Personal Values so it feels unique and motivating to you. If you fly through this exercise and write down words without putting in the necessary thought, it's not going to help you with your Portfolio Strategy, or anything else. If you have to, you can step away from your list and revisit it in the future to tweak it. This list doesn't need to be perfect—but you do want it to be an accurate depiction of what you want and why you're investing so it can inform the rest of your Portfolio Strategy.

 Once you have your list, write it down in your *PREP.* This will be the first of many things you write down as part of your Personal Real Estate Portfolio.

Congratulations on this important first step! This is a powerful activity, and you should finish it feeling energized and motivated. As you proceed through this book, always keep your Personal Values in mind, as they are the lens through which all remaining decisions should be made. For example, you will soon face questions like "Should I quit my job to invest in real estate?" or "Should I flip houses or buy rental properties?" Consulting your Personal Values list should help answer these important investing questions.

Now let's move on to the next part of your Vision, where you'll think through the role your job and transactional income play in your Portfolio Strategy: your Transactional Income Plan.

Chapter 11
TRANSACTIONAL INCOME PLAN

Although most people start investing in real estate to build residual income and achieve financial freedom, transactional income serves a crucial role in Portfolio Strategy. As a reminder, transactional income is earned by trading time and expertise for money (as opposed to residual income, which uses money to make more money).

Most people earn transactional income though a traditional job and continue to earn transactional income even as their portfolio grows. Transactional income can provide capital to invest. It also pays for your lifestyle while your portfolio grows large enough to cover expenses. Even the people I know who are financially free almost always choose to keep earning transactional income due to these benefits. Residual income will help you retire eventually, but don't dismiss how helpful a traditional job/transactional income is in your Portfolio Strategy.

For real estate investors, the question of if and how to earn transactional income is very important. Transactional income, by definition, is time intensive. But time is finite, so you need to think strategically about how to best use your time. Should you maximize your income at a job and use that to invest? Should you earn transactional income through real estate? Do you want to invest so you can stop earning transactional income altogether? There is no prescribed way to earn transactional income as a real estate investor. You don't have to quit your job or work full-time in real estate to be an investor. There are many approaches that work, and you get to decide how to use transactional income within your Portfolio Strategy.

In this chapter we'll discuss the key decisions you need to make regarding transactional income, and you'll create a Transactional Income Plan (TIP) that will go on your PREP. Of course, your TIP will change over time, so you don't need to plan your entire career out now in order to start building your portfolio. The point of this chapter is to help you figure out where you'll source the capital to invest in your portfolio, and how long you think you'll have that income for. If it changes in the future, so can your Portfolio Strategy.

FULFILLMENT AND RESOURCE ACCUMULATION

I've been working consistently since age 13 and have had dozens of different jobs in that time. Some jobs I've hated and some I've loved. Some have paid well, while others have paid terribly. Some have been easy, and others have demanded huge amounts of my time. I'm guessing this experience resonates with a lot of you. There is a big spectrum of ways to earn transactional income—some good, and others less so.

As I think back on my own career decisions, and those of the investors I speak with regularly, I've realized there are two primary variables in determining how to earn transactional income: fulfillment and resource accumulation. Fulfillment refers to how much you enjoy and find meaning in the work you do. Resource accumulation refers to resources you get for the work you do, be it capital, time, or skills. Each of these variables exists on a spectrum, and every way of earning transactional income (aka the job you have) can be plotted in one of four quadrants along these two spectrums.

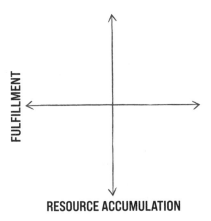

Some people strongly prioritize fulfillment, while others focus solely on prioritizing resources. Many look for a balance of the two. To help you think through how you want to use transactional income for your portfolio, let's dig into this idea a little further.

The Fulfillment Spectrum

In American culture, we are often told to find a job we love. To earn money by doing something that inspires and fulfills us. To find personal meaning from our work. If you have found this, that's wonderful—it can be difficult to find! You are at the upper extreme of the fulfillment spectrum. High-fulfillment jobs can come in any industry—it doesn't matter if it's medicine, technology, social work, landscaping, or anything else. If you enjoy and are motivated by your work, you're on the high end of the fulfillment spectrum.

On the other end of the spectrum are people who are absolutely miserable in their jobs. In contrast to feeling fulfilled by their work, these people feel drained by their jobs and often dread clocking in. If this describes you, I'm sorry to hear it. You're at the low end of the fulfillment spectrum, and it's not a good place to be.

I find that most people are somewhere in the middle—not quite in love with their job, but not entirely miserable either. I think most people are able to earn transactional income in a way that provides them with at least some sense of meaning and fulfillment.

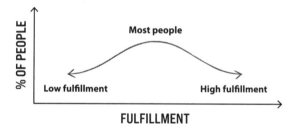

The Resource Accumulation Spectrum

The second variable in choosing how to earn transactional income is how well the job generates resources. Most of you are probably associating this with money, which is obviously very important, but remember, in the context of Portfolio Strategy, time and skills are also key resources. I encourage you to consider what a job offers you in terms of all three resources: capital to invest with, time to focus on building your portfolio, and skills to make your portfolio more profitable.

On one end of the spectrum is a job where you are well compensated with all three resources. You're paid well, you work a reasonable number of hours, and you learn a lot. I hope you've found one of these jobs—but they're exceedingly rare. Not many transactional income sources are strong in all three resources, but if you've found one, you're at the absolute top of the resource accumulation spectrum.

On the other end of the spectrum is a job that pays poorly, requires a ton of time, and teaches you nothing. I've had these jobs—they're awful. I hope you're not in this situation, but if you are, you're at the low end of the resource accumulation spectrum.

Just like with the fulfillment spectrum, most people fall somewhere in the middle. There are many jobs that pay poorly, but you learn a lot. Other jobs pay very well but are extremely demanding of your time. Hopefully you're getting at least some solid resources from your current transactional income source.

The Four Job Types

When you combine the fulfillment spectrum and the resource accumulation spectrum, you can see four distinct quadrants in which every transactional income source (job) falls.

- Quadrant 1 is people who are high on the fulfillment spectrum but low on the compensation spectrum.
- Quadrant 2 is where everyone aspires to be (but not many are)—fulfilled in their work and well compensated for it.
- Quadrant 3 are jobs where you're unfulfilled but well compensated.
- Quadrant 4 is the worst possible option—unfulfilled and poorly compensated.

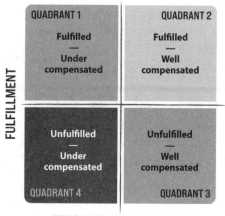

Even though some jobs offer few, or less obvious, benefits to your portfolio, I encourage you to fully consider how your transactional income source can help you invest in real estate. To assist with this, I plotted out a selection of the transactional income sources I've had over the years. As you can see, I've had at least one job in every quadrant. Each job, with the exception of cold-calling, provided some benefit to my portfolio, even if it wasn't directly.

I waited tables after college, which paid well and gave me a ton of free time, even though I didn't find the work particularly fulfilling. Being a server gave me the time resources I needed to get into real estate. Money isn't the only resource that matters in this exercise! For a brief time, I directed a venture fund for educational start-ups. This was a personally fulfilling job, but didn't provide me with a ton of learning, money, or time. I left pretty quickly because I wasn't growing enough (one of my personal values!). One of my first jobs was cold-calling for a commercial real estate tenant representative. I hated it, was paid minimum wage, and really didn't learn anything. This didn't help me in any way.

Ultimately, unless you're one of the lucky few in Quadrant 2, you need to decide what to prioritize. Some people are okay being unfulfilled in their transactional income source, as long as it provides them with resources. For others, having a fulfilling job is more important than the growth prospects of their portfolio. Both answers are okay, and we'll work through your TIP shortly.

But first, I want to address one of the most common questions I get from aspiring and active real estate investors: "Should I work full-time in the real estate industry?" Many investors who are unhappy in their work or want to gain more resources assume they should go into real estate full-time. This can be a good idea for some, but it's not for everyone.

REAL ESTATE AS TRANSACTIONAL INCOME

To me, whether or not you should consider earning transactional income in the real estate industry comes down to the fulfillment and resource allocation spectrums. Will working full-time in real estate give you improved resources? Will it bring you more fulfillment? Will it improve your overall transactional income situation? If the answer to all of these questions is no, then you shouldn't do it! Why would you work full-time in real estate if it's not more fulfilling or lucrative for you? That makes no sense. If you answered yes to any of these questions, then you could consider real estate as full-time work.

Different jobs in real estate offer different levels of resources. The one thing almost all of them have in common is that they offer excellent skill development. Below I will provide a quick overview of different real estate jobs. If you're seriously considering pursuing one of these transactional income sources, you should learn far more about them than I can describe here.

Real Estate Services

These are jobs that help people transact on and manage real estate: real estate agents, loan officers, appraisers, property managers, inspectors, and more. Real estate service jobs are popular among investors because you are surrounded by real estate—making them a great way to build a network and learn the business.

Contracting/Construction

Another great way to learn the industry is to go into construction or one of the trades like plumbing, HVAC, electrical work, or becoming a handyman. A huge part of being a real estate investor is assessing the condition of potential deals, managing risk, making repairs, and adding value to properties you invest in. Working in construction or one of the trades is the perfect job to learn these skills while building a network.

Wholesaling

Wholesaling is a business where the operator (known as a wholesaler) puts a seller's home under contract and then "flips" it to a buyer. It's basically arbitrage for selling homes. The wholesaler looks to secure the property for under market value and then sell it to another investor for an "assignment fee."

Wholesaling is a controversial business, and each state has different laws about what rules wholesalers must follow. But when done ethically and legally, wholesaling can be a good way to learn the industry. As with the other two options, it's an excellent way to build relationships and become an expert at underwriting (analyzing) deals. Many investors wholesale, or work with wholesalers, but make no mistake—wholesaling is not investing, it's transactional income.

House Flipping

Although flipping houses is a very popular way to invest in real estate, it is transactional income. There is no residual income earned on a flip. Of course, there are varying degrees of involvement in flips. You can passively invest in a flip, or, on the other end of the spectrum, you can be on-site every day managing subcontractors and even swinging a hammer yourself. So, it is possible to earn transactional income as a house flipper without making it your full-time job, but just remember, no matter your personal involvement, flipping houses is transactional income. As we progress through this book, we will continue to talk about flipping houses—because it's an investing strategy with great profit potential—but remember that flipping is just one of many ways that you can earn transactional income and is not going to contribute to any residual income or cash flow goals you develop in this book.

Real estate services, contracting/construction, wholesaling, and flipping are just a few of the many transactional income options for real estate investors. If you're interested in pursuing a full-time career in any of these options, I recommend you learn more about them. BiggerPockets has books about becoming a real estate agent and flipping houses, and the internet is full of other resources where you can learn about these potential career paths.

PREP WORK
TRANSACTIONAL INCOME PLAN

STRATEGIC DECISION: To complete the Transactional Income Plan section of your PREP, set an intention for how you will earn transactional income over the coming years. This doesn't need to be very specific, but must inform what, if any, resources you plan to bring to your portfolio through your job. For exercises and more information about your Transactional Income Plan (TIP), see below.

Now that we've reviewed some of the trade-offs and decisions that go into earning transactional income, it's time for you to work on your TIP. The point of your TIP is just to write out a sentence or two about how you plan to earn your transactional income going forward. It can be as simple as "Stay at my current job indefinitely" or could entail a complete career change.

If you haven't already done so, take a moment right now and figure out which quadrant your current jobs fall into. How fulfilling is your current job? Is it providing you with resources you can contribute to your portfolio? If you're not currently employed, think about prior jobs or jobs you're interested in.

No matter where you find yourself, remember not to get discouraged. It's okay if you're not where you want to be right now. The most important thing is not where you are—it's diagnosing your situation and coming up with a plan to move forward. Here are a few tips based on which quadrant your current transactional income source falls into.

- The best position in which to build a portfolio is Quadrant 2. If you're accumulating resources and you're fulfilled in your job, you're in a great spot. Liking your job means you probably want to stay in it—and therefore can continue to bring strong resources to your portfolio.
- Quadrant 3 provides resources but not fulfillment—a perfectly fine place from which to start building a portfolio. Frankly, your portfolio doesn't care if your resources come from a fulfilling job or not; it just needs resources. The

question for this quadrant is whether your transactional income is sustainable. If the job is unfulfilling, can you keep at it long enough to fuel your portfolio or should you consider other options?

- People in Quadrant 1, who are fulfilled but lacking resources, need to think hard about how they plan to grow their portfolio. You need resources from somewhere. If building a real estate portfolio is a large enough priority to you, you could consider switching jobs to a more resource-intensive job. On the other hand, finding a fulfilling job isn't easy, and if you've found one, staying in that job may very well be the right choice. Often a hybrid approach is possible. Can you stay in your job and get resources from outside your job, like a side hustle? Could you reduce hours to free up your time resources? Can you work part-time for an investor to learn some skills? One way or another, you need resources to contribute to your portfolio.
- Quadrant 4 is the hardest place to start because it lacks fulfillment and resources. Ideally, you can find a new source for transactional income, but that's not always easy to do. Not everyone can just go find a better job with ease. But I encourage people in this quadrant to think about ways they can improve their resource accumulation or their job satisfaction over time. Even if a new job isn't readily attainable, look for small ways to free up some time, learn a new skill, or identify ways to improve your transactional income situation over the long term.

From here, you need to write out a Transactional Income Plan on your PREP. Your TIP does not need to be as detailed as some of the other parts of your PREP. For example, you can write "Transition to a higher-resource job within the next three years." That's an excellent plan! Or "Stay with current job until I reach $3,000 per month in residual income, then go part-time." You don't need to know the exact job you want today, nor do you need to make any changes immediately—but if you can get specific, go for it! The whole point of this exercise is to help you think through what resources you will contribute to your portfolio. The examples above work because, for Portfolio Strategy purposes, you can count on your current resource levels for the next few years but anticipate greater resources a few years out.

If you're planning a career change, don't make that decision lightly. You should talk to your family and community, consult people in the industry, think through whether you'll be good at the job, and seriously consider what benefits and risks there are in a potential change.

If you're developing your Portfolio Strategy with a partner or spouse, make sure to consider if and how each person will contribute transactional income. One partner can focus on resources, while the other works at a fulfilling job. One partner can go full-time into real estate while the other continues at a job with great benefits. One can earn transactional income while the other one doesn't. The choice is yours—just make sure to write the plan for each partner.

If you need additional help with writing your PREP, here are a few questions to consider.

- What do my values tell me about how I could and should be earning transactional income?
- Do I find my current work meaningful beyond the resources it provides me?
- Does my current means of earning transactional income provide me with resources that will help me build a real estate portfolio?
- Is my current source of transactional income stable and secure? Is that a priority (maybe even a higher priority than a real estate portfolio) to me and my family?
- How difficult would it be for me to find a transactional income source that paid better? Or offered me more fulfillment?
- Would transactional income from the real estate industry put me in a better position to build my portfolio?
- Would a real estate job like flipping, wholesaling, or real estate services offer the same benefits (healthcare, paid time off, etc.) as my current job? Would it make it easier or harder to get a loan? Find partners?
- Do I want my entire career to be dependent on one industry, which can be cyclical? Or do I want to hedge my income streams by working across industries?
- Can I augment my resources through gig work, part-time work, or volunteering, above and beyond my current job?

While these are big, important questions for your portfolio, you don't need all the answers right now. For the purposes of your Portfolio Strategy, as long as you have a general idea of how much transactional income you'll be earning, you're doing great. Once you've thought this all through, write it down in your *PREP* in the Transactional Income Plan section.

Now that you've determined if and how you intend to earn transactional income, it's time to evaluate the specific resources you intend to contribute toward your real estate portfolio. To do this, we'll return to the concept of the Resource Triangle we discussed in Part 1, but we'll make it more personal. In the next chapter you'll do a Resource Audit to determine what time, skill, and capital you will contribute to your Portfolio Strategy.

Chapter 12
RESOURCE AUDIT

Every portfolio needs the same three resources: time, skill, and capital. But remember, you don't personally need to have all three. As long as you have one resource, you can exchange it for the other two. For example, if you have time, you can exchange it for other people's capital or skill. If you have capital, you can trade it for someone else's skill or time—and so on.

As you develop your Portfolio Strategy, it's important to assess which resources you have currently, and which of them you realistically can contribute toward your portfolio. To do this, we're going to conduct a Resource Audit. Over the coming pages we'll go through each resource individually—time, skill, and capital—and do a thorough assessment of how much of each you have today, and what you can contribute to your portfolio.

As you go through the Resource Audit, remember it's common and perfectly fine if you lack any (or all) of these resources right now. Good strategy doesn't come from having the most or the best resources. Good strategy comes from putting the resources you have to the best possible use. The point of this exercise is for you to take an honest look at your current situation and create an accurate assessment of the resources you have. The same can be said about the resources you *want* to commit to your portfolio. For example, if you have a lot of time on your hands, but your values dictate that you want to maximize family time, make sure to conduct your Resource Audit accordingly and don't commit all your time to real estate. The key here is to accurately assess what resources you can, and want to, commit to your real estate investing portfolio.

If you intend to simultaneously invest in other assets like stocks or bonds alongside your real estate portfolio, you can still use the frameworks in the Resource Audit. Conduct these exercises and then simply subtract the resources you will devote to other asset classes. For example, if you have $50,000 to invest, but want to allocate $10,000 to the stock market, simply put $40,000 into your PREP. The same goes with time and skills. Only put the resources you intend to dedicate toward real estate into your strategy.

TIME

Every person reading this book will value the three resources in the Resource Triangle somewhat differently. For me, the most valuable resource is time. Time is finite. Unlike capital and skill, you cannot "scale" how many hours you have in a day. None of us knows how many years we'll live, but while we're here, we all get the same number of hours in a day and days in the year. With a resource as scarce as time, it's important you spend it wisely .

To build a real estate portfolio, you need to commit at least some time. As we discussed in Part 1, although you may often hear the term "passive investing," there isn't any form of real estate investing that is truly 100 percent passive. If you're not managing deals yourself, you still need to at least be tracking the performance of the deals people are managing on your behalf. Even when you invest in a syndication, you should be doing due diligence, attending status calls, and reviewing financial performance. There are many moving pieces to a portfolio, almost all of which require some amount of time. You don't need to do everything yourself, but you do need to figure out how much time you want to commit to real estate. Once you know that, you can determine where to focus your time and what you'll need to outsource to others.

What Time Can I Invest?

The more specific you can be about the time you intend to give to your portfolio, the better. If you're thinking, "I'll work on my portfolio when I can," I would caution against that approach for two reasons:

First, life is busy and unpredictable. Competing priorities come up all the time. Think about how hard it is to get to the gym or run an errand after work, given all the demands on your day. Setting an intention and carving out time blocks to build your portfolio is the best way to maximize your chance of success. If something is important to you, you have to make room for it. For example, because one of my Personal Values is mental and physical health, I set aside time to exercise every day. If building your portfolio is important to you, you have to set aside at least some time to pursue it.

The second reason you need to assess your time resource is because the time intensity of a real estate deal varies significantly by the Deal Design you choose. For example, flipping houses is time intensive, house hacking requires a moderate amount of time, and investing in passive note funds requires minimal time. Knowing how much time you are willing to commit to real estate investing will help you pick tactics that fit your schedule and goals. If you have minimal time but choose to start flipping houses, your chances of success are low. Those two ideas are not aligned. You need to pick tactics that work within your time constraints.

I started my investing career with plenty of time (more than ten hours per week). This allowed me to actively manage deals and do a lot of repairs and maintenance myself. Over the years, my career has shifted, and now I have far less time to dedicate to my investments. As such, my tactics have changed. I hire property managers, invest in funds and syndications, and outsource all of my bookkeeping. If I tried to actively manage a new property now, I would fail. I have to align my portfolio with the time I can contribute to it. You need to do the same.

PREP WORK
TIME AUDIT

STRATEGIC DECISION: To complete the Time piece of your PREP's Resource Audit, set an intention for how much time you will commit to your real estate portfolio on a monthly basis. For help and exercises to think through your time commitment, see below.

To complete the Time Audit, all you need to do is commit a number of hours per week to your real estate portfolio. The idea here is that once you know the amount of time you can put into your portfolio, you can select the types of deals that work within your schedule when we move on to Part 3.

For some people, finding time to commit to real estate may be relatively easy; for others, it could prove difficult. Either way, I encourage you to try to find some time for your portfolio. Especially in the beginning, you need to learn and be hands on. You can become more passive over time, but I strongly encourage people to start by working on their business at least a few hours per week.

Although time is finite, I've found it's one of the resources that is easiest to reallocate. It can take years to substantially increase your income or to learn a new skill. But for many people, they can reprioritize some free or personal time toward real estate. I know this is not true for everyone—some people are already stretched thin, and it will be very difficult to find the time to invest. But if this is important to you, talk to your family, friends, and support group to find a way to commit *some* time toward investing. Remember, you cannot build something out of nothing, and even the most "passive" investments require some time. If you want to build a portfolio, you need to dedicate some time to it .

To help you think through your time commitment, below are some questions and ideas to consider.

- If building your portfolio is important to you, try to allocate as much free time toward real estate as possible, especially in the beginning. The more time you put in, the faster your portfolio is likely to grow.

- Generally speaking, the less capital and skills you have, the more time you'll need. Remember the Resource Triangle. If you don't have enough capital for a down payment, you'll likely need to trade your time for someone else's capital. Make sure you allocate time for that. The more time you're willing to allocate, the easier time you'll have finding capital partners to trade with.

- With most investments, time intensity varies over time. You'll need to commit much more time when you're in "buying mode" and for the first few months you own any new property. Between acquisitions, the time you'll need to spend on your portfolio should decrease. However, I recommend you don't reallocate that time away from your portfolio. Instead, spend that time learning, gaining new skills, and preparing for future deals.

- If you want to be actively involved in your investments (because that generally earns higher returns), you should probably allocate at least twenty hours per month toward your portfolio—and ideally more than that if you're just starting out. When you're first getting started, you need to allocate time both toward improving your skills and actually doing deals. If you want to get your first deal fast (which you should!), I'd allocate at least ten hours per week to learning and searching for deals.

- If you want to invest on the low-time-intensity, "passive" side of the involvement spectrum, you need capital. The minimum investment for syndications or funds is high. Typically, the minimum investment is around $25,000, and some have a minimum of $100,000 or even more. There are reasons for this, which we'll explain later, but for now just factor this into your thinking. If you have only $10,000 to invest, the most passive options won't work. You'll need to allocate more time to help yourself find a capital partner.

Hopefully the guidelines above, coupled with some self-reflection, have allowed you to come up with a set number of hours per week you can commit to real estate investing. If you're still struggling to nail down a number, or you need freeing up of some time, I have created an additional resource for readers of this book called the Time Budget. This tool will help you reflect on how you spend your time currently and prioritize your weekly commitments. You can find the tool and instructions in the Strategy Tool Kit that accompanies this book at www.biggerpockets.com/strategybook.

Once you have your number, write it down in your *PREP* under the Resource Audit section. Having an idea of the time you want to commit to real estate will make selecting markets, a management plan, financing options, and everything else much easier in the coming chapters.

Now, let's turn to the next resource: skill.

SKILL

Being a successful real estate investor requires specialized skills. If you're new to real estate, it may seem like investing is simple—all you're doing is buying property and collecting checks, right? Not exactly. Don't get me wrong, real estate isn't rocket science—it's a pretty logical business that nearly anyone can master—but it takes a diverse skill set applied appropriately to do well. The more skill you bring to a deal, and to your portfolio, the higher your potential rate of return, and the higher your probability of success.

Luckily, you don't need to possess every skill of an investor. There are just too many things to do yourself. As such, most investors trade capital or time for the skills of others, as we've discussed. In the previous section you determined how much time you can commit to your portfolio; in this section you'll think through how to use that time as efficiently and effectively as possible.

As we'll discuss at length in Part 3, each real estate tactic requires different skills in varying degrees of intensity. But to complete your Resource Audit, you need to get a basic understanding of the spectrum of skills that real estate investors may need to call upon during their career. Here is a list of the broad categories of skills that investors need to tap into.

- Portfolio strategy
- Deal flow
- Deal analysis
- Operations
- Networking
- Securing financing
- Finance and tax
- Market analysis
- Tenant management
- Repairs and maintenance

- Construction and capital improvements
- Transacting

Below I will explain the basics of each skill and why it's important. But know that this list of skills is far from exhaustive. There are far too many skills for me to list here, and I've bucketed a few big categories together for simplicity's sake. Within each of these categories there are many vital subskills and specialties, most of which we won't be able to cover in this book.

The purpose of the following explanations is not for you to get a full grasp of each skill, but rather to familiarize yourself with the many broad disciplines that real estate investors will call upon over the course of their career. Start thinking about which skills you can contribute as a resource to your portfolio and which you'll need to trade capital or time for.

Skill: Portfolio Strategy

Portfolio Strategy is the skill of allocating your resources in service of your long-term goals—and is what this book is about! This is a skill everyone needs to have and contribute to their portfolio. It's nearly impossible to outsource Portfolio Strategy. Luckily, since you're reading this book, you're already contributing this skill to your portfolio. Just remember, Portfolio Strategy requires continued attention throughout your investing career. You need to constantly be evaluating your tactics and updating your Portfolio Strategy to meet your ever-changing goals and circumstances. If you were to pick just one skill to devote time to mastering, this is the one I'd recommend.

Skill: Deal Flow

Deal flow is the skill of identifying opportunities for investment. This can be finding individual properties to buy, picking great syndication opportunities, or finding a reliable turnkey operator. Finding great investments is often a numbers game—the more potential deals you look at, the better deals you find, and the better your chance of success. I typically recommend investors develop this skill for themselves because it's so important, and it's difficult to outsource. You will always know your strategy best, and I find it very worthwhile to be able to generate deal flow that is well aligned to your strategy. How you get deal flow will depend on your broader strategy. If you're a very hands on, active investor, you're going to want to be looking at tons of different on- and off-market deals.

If you're more of a passive investor, deal flow will come from networking and building relationships with high-quality operators.

Skill: Deal Analysis

Deal analysis is projecting the performance of a potential real estate deal (also known as "underwriting" a deal). This is the skill of "running the numbers" on a prospective deal to understand the likely return the investment will generate. Depending on the type of investment, analyzing a deal will tell you key metrics like the projected **cash-on-cash return**, **return on investment**, **internal rate of return**, and more.

Everyone needs to be able to analyze deals, at least at an intermediate level, to be a successful investor. Sure, you can have someone on your team or in your network who helps you with deal analysis, but you need to know the basics. Otherwise, how will you know if the person on your team is even good at deal analysis? At the end of the day, the success of your Portfolio Strategy will come down to the performance of the individual deals you invest in. You need to understand which deals are going to deliver the returns you're seeking.

Deal analysis is not difficult, but it can be intimidating for those who have never analyzed an investment before. I wrote an entire book on this topic with J Scott to make it easy for real estate investors to become pros at deal analysis; it's called *Real Estate by the Numbers*, and I recommend it for those want to master this skill.

Skill: Operations

Operations is the running of the day-to-day activities of a business. This entails everything from hiring and managing employees to doing paperwork, ensuring compliance, and managing projects. It also includes managing the many partners and contractors you'll inevitably work with as you grow your portfolio. "Operations" is somewhat of a catchall term for "making your business work."

Every investor needs some operational skill, but the complexity will depend largely on your portfolio size and ambition. If you're intending to operate a modest portfolio of simple investments, you can likely learn and contribute the operations skills yourself. If, however, you want to grow a large team, take on big capital improvement projects, or diversify across many types of deals, you may want to bring in operational support.

Operations is one skill I find real estate investors often overlook or underestimate. There are tons of little administrative (and yes, sometimes boring) things that need to be done to run your business, but they are important and will have an outsized impact on your portfolio's performance. Make sure you or someone on your team knows how to operate your business well.

Skill: Networking

Networking is the skill of developing relationships with people across the real estate investing industry. As an investor you need personal relationships with people who are going to help you succeed, like agents, property managers, contractors, lenders, and, of course, other investors! It's not always obvious, but real estate is a relationship business. Having smart, competent people around you is one of the easiest ways to increase your chances of success.

Networking is not really a skill you can outsource. No one can build personal relationships on your behalf. To be a successful investor you need at least some basic networking skills. Luckily, networking isn't super hard. BiggerPockets provides an online community of several million investors where you can network and learn for free. There are real estate investing meetups in almost every city in the U.S., and plenty of conferences to attend. Depending on your personality type, some networking formats can be intimidating, but I encourage everyone reading this to find some way of networking that is comfortable to them—whether that's online or in person.

Remember that networking is a two-way street. Don't just approach people with the intention of finding out what they can do for you—look for ways to help those around you too. Whether that's teaching someone a skill you know, sending a referral for a contractor who did a great job, or whatever else you can think of, you should try to add as much value as (or more than!) you take. Networking is all about finding mutual benefit.

Skill: Securing Financing

Very few real estate investments happen with the cash of just one investor. Instead, most investments require some kind of financing. The skill of securing financing involves obtaining loans, private capital, or other sources of funds to purchase real estate investments. This can be as simple as applying for a conventional mortgage at a major bank, or as complicated as raising millions of dollars from dozens of individual investors to purchase a large multifamily complex.

If you're looking to actively purchase a few residential properties, this is a skill most investors can and do contribute for themselves. It's not so hard to figure out how to get a bank loan if you have a stable job and reasonable credit. However, if you want to raise money from private investors, want to use creative finance, or won't easily qualify for a bank loan, securing financing can be more complex and therefore a worthwhile skill to master.

Skill: Finance and Tax

The skill of finance and tax entails managing the flow of money in and out of your investments. This means everything from collecting revenue to categorizing expenses, paying contractors, bookkeeping, preparing tax documents, and tax strategy. Every investor needs this skill in their business, but this is one skill commonly outsourced to a professional bookkeeper or a certified public accountant (CPA).

Learning the tax code is pretty tough. Unless you're already a CPA or have just a rental property or two, I recommend you find a professional to help with your tax preparation and planning. Learning the bookkeeping side can be relatively simple with the help of software (something like QuickBooks) for people who want to DIY their finances, but if you're not going to do it diligently, I'd recommend outsourcing your bookkeeping. Whatever you do, just make sure you keep excellent records. Trust me (and the thousands of other investors who have downplayed the importance of bookkeeping)—do this one right.

Skill: Market Analysis

Market analysis is the skill of identifying which markets and specific neighborhoods to invest in. It plays a large role in the performance of your investment. As we'll discuss at length in Part 3, where you invest plays an important role in your deal performance, and this skill allows you to identify markets that are well aligned with your overall strategy.

Luckily, learning market analysis isn't difficult if you're fairly analytical in nature and educate yourself on the macroeconomic factors that drive local economies. This is a skill that most investors can learn quickly and take on for themselves. You'll learn much of what you need to know for this skill in Chapter 22. If you aren't interested in learning this skill, I personally put out analyses of many different cities and regions around the country, as do other analysts. Just make sure you work with objective analysts who don't have a financial interest in selling you one market over another.

Skill: Tenant Management

Tenant management is the skill of working with the individuals, families, or businesses that occupy your investments. For rental properties and commercial properties, this is typically a "tenant," while for short-term rentals, you're working with "guests." Tenant management is a very broad skill set and involves everything from marketing your units to screening tenants, managing leases and documents, communicating with tenants, and managing relationships. It can also unfortunately mean managing uncomfortable situations, or even an eviction if things go really wrong.

Tenant management is a skill that can easily be done by you, but is also easily outsourced. The individual activities undertaken to manage tenants are easy: posting listings to online marketplaces, communicating with tenants, managing leases, screening tenants. This stuff isn't conceptually difficult, but it takes time and appeals to a certain personality. Do you like talking to people? Are you good at building long-term, constructive relationships? Are you comfortable talking to people who are upset or agitated? If so, contributing tenant management could be an easy and profitable option for you. If you answered no to the above questions, you may want to consider flipping (which doesn't have tenants at all!), hiring a property manager for this skill, or seeking more passive options for investing.

Skill: Repairs and Maintenance

Repairs and maintenance is the skill of keeping a property functioning as expected. This includes keeping the lawn mowed, repairing broken appliances, painting the walls, and everything else in between. It also entails fielding calls/requests from tenants, conducting other communication with tenants, and managing contractors. It does not include improving the property (renovating a kitchen, etc.)—that is a separate skill we'll discuss shortly

This is a skill required for all deal types that you hold for a long period of time (commercial, rentals, STRs). Things break—it's just a fact of life. It is your responsibility to keep your units in the same working condition as they were when your tenants signed a lease (or better!). This is another skill that can be easily outsourced or done yourself. If you're handy and know how to fix things, you can contribute this skill to your portfolio. It can be tempting to try to fix things yourself to save money, but is this actually a good use of your time or are you better off focusing your efforts on an area of your portfolio you're more proficient in? If you struggle with fixing things, or simply don't want to do repairs yourself, you can typically hire out repair and maintenance work easily. Many investors choose a "hybrid" approach to this skill—doing some easy maintenance work themselves, while hiring out the more complex work.

Skill: Construction and Capital Improvements

Construction and capital improvements is the skill of adding value to your properties through construction or renovation. Recall that repairs and maintenance mean keeping your property up to standard. Capital improvements are similar, but instead of maintaining the status quo, they're investments you make to improve the quality (and value!) of your property. This can be something as simple as a kitchen renovation or adding an extra bedroom, or as complicated as ground-up construction or adding an accessory dwelling unit (ADU).

This is a skill not required for every deal. But if you plan to take advantage of the value-add profit driver, you'll need this skill in your portfolio. Construction and capital improvements are time-intensive activities that take attention and experience to do well. That said, they're also one of the best ways to generate returns as a real estate investor. Whether you're doing ground-up construction, flipping houses, or adding value to a rental property, capital improvements (done well) are a proven moneymaker.

Given the potential for profits and the complexity of the skill, most investors choose to hire out this skill to experienced contractors, architects, designers, etc. Of course, you can do it yourself, but make sure you can do this well! Construction is capital intensive, and you want to make sure you're putting your capital in good hands. If you intend to contribute this skill but are new to it, I encourage you to start small to learn, and gradually build up to larger (and hopefully more profitable) projects.

Skill: Transacting

Transacting (the actual buying and selling of real estate) requires a host of specialized skills. You'll typically need the skills of an agent, appraiser, inspector, title company, loan officer, and more to close on a property. That said, most of these skills are typically outsourced to professionals I'd only recommend learning and contributing these skills yourself if it aligns with your Transactional Income Plan. As discussed earlier in the book, pursuing these skills as a full-time job can be a great way to learn about real estate and generate money to invest with, but they are not "investing." Unless you want this to be your transactional income, I'd recommend hiring an experienced person and leveraging their transacting skills for your investing.

Now that you have a broad sense of what skills you'll need to execute on your Portfolio Strategy, it's time to identify which ones you'll contribute yourself and which you'll source from a third party.

PREP WORK
SKILL AUDIT

STRATEGIC DECISION: To complete the Skill part of your PREP's Resource Audit, determine what skills you'll be dedicating to your portfolio yourself and which you will source externally. On your PREP, only write the skills you will commit. For help and exercises to think through your skill contributions, see below.

Before we start selecting the skills you can bring to your portfolio, let me just say that I think this exercise is one of the most important, but often overlooked, parts of developing your Portfolio Strategy. When you first get into real estate, there are so many things to learn, and it can be very tempting to try to learn and do everything yourself because it's cheap. I'd caution against that approach. Learning and doing everything yourself may save you some money in the short run, but it will cost you valuable time, and your deals will have less skill contributed to them.

One of the most common regrets I hear from other investors is "I should have built a team sooner." The reality is you cannot possibly master all the skills an investor needs. You might be able to learn the basics of many of these skills, but you cannot do them all well. You have to carefully consider how you are allocating your resources.

In the Skill Audit exercise, you will go through each broad skill category and consider how you intend to acquire or implement that resource. Do you already have any of these skills? How hard would it be for you to learn each skill? Do you want to learn it, or would it be better to trade either your time or money resource for that skill?

There are a couple of skills that I strongly recommend you become proficient at yourself. Those are the first five listed above: portfolio strategy, deal flow, deal analysis, networking, and operations. To run a portfolio, it will help you to at least know the basics of these skills. You can still get help with them (I certainly do!), but I wouldn't recommend trying to acquire these skills entirely from external sources.

Beyond these are skills you can outsource some or all of. Think about which skills you can realistically contribute to your portfolio today, or in the near future. You don't need to have each skill that you contribute perfected right now—but you should be able to reach proficiency within three to six months if you're going to contribute it.

Use the table below to evaluate each skill for yourself.

SKILL	CURRENT SKILL LEVEL	DIFFICULTY TO LEARN	CONTRIBUTE/ ACQUIRE
Portfolio Strategy			
Deal Flow			
Deal Analysis			
Operations			
Networking			
Securing Financing			
Finance & Tax			
Market Analysis			
Tenant Management			
Repairs & Maintenance			
Construction & Capital Improvements			
Transacting			

First, in the Current Skill Level column, write down your current skill level in the category as high, medium, or low. If you have no experience in a category, just put low. If you feel like you could contribute this skill to a real estate deal in most circumstances, put medium. If you are a genuine expert in one area, mark it as high.

Note that you shouldn't be medium or high in very many categories. If you're starting out, you might be low in every single category, and that's okay. Try to put your ego aside here. It's not a failure to be low in many categories, and, in fact, I recommend you err on the side of underselling yourself. Admit where you are not an expert and where someone else's expertise will benefit you. Remember, these resource exercises are all about understanding where you are today—not about the future. It's not reasonable or expected for you to be an expert in each area, and you can always acquire new skills. That said, if you have a lot of skills today, more Deal Designs and tactics will be available to you in the near future.

Next, go through the Difficulty to Learn column and mark down how hard it would be for you to learn the skill as high, medium, or low. If there is a skill category you have marked as high for the Current Skill Level, you can just leave the Difficulty to Learn column blank. If you're already an expert, I am going to presume you won't have trouble staying on top of your game. Again, be honest with yourself about what you're good at and what you'll enjoy doing. I find it helpful to think about what you do with your free time and how you earn transactional income. Are there related skills from elsewhere in your life that you can apply to your portfolio? For instance, I have a master's degree in business analytics, so deal analysis and market analysis come easily to me. You may be great at operations or bookkeeping from a job, or perhaps your hobbies include working with your hands and you'd be good at repairs and maintenance. From the descriptions of the skills above, you should have a decent idea of what skills you're well suited to pursue.

The last step in the Skill Audit is to decide if you're going to learn and contribute each skill yourself or acquire it from someone else. The options to mark down here are Contribute (I am going to do this myself), Acquire (I will hire this out), Hybrid (I will contribute some and acquire some), and N/A (I don't need this skill right now). This evaluation should be done by thinking through both your Current Skill Level and your Difficult to Learn columns. If you can and want to contribute a skill, do it! If you are not good at something, and it would be difficult for you to learn, acquire it! There is nothing wrong with acquiring skills from third parties (using either your time or your capital). Being honest about what skills you can contribute will help you scale faster and reduce risk. Although acquiring the skills of others can cost money in the short run, I am quite confident it will improve your returns over the lifetime of your portfolio.

Remember that the skills you choose to contribute can be used for your own deals, but you can also use them to trade for the resources of others. As an example, you may be able to contribute your transacting skills or repair skills to someone else's deal in exchange for equity or cash. Make sure to consider what skills you have that may be of use to other investors and can contribute to your Portfolio Strategy beyond just your next acquisition.

To help you think through your Skill Audit, let's take a look at mine.

SKILL	CURRENT SKILL LEVEL	DIFFICULTY TO LEARN	CONTRIBUTE/ ACQUIRE
Portfolio Strategy	High		Contribute
Deal Flow	Medium	Medium	Hybrid
Deal Analysis	High		Contribute
Operations	Medium	Medium	Contribute
Networking	Medium	Medium	Contribute
Securing Financing	Medium	Low	Contribute
Finance & Tax	Low	High	Acquire
Market Analysis	High	Medium	Contribute
Tenant Management	Medium	High	Hybrid
Repairs & Maintenance	Low	High	Acquire
Construction & Capital Improvements	Low	High	Acquire
Transacting	Low	High	Acquire

As you can see, even though I am an experienced investor, I rate myself as high in very few categories, because I know I can easily hire more skilled people than I am in most categories. Next, I recognize that most of the skills for which I have only a low/medium Current Skill Level would be hard for me to learn, given my time constraints and abilities. Last, I seek balance between the skills I contribute and skills I acquire. Notice that outside the first five skills, I only contribute two skills fully. This is intentional. Even though acquiring skills externally can cost money or time, it allows me to focus on the things I am good at, while outsourcing the rest. This will *save* me time and money in the future.

 Take some time to complete the Skill Audit now. Write down the skills you plan to contribute on your *PREP*.

As we proceed through this book, the results of your Skill Audit will be very beneficial in your Portfolio Strategy. In Parts 3 and 4, you will be selecting tactics and making an Action Plan. As you do this, think back to your Skill Audit. Which tactics will be easy for you to pull off, given your current skills? Which will require a lot of external skill that can be complex and expensive to acquire? As you put together your strategy, consider how you can put your skill resources to the best possible use.

CAPITAL

Capital, as a resource, has very different characteristics than time or skill. While time is finite, and there is a practical limitation on what skills you can realistically contribute to your portfolio, capital is the opposite. The amount of capital any one individual can have is theoretically only limited by the total monetary supply on earth, and each person reading this book will have different financial resources at their disposal.

How much capital you can contribute to your portfolio today will play a big role in your Portfolio Strategy. Remember, you can get started even with little or no capital—but the amount of capital you put toward your portfolio will dictate which tactics you select in Parts 3 and 4.

I'll be frank: The more capital you have when you get started, the easier it will be to build your portfolio. As Benjamin Franklin said, "Money makes money. And the money that money makes makes more money." This is the basic premise of investing—using money to make more money. When you have capital to begin with, you'll be able to consider more tactics and start compounding your money sooner. This is one of the reasons you may want to prioritize earning transactional income with the highest earning potential: more and faster access to capital.

If you don't have tons of capital to invest right now, don't worry. This is very common. Throughout my time at BiggerPockets, I have witnessed thousands of investors starting with little to no money build successful portfolios. You can do it too. As I hope you can see by now, it's totally fine to have little or no money as long as you have one of the other resources. You'll just have a narrower set of tactics to choose from at the outset.

Regardless of where you're starting from, it's absolutely essential to assess your overall financial position. Conducting a Capital Audit and understanding your current financial situation will help you in two important ways: First and foremost, it will help you pick the most beneficial and achievable real estate investing tactics for your portfolio in Parts 3 and 4. Second, measurement is essential to growth. If you don't know where you are right now, how will you know whether or not you've improved? Imagine wanting to build your social media presence but not knowing how many followers you have to begin with. How would you know if you're achieving your goals? The same is true with your financial situation.

The specific financial measurements you'll need for your PREP are:

- Discretionary income
- Net worth
- Investable assets

Below I will explain each metric and give an example using an investor named Chloe, who works full-time as a graphic designer. Later in the chapter, I will provide instructions and tools for you to calculate these metrics for yourself.

Discretionary Income

- **What it is:** The monthly income you have left over after covering expenses
- **How to calculate it:** Total Income – Total Expenses
- **Why it matters:** Calculating your discretionary income unlocks many insights: your current income, spending patterns, and how much capital you can commit to your portfolio on a monthly basis. It will also help you decide how much of your investing income to reinvest, what profit drivers to prioritize, and what deals to choose. You will use your discretionary income to help set your financial goals in Chapter 14.

Example: Let's take a look at Chloe's discretionary income. To calculate this, first Chloe adds up her post-tax income, which includes both her W-2 job and some freelancing she does. In total she earns $5,100 per month after taxes. Next, Chloe sums her monthly expenses, which come out to $3,638 per month. To calculate her discretionary income, Chloe simply subtracts her expenses ($3,638) from her income ($5,100) and gets a total discretionary income of $1,462 per month.

From this exercise, Chloe knows that even after all of her expenses, she has $1,462 that she can use at her discretion (hence the name!). She can choose to invest that into her portfolio, save it, or spend it.

DISCRETIONARY INCOME: CHLOE FRANKLIN
As of December 31, 2023

Income	Estimated Value	Expenses	Estimated Value
Salary	$4,500	Mortgage	$1,623.00
Freelancing	$600	Car payment	$325.00
		Student Loan Payment	$280.00
		Food & Groceries	$400.00
		Entertainment	$350.00
		Gym	$60.00
		Gas	$100.00
		Misc	$500.00
Total Income	**$5,100.00**	**Total Expenses**	**$3,638.00**
Discretionary Income			**$1,462.00**

Net Worth

- **What it is:** The total value of everything you own (assets) minus everything you owe (liabilities)
- **How to calculate it:** Total Assets – Total Liabilities
- **Why it matters:** Your net worth is an important measurement of your financial position and stability. It gives you a scorecard to track your financial position over time, including the value of your real estate holdings and any debts outstanding. You will set a goal for your net worth in Chapter 14.

Example: Chloe has a list of assets that includes her cash, her investments, her home, and really anything else of value that she owns. Her list of liabilities contains all of her debts including her mortgage, car loan, student loans, and credit card debt.

Now all we have to do is subtract the total liabilities from the total assets and we have our net worth. In the case of Chloe, her assets amount to $130,000 and her liabilities add up to $318,800. When we subtract the total liabilities from the total assets, we get a net worth of $119,200.

PERSONAL FINANCIAL STATEMENT: CHLOE FRANKLIN
As of December 31, 2023

Assets	Estimated Value	Liabilities	Estimated Value
Cash or Cash Equivalent		**Loans**	
Cash on Hand	$500.00	Mortgage - Personal Residence	$248,000.00
Bank - Checking Account	$2,500.00	School Loan	$55,000.00
Bank - Savings Account	$18,000.00	Car Loan	$14,600.00
Retirement Accounts		**Revolving Debt**	
Self-Directed IRA	$22,000.00	Credit Cards	$1,200.00
Investments		**Other**	
Stocks	$24,000.00		
Bonds	$6,000.00		
Real/Personal Property Owned			
Personal Residence	$345,000.00		
2018 Nissan Altima	$18,000.00		
Jewelry	$2,000.00		
Assets Total	**$438,000.00**	**Liabilities Total**	**$318,800.00**
Estimated Net Worth:			**$119,200.00**

Through this exercise, Chloe can now see her complete financial situation. If she were to sell everything of value she owns, and pay off all of her debts, she would be left with an impressive $119,200. This information will help Chloe set her financial goals and give her an important metric for tracking her progress over time.

Investable Assets

- **What it is:** The capital you have today to invest in real estate
- **How to calculate it:** Liquid Assets – Emergency Reserves
- **Why it matters:** Investable assets are key to Portfolio Strategy, as they provide a snapshot of what your capital resources are today. You absolutely need to know your what your investable assets are in order to choose tactics throughout this book. Even if this number is zero, or smaller than you'd like, you need to know what it is.

Example: For Chloe to get her list of investable assets, she first needs to figure out what assets she is willing and able to invest into real estate. She decides she is willing to invest her cash and her stock and bond portfolio, which comes out to $51,000.

Next, she needs to subtract her emergency reserves. Even though she is willing to invest the entirety of her cash, as well as the value of her stock and bond holdings, doing so wouldn't be wise. She needs reserves in case of an emergency (remember, liquidity is key!). Chloe decides she needs three months of expenses as reserves, which comes out to $10,914.

Last, she subtracts her total reserve ($10,914) from her committed assets ($51,000) and gets investable assets of $40,086. Chloe now knows she can responsibly invest $40,086 of capital into her portfolio. Knowing this number will be a huge help for her when she selects tactics and specific deals to go into her portfolio.

INVESTABLE ASSETS: CHLOE FRANKLIN
As of December 31, 2023

Assets	
	Estimated Value
Cash or Cash Equivalent	
Cash on Hand	$500.00
Bank - Checking Account	$2,500.00
Bank - Savings Account	$18,000.00
Investments	
Stocks	$24,000.00
Bonds	$6,000.00
Committed Assets	$51,000.00
Total Reserve	$10,914.00
Investable Assets	**$40,086.00**

Understanding your own discretionary income, net worth, and investable assets will put you in a great place to set financial goals, keep track of your progress over time, and start designing deals in Part 3.

PREP WORK
CAPITAL AUDIT

STRATEGIC DECISION: To complete the Capital part of your PREP's Resource Audit, calculate your discretionary income, net worth, and investable assets. These are all essential numbers you'll need to grow your portfolio. If you need assistance in calculating these metrics, use the exercises below and the Financial Assessment sheet in the Strategy Tool Kit that accompanies this book.

While calculating discretionary income, net worth, and investable assets for yourself may sound like a lot, don't worry. There is no complex math here, and all of the inputs are numbers you already know or have easy access to—like your salary, housing costs, car payments, etc.

The exercises that follow will help you understand the concepts and math to track your personal finances. If you want to do these calculations yourself, you're welcome to, but I've also created a tool that will do all the math for you. Just go to the Financial Assessment tab on the accompanying Strategy Tool Kit (find it at www.biggerpockets.com/strategybook). Even if you're using the Excel doc, read the explanations below so you understand the concepts behind these metrics, and to ensure you use the tool correctly.

Discretionary Income

Discretionary income is how much money you make after expenses each month. You calculate your discretionary income the same way you calculate the cash flow for a real estate investment. You add up all of your income and subtract your expenses. The result is your discretionary income. You may also hear this calculation called "disposable income"—which isn't exactly wrong, but I encourage you not to think of this income as "disposable"!

If you're a diligent budgeter, you may already know your monthly discretionary income, and if that's the case, feel free to write down your monthly discretionary income on your PREP and skip to the next section. I have to admit—I am terrible at budgeting. I've never really kept a detailed budget, and probably never will. So if you're like me, you may need some guidance, which you can find below.

Income

- If you are a salaried employee, just look at your last few paychecks and identify your post-tax income.
- If you have an hourly job, or one that has variable income each month like gig work, figure out your average income over the last three months.
- If you have more than one source of income, make sure to write down your income for each source. For example, if you own an existing rental property, have a side hustle, receive stock dividends, or anything else, make sure that is accounted for.

- If you're creating a Vision as a couple, make sure to include the income sources for both people.

Once you know your monthly income, write that down in the Excel file or wherever you're doing your calculations.

Expenses

- Start with the fixed expenses (costs that don't change month to month). These are things like rent/mortgage payments, car payments, childcare, debt payments, etc. You should hopefully have statements for these big-ticket items regularly available.
- Next, move to the variable expenses and try to come up with an average from the last three months. These are things like groceries, eating out, gas, entertainment, clothing, etc.
- Last, I like to make a generalized "miscellaneous" category. In my opinion, it's not necessary to make a line item in my expenses for every little thing. If I spend less than $100 per month on average, it all goes in the miscellaneous category. It's not that these expenses aren't important—they are—I just don't want to have fifty expense categories on my budget. Try to figure out what those small expenses added up to on average over the last three months.

Results

Now that you have your total income and total expenses figured out, simply subtract your expenses from your income, and you have your discretionary income. Whatever the results of your calculation, it's okay. That said, your next steps will depend on whether your discretionary income is positive or negative.

Negative Discretionary Income: Fix This First

Having negative discretionary income is not ideal. By spending more than you're making, you are racking up (bad) debt, and I recommend you address this as soon as possible. You can continue to craft a strategy, but I don't recommend making your first investment until you are earning more than you spend. It will be nearly impossible to get a conventional loan with negative discretionary income and challenging to find a partner (though theoretically possible).

Improving your budget is beyond the scope of this book, but if you find yourself with a negative discretionary income, I suggest you turn to one of many free online resources that can help you with budgeting and saving money and teach you ways to increase your income. I also recommend the book *Set for Life* by Scott Trench, which can help you with your personal finances.

If you have negative discretionary income, you can still complete your PREP! Write down $0 as your discretionary income and keep reading. You can still use the concepts in this book to start planning your portfolio, even if you can't make your first investment right away.

Positive Discretionary Income: How Much Will You Invest?

If you have positive discretionary income, you need to figure out how much of that discretionary income you're planning to invest. There is no right answer to this question, but financial advisors generally suggest investment rates according to the age at which you start investing (remember, if you start early, you have more time to compound and don't have to save as much).

Start in your:

- 20s: 10–15 percent
- 30s: 15–20 percent
- 40s+: 25–35 percent

These rules of thumb are based on retiring at a traditional age, in your mid-60s. So, if you want to retire sooner than that, or want to maximize your wealth, try to invest as much as you can as soon as you can.

Once you have decided how much of your discretionary income you want to contribute to your portfolio, write it down on your *PREP*.

Net Worth

To measure your net worth, the first step is to count up everything of value that you possess. And while I don't mean every individual thing, I do mean anything that is worth more than a few hundred dollars. Own a car? That's an asset. Contribute to a 401k? That's an asset. Jewelry? Also an asset.

A few quick tips:

1. You may have some items of value like a laptop, a TV, expensive clothing, or something else valuable—all of which are technically assets—but if you use those items and don't intend to sell them, you can leave them off your list of assets.

2. Even if your asset has a loan against it, it is still an asset (this is called an "incumbered asset"). So, if you own a home that is worth $400,000, but you have an outstanding mortgage on it, it's still an asset. Add the $400,000 to the Assets column of your Net Worth spreadsheet. We'll talk about the loan in the Liabilities column.

3. Don't overthink what is an asset and what's not. While some people say that a car is not an asset because it declines in value, that is incorrect. It's still an asset, just a depreciating asset. There's a very famous real estate book, *Rich Dad Poor Dad*, that says your personal home is not an asset because it doesn't make you money.

While well-intentioned, it's actually incorrect. If you can sell it for cash, it's an asset. Whether or not an asset is a good use of capital is a totally different question and has no bearing on whether or not it's an asset in the first place. For the purposes of calculating your net worth (and legal accounting!), anything that can be exchanged for cash is an asset.

Once you've completed your list of assets, write down all your liabilities. Remember, liabilities are debts that you owe other people. Here are a few things to think about.

- Common liabilities are a mortgage, student debt, car loans, credit cards, or even money you owe a friend or family member.
- This is where you account for any incumbered assets (assets with a loan against them). If you own a home, you should have listed the full property value as an asset, but you also need to list the outstanding debt as a liability. Same goes for a car.

Results

Once you have your lists, simply subtract your liabilities from your assets and you will have your net worth. If your net worth is already positive, that's great. If your net worth is currently negative, it's nothing to worry about. I started this way! As long as you have positive discretionary income, you should be able to start building your portfolio.

Take a minute to write down your net worth on your PREP, under the Capital Audit section. Knowing your net worth will help you set future goals and track your financial progress over time.

> **ACCREDITED INVESTOR:** *Before moving on, take a minute to figure out if you qualify as an accredited investor. An accredited investor is defined for an individual as anyone who has made at least $200,000 per year for the last two years and has a reasonable expectation to make that much money again this year or has a net worth of at least $1,000,000. For married couples filing together, the income requirement goes up to $300,000 per year, but the net worth requirement stays at $1,000,000. There is actually a whole list of ways to qualify as an accredited investor, but these are the two most common. Now that you've calculated your income and net worth, see if you qualify. If you meet either of these criteria, you are likely an accredited investor and will legally be able to invest in almost any type of real estate offering, whether passive or active.*

Investable Assets

To calculate your investable assets, you need to do a few simple calculations. First, you need to figure out your liquid assets, and how much of them you want to contribute to your real estate portfolio.

- As a reminder, liquid assets are assets that can *easily* be converted into cash. There's really no definition of what "easily" means, but I generally define it as anything you can turn into cash in less than a week.
- Under this definition, any cash or cash equivalents you have in the bank, stocks, bonds, and even a car could potentially be a liquid asset. On the other hand, your 401k or retirement account, your home, or your stake in a business would be considered illiquid.
- For the purposes of Portfolio Strategy, you can omit any liquid assets you don't want to invest into real estate. For example, if you have a car, jewelry, or a stock portfolio that you don't want to put into your portfolio, don't list it. These are technically liquid assets, but in this book, we're not going to talk about assets you keep outside of real estate.
- Recall our conversation from Chapter 8 on liquidity. You need to maintain cash reserves for your investments, and cash reserves, although liquid, are not investable assets!

Once you have your list of liquid assets, you need to calculate your personal reserves. This is the cash you keep on hand to cover any emergency expenses you incur as an individual (as opposed to reserves you keep for your business). Most people choose to calculate their reserves by thinking about how many months of expenses they want to have on hand in case of an emergency. Here are some guidelines for determining how much to keep in reserves.

- Most budgeting experts recommend you keep three to six months of expenses on hand in case of an emergency.
- Where you fall within that range is up to you. If you have a relatively stable job and are single, three months is likely enough. If you have a job with variable income or you have children, you probably want to be more conservative and keep closer to six months of expenses in reserves,
- You should also factor in economic conditions. If there is an impending recession or your employer is facing difficult times, you may want to up your reserves.

To calculate your reserves, simply multiply your monthly expenses (which you figured out when calculating your discretionary income) by the number of months of reserves you desire. Once you have that, subtract your monthly reserves from your liquid assets, and you have your investable assets.

Results

The results of your investable asset calculations will help you make key decisions about your Portfolio Strategy. If you don't have any investable assets, that's totally okay. Remember, you can trade either your time or your skills for other people's capital. That's what I did. Knowing that you don't currently have investable assets simply means that you'll want to focus on partnerships, and perhaps increasing your discretionary income over time, to get started.

If you have investable assets, think through the calculation one more time to make sure you want to commit these assets to your portfolio. To get the most out of your PREP, you need an accurate number for your investable assets. Here are some final thoughts on how to allocate these assets.

- The more you invest now, the better your financial position will be over the long run. If your goal is to grow as quickly as possible, you'll want to invest as much of your liquid assets as possible.
- If you have under $20,000 in investable assets, you won't have many options for direct ownership (owning a property yourself). It's technically possible, but you may want to think about partnerships to get started. If you have more than $20,000 in investable assets, you can consider most tactics, depending on where you want to invest and your tactics (more on that later).
- If you don't have a proper emergency fund, you should start there. It's extremely risky to invest in anything if you don't have an emergency fund established. While this will slow down your investing at first, it will empower you later to take on the necessary risk needed to build a great portfolio.
- At this point, many people ask if they should use their assets to pay down debt. This can be a controversial topic, but I don't think it needs to be. I think that for most people there is a pretty simple rule of thumb to follow: If the interest rate on your debt is higher than the rate of return on a potential investment, pay it down. For example, if you can earn 12 percent on a rental property, but you have credit card debt with an interest rate of 20 percent, you're

better off paying down the credit card debt. However, if you can earn 12 percent on a rental property, but your student loan debt is just 6 percent, invest in the rental property!

Once you feel comfortable with the investable assets you want to commit to your real estate portfolio, write them down on your PREP.

You're now done with the Capital Audit! I know these Resource Audits were a bit of work, but they're absolutely crucial. With these assessments completed, you should have a general sense of the capital resources you have to commit to your real estate investing portfolio. You should be encouraged and proud that you've completed these exercises, even if the results of your audit don't reflect the reality you want to see in the future. Remember, good strategy is not about the resources you start with—it's about how well you use the resources you have!

As your resources change in the future, make sure to update this portion of your *PREP*. Maybe you get a raise and have more capital to invest. Or you have to take care of a loved one and need to reduce time spent on your portfolio. Maybe you commit to learning new skills. These changes in resources are inevitable. Remember that your Vision and your portfolio are meant to be flexible and to adapt to your changing life.

Knowing the resources you can contribute to your portfolio is an important step in creating your Vision and Portfolio Strategy. This will inform how you allocate resources in future parts of the book. But before we get to resource allocation, we need to next talk about how much risk you're willing to subject your resources to.

Chapter 13
RISK ASSESSMENT

Risk is an essential component of investing, but not all portfolios contain the same level of risk. As part of your strategy, you need to decide what levels of risk are appropriate for your portfolio. In the previous chapter, you decided what resources to contribute to your portfolio—now you need to decide how much risk you're willing to subject those resources to.

In this chapter we're going to conduct a Risk Assessment and develop your Risk Profile—a key component of your Vision. A strong Risk Profile will enable you to select the deals and tactics that are aligned with your risk preferences, and it will help you act more confidently. If you thoroughly understand and accept the risks you're taking, and know exactly how to mitigate those risks, it should reduce fear and encourage action.

Your Risk Assessment is made up of three components: **time horizon, risk tolerance,** and **risk capacity**. Each of these components is important by itself, but will also be combined into a unified Risk Profile. Your Risk Profile will give you crucial and actionable information to build out your Vision. With this information in hand, you'll have a much easier time working through Deal Design in Part 3, and choose the appropriate Portfolio Management decisions to employ in Part 4.

Below, I will explain and provide examples of each component of your Risk Profile, and how to unify them. Then, you will set your own Risk Profile in the PREP Work section at the end of this chapter. Throughout this chapter I will be referencing two different tools I've built to help you develop your Risk Profile, and I encourage you to try them. You can access the Time Horizon and the Risk Assessment tools for free through the Strategy Tool Kit Excel file that accompanies this book.

TIME HORIZON

Back in Chapter 7, we discussed the strategic implications of your time horizon. As a reminder, the longer your time horizon, the longer you have to compound your returns, and the more risk you should be comfortable taking. In that chapter, we also defined time horizon as the "period of time you intend to operate your portfolio for," expressed as a number of years. This is a correct definition, but it can mean different things to different people. Some investors see this as the day they sell off their portfolio and truly "retire." Some see it as the day they stop adding new deals to their portfolio. Others see it as the date they want to become financially free, even though they continue to manage their portfolio. All of these are worthwhile definitions, but for the purposes of your Portfolio Strategy, I propose standardizing how we think about time horizon.

To me, time horizon is the point at which you *can* live off your portfolio's residual income, even if you *choose* to keep growing your portfolio or earning transactional income. In other words, I think of my time horizon as the day I will be financially free—the point at which my residual income exceeds my desired living expenses.

I like this definition because it focuses your time horizon on your residual income (as opposed to transactional income or net worth), which is what you need to reach financial freedom, retire, or become work-optional. It also doesn't say that you have to stop working—it just states that you could stop working at this point if you choose. As an investor, you may choose to hold and operate your portfolio past your time horizon, and even until your death. That's a pretty common approach. But for the purposes of planning your portfolio, you cannot have an "unlimited" time horizon—hence the above definition.

Let's take a quick look at examples of time horizons from two investors, Alex and Vanessa. Alex is 37 years old, has a young family, and is brand new to real estate investing. He isn't very satisfied in his career, so rather than waiting until age 62 to retire, Alex wants to use real estate to retire ten years early, at 52. His time horizon is fifteen years (52 – 37 = 15 years). Vanessa is 55 years old, has a portfolio of five rental properties, has adult children, and is content in her current job. She plans to retire at age 65 and is on track for her goal. Her time horizon is ten years (65 – 55 = 10).

Both Alex and Vanessa can choose to continue to operate and even grow their portfolios past their respective time horizons—but they need a target date at which they could live off their portfolio. That's their time horizon.

RISK TOLERANCE

Risk tolerance is a subjective evaluation of how comfortable you are with risk. Knowing that there is a trade-off between risk and reward for every investment, where do you fall on that spectrum? Are you willing to expose yourself to high levels of risk to pursue maximum returns? Or do you prefer the comfort of low-risk investments, even if that means lower returns? Ideally, every investor wants excellent returns, but what if the potential for great returns comes with worry, anxiety, and fear? You need to be able to sleep at night!

Because risk tolerance is a subjective evaluation, there is no defined way to measure it. For the purposes of this book, we're going to use a subjective numerical scale from 1 to 5.

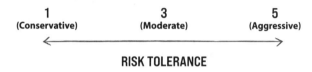

RISK TOLERANCE

A risk tolerance of 1 is very low comfort with risk, and a risk tolerance of 5 is extreme comfort with risk. I use a numerical evaluation because it will help you track your portfolio's risk levels over time, which we'll discuss more in Part 4.

An investor with an aggressive risk tolerance is a person willing to risk principal loss to maximize the potential for returns. Investors with a moderate risk tolerance are people who want solid returns while only exposing themselves to modest risks. This is the most balanced approach to investing and is how the majority of investors categorize themselves. Someone with a conservative risk tolerance is an investor driven primarily by their desire to avoid volatility and principal loss. These investors will earn lower returns, but they're willing to accept that because their risk of loss is also low.

Returning to our examples of Alex and Vanessa above, we can see how two different investors have two different tolerances for risk. For Alex, who doesn't like his job and has a time horizon of fifteen years, he is fairly comfortable with risk. He really wants to move up his retirement date by ten years and is willing to endure fluctuations in his portfolio value to achieve his goal. He scores his risk tolerance as a 4 out of 5.

Vanessa is even more comfortable with risk. Outside of her job, she is a thrill seeker and subscribes to the "nothing ventured, nothing gained" life philosophy. She has taken many financial risks in her life and is okay with the results, win or lose. She rates herself as a 5 out of 5 for risk tolerance.

RISK CAPACITY

Risk capacity is a measurement of how much risk you can responsibly take, given your personal financial situation. While this is often combined, or confused, with risk tolerance, they are separate things. Your risk *tolerance* is your comfort level when it comes to risk. Your risk *capacity* is your actual ability to take on that risk—regardless of comfort. Risk capacity, in this book, will be evaluated on a 1 to 5 scale, just like risk tolerance.

Our example investor Alex has a relatively low risk capacity. He is new to real estate investing and is putting a lot of his net worth into his first deal. Additionally, he has a family he needs to provide for and doesn't want to risk their financial stability. Even though Alex can *tolerate* more risk, his current risk *capacity* is a 2 out of 5.

For Vanessa, her risk capacity is much higher. She has an existing portfolio, she is happy in her current job, and her children support themselves. Vanessa doesn't want to do anything to jeopardize her retirement in ten years, but she is able to take on significant risk in pursuit of her financial goals. She scores her risk capacity as a 4 out of 5.

RISK PROFILE

For the purposes of Portfolio Strategy, you need to combine the various components of risk into one single Risk Profile. Of course, it's helpful to know your time horizon, risk tolerance, and risk capacity individually, but when you're looking at deals, you want just one policy about risk in your Vision. That's your Risk Profile, and is again evaluated on a scale of 1 to 5, with 1 being the lowest risk and 5 being the highest.

For our sample investor Alex, his Risk Assessment determined a time horizon of fifteen years, a risk tolerance of 4, and a risk capacity of 2. So, what's his Risk Profile? That is, of course, up to him, but I would say it's a 2.

Time Horizon	15 Years
Risk Tolerance	4 (Moderately Aggressive)
Risk Capacity	2 (Moderately Conservative)
Risk Profile	**2 (Moderately Conservative)**

Alex has a conflict between his risk tolerance and his risk capacity. This is quite common, and in these situations, I recommend deferring to the lower of the two. It's nice that Alex is tolerant of risk, but his risk capacity implies that taking on a high level of risk right now would be irresponsible. I recommend that if you're in doubt, you should take less risk.

When we look at Vanessa, her Risk Assessment has more alignment. She has a time horizon of ten years, with a risk tolerance of 4 and a risk capacity of 5.

Time Horizon	10 Years
Risk Tolerance	4 (Moderately Aggressive)
Risk Capacity	5 (Aggressive)
Risk Profile	**4 (Moderately Aggressive)**

Vanessa's risk capacity is high, but given her slightly lower risk tolerance (4), and her moderate time horizon, she has chosen a Risk Profile that is aggressive, but not excessively so. She doesn't need to take on super-high risk to reach her goals, and therefore doesn't.

Note that for those just starting out, it's very common for your risk tolerance to exceed your risk capacity. When you only have one deal and you're putting the majority, or all, of your principal into a single deal, you shouldn't be taking on a lot of risk. But you don't need to invest conservatively forever. As you grow your portfolio, your risk capacity and Risk Profile will change. Once you get a few deals under your belt and diversify your investments, you'll be able to adopt a more aggressive Risk Profile.

Similarly, your Risk Profile number may decline as you approach your time horizon (as long as you're on track to hit your goals). This is the situation I am in right now. I have a high risk capacity, but I am tracking ahead of schedule against my goals, so there is really no reason for me to take on a ton of risk. I can take on moderate risk and still hit my goals comfortably.

There is no one answer for your Risk Profile. You need to evaluate your Risk Assessment holistically and figure out the right strategic approach for your situation. A completed Risk Profile is an essential component of your Vision and your overall Portfolio Strategy. Your Risk Profile will dictate which deals you should do, the types of financing to pursue, how to manage your deals, and much more. While taking on risk offers better potential for returns, it's not the right solution for everyone. You need to be comfortable with the level of risk in your portfolio—and your Risk Profile should help provide that comfort. As you build your strategy, make sure that your deals and your overall portfolio's risk level are aligned with your Risk Profile.

PREP WORK
RISK ASSESSMENT AND RISK PROFILE

STRATEGIC DECISION: Define your time horizon, risk tolerance, and risk capacity. Then consolidate them into a guiding policy on how you'll use risk in your portfolio. Once you've done that, write them in the Risk Profile section of your PREP. For assistance, read the instructions below, and consider using the Time Horizon and Risk Assessment tools in the Strategy Tool Kit.

To determine the appropriate level of risk for your portfolio, you need to complete a Risk Assessment and unify the results into a Risk Profile. There are two tools in the Strategy Tool Kit that can help in these efforts: the Time Horizon tool and the Risk Assessment tool. In addition to these Excel files, below you will find commentary and open-ended questions that will help you evaluate the level of risk that belongs in your strategy.

Risk Assessment: Time Horizon

As mentioned earlier, your time horizon is your goal for when you can live off your portfolio's residual income and is expressed as a number of years from now. If you've never thought through your time horizon, I recommend you take some time to play with the **Time Horizon tool in the Strategy Tool Kit**. Go to the tab called Time Horizon, where you can enter some information about your financial situation from your Resource Audit and see how different time horizon scenarios impact your portfolio. Additionally, below are some questions to help you think about your time horizon.

- Is retiring your primary objective for real estate investing? Or are you willing to work longer to reduce risk and improve growth potential?
- How ambitious are your financial goals? The more ambitious you are, the longer your time horizon will need to be.
- Do you want to stop working altogether or are you more interested in being "work-optional"?
- Are you comfortable with a relatively common retirement age of 65 or would you prefer to move it earlier? Or do you love your work and plan to work beyond a traditional retirement age?

 When you've completed your evaluation, write down your time horizon (in years) on your *PREP.*

Risk Assessment: Risk Tolerance

Risk tolerance is a subjective measurement of your comfort in taking on risk. Remember, this isn't how much risk you necessarily *will* take—it's how comfortable you are with the idea of risk. Think through the open-ended questions below and determine your own risk tolerance on a scale of 1 to 5 (1 being low risk tolerance, 5 being the maximum).

- How do you feel about risk in non-investment parts of your life? Are you a thrill seeker or do you prefer to play it safe most of the time?
- What is more important to you: protecting the money you have or maximizing your returns? The more you look to maximize your returns, the more risk you will need to take.
- Are you willing to accept principal loss in order to maximize returns?
- If you saw your portfolio value decline by 10 percent or more, what would you do? Would you sell to avoid further losses or would you ride it out?
- How would you feel if the housing market experienced high volatility for a year or two? Are you comfortable riding out volatility in the service of long-term benefit?

 When you've completed your assessment, write down your risk tolerance as a number between 1 and 5 on your *PREP.*

Risk Assessment: Risk Capacity

Risk capacity measures whether you're capable of taking on risk, independent of your tolerance of risk. Again, this is a subjective analysis, and you should rank yourself on a scale of 1 to 5 (1 being low risk capacity, 5 being the maximum).

- How experienced are you in real estate investing? The more experienced you are, the higher your risk capacity. If you've never done a deal, or are on your first one, you will likely have a low risk capacity.
- What is your transactional income and personal cash flow situation? How stable is that income? The more cash you generate from outside your portfolio, and the more stable that income, the higher your risk capacity.
- How much principal do you plan to add to your portfolio? The more principal you plan to add over the course of your time horizon, the higher your capacity for risk.
- What is your family situation? Do others depend on you for financial stability and support? If you need a good deal of liquidity to support your lifestyle, your capacity for risk will be low.

 When you've completed your assessment, write down your risk capacity as a number between 1 and 5 on your *PREP.*

Your Risk Profile

Now that you've determined your time horizon, risk tolerance, and risk capacity, it's time to combine these three components into a single Risk Profile. This isn't complex—it is just a categorization of your overall approach to risk. You can do this in one of two ways:

The first option is to use the Risk Assessment tool in the Strategy Tool Kit Excel file. You can find this at www.biggerpockets.com/strategybook. This is a questionnaire that measures the different components of risk and delivers you a simple Risk Profile on a 1 to 5 scale. It's super easy to use.

The other option is to write out your time horizon, risk tolerance, and risk capacity, and perform your own analysis. The main things you want to look for here are inconsistencies and conflicts. For example, if you have a high risk tolerance, but a short time horizon, how will you resolve that conflict? Or if you have a long time horizon, but a high risk tolerance and high risk capacity, could you shorten your time horizon and work less?

Recall our example of Alex from earlier in the chapter. He had a conflict between his risk tolerance and his risk capacity, and decided to defer to his lower score (as I recommend). But that's not the only option. Alex could have addressed his conflicts in other ways. He could have lengthened his time horizon to, say, twenty years, to address this conflict. Or he could have decided to use a Risk Profile of 3 by averaging his scores for risk tolerance and risk capacity. There's no right answer here, but you need to come up with a level of risk that supports your strategic goals while allowing you to sleep at night.

Time Horizon	15 Years
Risk Tolerance	4 (Moderately Aggressive)
Risk Capacity	2 (Moderately Conservative)
Risk Profile	**2 (Moderately Conservative)**

Whether you use the Excel tool or a more subjective analysis, you need to put one consolidated Risk Profile number on your PREP. This should be a score of 1 through 5. Once you have it, write that down on your *PREP* under the Risk Profile section.

Knowing your Risk Profile is a key piece of your Vision and overall strategy. It will help you select the right deals, manage your portfolio well, and set realistic financial goals in the following chapter. Although it can be tempting to set wildly ambitious goals; you'll want to make sure that the financial goals you set are aligned with your Risk Profile. Pursuing ambitious financial goals that are in conflict with your Risk Profile lowers your probability of success and can add unnecessary stress to your investing.

Chapter 14
GOAL SETTING

Your Vision is starting to take shape. You've identified your Personal Values and created your Transactional Income Plan, Resource Audit, and Risk Profile. Now it's time to finish out your Vision with what I believe is the most exciting part: setting goals. In this chapter we're going to turn everything we've done so far into a set of clear, motivating, and achievable goals.

The importance of having specifically defined goals cannot be overstated. Before you start working on a big project like building a real estate portfolio, you need an idea of where you want to end up. That's where your goals come in. Well-structured goals help you make consistent progress toward what you want most in life. Good goals are motivating, empowering, and fun. And, best of all, by using the frameworks in this book, your goals will be achievable.

In this chapter we'll review a common goal-setting framework known as SMART goals, which will teach you how to set high-quality, motivating goals you're likely to stick to. Next, we'll walk through a set of exercises to help you set the two types of financial goals you'll need for a great Portfolio Strategy: cash flow goals and portfolio value goals.

SMART GOALS

There are many popular goal-setting frameworks out there. I've tried a handful and recommend the SMART framework. Here's how SMART goals work:

SMART is an acronym that stands for **S**pecific, **M**easurable, **A**chievable, **R**elevant, and **T**ime-bound. Each goal you set should have these five characteristics.

Specific

Every goal needs to be written in a way that makes explicitly clear what you're trying to achieve. A good goal leaves no ambiguity about what constitutes success or failure. For example, a specific net worth goal could be written as "Grow my net worth to $2,000,000 within ten years," as opposed to a goal written as "Become financially free." The first example is specific, and you'll know exactly what you're shooting for. The second goal is not specific and is open to interpretation.

Measurable

Goals should be quantifiable. Part of the purpose of writing down your goals is to keep track of progress and know when you've achieved your goal. Making your goals measurable enables you to keep score. If you write a goal like "Get enough cash flow to retire early," that's neither specific nor measurable. How will you know when you get there? Instead, you could write a similar goal as "Generate $100,000 per year in cash flow within the next five years." Writing the goal this way allows you to keep track of your progress, which will help motivate you and inform your investing decisions.

Achievable

You need to be realistic about your goals. There is nothing more discouraging than setting a goal that you cannot realistically hit. If you're starting with $10,000 in net worth and make $50,000 per year, a goal of "$2,000,000 in net worth within three years" is not achievable. No realistic investment could earn that rate of return.

The key here is to strike the right balance between ambition and reason. Don't make your goals so easy that you're selling yourself short, but don't make them impossible either. For me, I know I have the right balance when I am mildly uncomfortable with the goal. This is a very unscientific tip, but I think a good goal leaves you feeling 80 percent confident and 20 percent nervous that the goal is too big. To me that's the magic formula for motivation, but it could be different for you. Some people advocate for setting hugely ambitious goals, because even if you miss, at least you've made progress. That's never worked for me, and I personally recommend working toward goals you feel happy about and that are achievable.

Relevant

Your goals need to carry personal meaning to you if you want to stick to them. If your Personal Values consist of time with family, community, and balance, etc., then setting a goal to "Amass a fortune of $10,000,000 in the next three years" isn't really aligned. On the other hand, a goal like "Earn an extra $20,000 per year in cash flow so I can stop working overtime" might be a very relevant goal for you. Set goals that are aligned with your values and where you want to be—it's the only way you'll actually stick to them. Remember your why!

Time-Bound

Your goals need to be confined to a specific time period to keep you focused and on task. Open-ended goals never work, in my opinion. Notice that all of my examples above have a time frame in them. Instead of just writing "Generate $100,000 in cash flow per year," write "Generate $100,000 in cash flow per year, within the next five years." If you don't include a time frame, it's easy to procrastinate and deprioritize your goals in favor of more short-term issues that need your attention. Hold yourself accountable to a time period.

I've found that using SMART goals has improved my goal completion rate, both within and outside my portfolio. For example, when I set out to write this book in early 2022, I set a SMART goal for myself. I wrote down: "Write a top-ten best-selling real estate investing book about portfolio strategy by December 31, 2023."

This goal has every required component of a SMART goal. It's specific—a book about portfolio strategy. It's measurable—I want it to be a top-ten best-selling book in the real estate investing category (thanks for your help!). It's achievable—I've written a book before, and I know I can do it again, even though it feels hard. It's relevant because it is aligned with my value of personal growth. It's time-bound because I included a deadline for finishing the writing.

SMART goals have been very helpful to me in my personal life and professional career, and I am confident they can help you set goals you are motivated by and stick to. As we work through your cash flow and net worth goals over the coming pages, I encourage you to make them SMART.

FINANCIAL GOALS

How much money do you want? It's a pretty straightforward question, but in my experience almost no one can answer it. I'm guessing you know you want more than you have today, but how much more? You need to answer that question. It's crucially important to determining which tactics to use and investments to make, and it will keep you focused on the big picture. You need a long-term goal.

In this part of your Vision, it can be tempting to just write down a huge number, or think to yourself, "I just want to make as much money as possible." I understand that desire but would caution you against it.

First, as we just discussed, your goals need to be specific, relevant, and achievable. If you just write down a huge number without much thought, it will probably not be any of those things. That will reduce your chance of success.

Second, it will help you avoid a common portfolio trap —what I call "moving the goal posts." When you're starting out, it's typically pretty easy to know why you're interested in investing in real estate. Perhaps you want to quit your job, help out a family member, or free up your time. Whatever it is, there are probably a couple things that drove you to read this book that feel tangible and urgent. As you start to build your portfolio and accumulate wealth, that focus can be hard to maintain. If you find success, it can also be tempting to want more and more. Often you can wind up in a cycle where you work extremely hard to achieve your goal, only to arrive there and be dissatisfied because you now want more than you did originally. To reach your new goal, you work even more and negate the whole reason you started investing in the first place!

I've fallen into this trap before. When I first started out, I thought, "If I could just get an extra $1,000 a month, that would really reduce my stress." That was my goal at first, but when I got there, I was not even remotely satisfied and set my goals higher. I didn't even take a half second to appreciate what I had accomplished. Then, when I achieved that second goal, I did the exact same thing. I wasn't setting thoughtful or meaningful goals, so I kept changing my goals. It was inefficient and held me back from optimizing my portfolios in the early years.

That's "moving the goal posts"—basically, as you start to approach a goal, you move it further and further out. This prevents you from allocating resources properly and can lead to missing the entire point of investing altogether. The whole point of building a portfolio is to use your financial independence to achieve the life you want, not blow past your financial goals and just keep making more money for the sake of it. Don't get me wrong; I don't think there's anything wrong with being ambitious, and I'm not judging the numbers you write down in this section. I just know from experience that the more accurate your goals are now, the more efficient your Portfolio Strategy will be, and the more fulfillment you'll feel when you hit your goals.

Financial goals come in different shapes, sizes, and time horizons. Paying off debt, becoming financially free, and saving for a down payment are all good financial goals. In this chapter, though, we're going to focus solely on long-term financial goals. Remember, this part of the book is all about setting your long-term Vision. Specifically, this means we're going to be setting goals for your cash flow and portfolio value. In Part 4, when you're developing your Action Plan for the coming year, we will discuss short-term financial goals. In that section we'll talk more about goals for saving money, paying off debt, starting a side hustle, etc.

Whatever you write down in your PREP at the end of this chapter is great—modest, enormous, simple, etc. The important thing is to select financial goals that are aligned with the rest of your Vision—your Personal Values, your Transactional Income Plan, your Risk Profile, and so on. This will help you stay motivated and increase your chances of success.

PREP WORK
FINANCIAL GOALS

STRATEGIC DECISION: To complete the Financial Goals section of your PREP, create a cash flow goal and a portfolio value goal. Think hard about what you actually want and need before setting these goals. You can use the exercises below, as well as the Goal Setting tool in the Strategy Tool Kit, to help you set your financial goals. Once you have them, write them in your PREP.

For most real estate investors, reaching a certain level of cash flow is the ultimate financial goal. Your net worth and your portfolio's equity value are both important, but the key to financial freedom is generating enough cash flow that you can cover all your expenses and live the lifestyle you want. So how much is that? How much cash flow do you actually need to achieve your financial and lifestyle goals? Once you figure that out, you'll have your cash flow goal. Remember, residual income and cash flow are related, but not the same thing. The goal we're setting here is specifically how much cash flow you need to generate to live off of.

Setting a cash flow goal isn't very hard, and you've already done the hardest part—figuring out your discretionary income—which we did in the Resource Audit. If you need to, take a minute to review that. That section was an audit that included a simple, factual accounting of how things stand today. Now it's time to determine what you want your income to look like in the future.

As with everything in this part of the book, the outcome of this exercise is personal. Some people may be perfectly happy with their current lifestyle. If that's the case for you, this exercise is going to be super easy. Your cash flow goal can be to maintain the same income you have today, but to generate that income residually, rather than transactionally. That's an excellent, achievable goal.

If you already have an idea of how much cash flow you want, you can skip the following exercise and just write it down on your PREP. However, if you want some guidance on setting a cash flow goal, I have written out some steps I recommend you follow. You can do this on your own or use the Goal Setting tool in the Strategy Tool Kit that accompanies this book.

Step 1: Reimagine Current Expenses

I find that the best way to determine your financial goals is to start with the baseline of where you are today. It tends to be easier to base your future expectations off where you are today rather than pulling a number out of thin air. Because this goal is designed to help you reach the point where your cash flow covers your expenses, let's start with an analysis of your current expenses.

Return to your Resource Audit and find your listed expenses. Then go line by line and think through how you see each expense changing over time. In other words, do you see your spending going up? Will your spending go down as you approach your time horizon? Or are you content with your current spending levels? It's probably going to be a mix of a few things. Maybe you are content with your car, but you want a bigger house. Or you want to significantly increase your travel budget and pretty much everything else. Or maybe you live a fast-paced and expensive lifestyle now, but you're aiming for a simpler and less costly life. Consider each expense category and estimate where you expect it to go in the future.

Make sure to consider your time horizon carefully as you estimate your future expenses. For example, will you still have student debt in fifteen years? Will you need a bigger car to support a growing family? Think through where you intend to be when you reach your time horizon, and plan accordingly.

Step 2: What's New?

Do you anticipate new expenses entering your life? What expenses do you want to add on top of your existing ones? These additional expenses can occur either due to circumstance or desire. Perhaps you're expecting a child, or to pay college tuition, and want to plan for those expenses. Maybe you'll need to pay for medical insurance once you stop working. Or perhaps you want a second car, or to have more money for hobbies, or to buy a second home.

I'm guessing that because you're reading this book, you're hoping that real estate investing will enable some additional spending in your life, which makes total sense! Think through what new expenses may come into your life and put them into your cash flow goals.

Step 3: Reinvestment

Just because you can live off your cash flow doesn't mean you have to withdraw 100 percent of your cash flow from your portfolio. Instead, you can choose to continue to reinvest some of your profits back into your portfolio as new principal. As you know, the more principal you feed into your portfolio, the better the growth potential, so continuing to reinvest beyond your time horizon will provide additional upside. Personally, I think it's wise to keep reinvesting. It ensures your portfolio keeps growing and gives you some additional cushion in case some of your estimations on expenses are off.

Step 4: Account for Inflation

Don't forget to account for inflation! If your goal is to have $100,000 per year in cash flow in today's dollars, that $100,000 won't buy the same amount of stuff in the future. As a general rule of thumb, inflation causes the spending power of money to halve every thirty years. That is a pretty rough average, though. In recent years we've seen inflation get extremely high, but that was preceded by a decade of low inflation from 2010–2020. There's no knowing where inflation will go in the future, but I find the general rule of thumb that spending power halves every thirty years is a good enough estimate to help you with your planning.

For example, if your goal is to have $100,000 (in today's dollars) thirty years from now, you actually need to double your goal, since the spending power of money will have roughly halved. In thirty years, you'll actually need $200,000 in cash flow to have the equivalent of $100,000 of spending power in today's dollars.

If your time horizon is fifteen years, you'll probably want to increase your goal by 50 percent (multiply your goal by 1.5). This doesn't need to be a precise calculation (although super-analytical people can do that!)—the point here is to make sure you're accounting for inflation. It would be very disappointing for you to spend decades building a portfolio, only to realize your target income buys significantly less than what you were anticipating during your retirement. I know this concept is a little abstract, but remember inflation is risk! You need to account for and mitigate inflationary risk.

In the Strategy Tool Kit Excel file that accompanies this book, under the Goal Setting tab, I have built a formula that will do this calculation for you. Just enter your time horizon and your expenses in current dollars, and it will give you a rough estimate of what your goal should be in future dollars.

Step 5: Make It SMART

Once you have your cash flow goal, turn it into a SMART goal. Remember, just knowing a specific number doesn't make it a SMART goal—it has to be specific, measurable, achievable, relevant, and time-bound. For example, your SMART cash flow goal might sound like "Earn $12,500 per month in cash flow by 2035 to support my family and spend more time traveling." Now that's a motivating goal!

Cash Flow Goal Planning Tips

- Your real estate investing portfolio isn't magic. You can set whatever goals you want, but the more you want to spend, the harder (and probably longer) you're going to have to work to achieve it. As you're conducting this exercise, remember that everything in your portfolio has trade-offs. Want a nicer car? That's great, but it might mean you need to spend another year at your W-2 job. Either choice is okay, just be aware of the trade-offs you're making.

- It can be tempting to just pick a huge number, like $500,000 per year, and not think through the specifics. I would caution against that, and instead recommend that you tie your personal cash flow goals to specific expected increases in expenses. If you know specifically what you're working and investing for, it will help motivate you and keep you on track. For example, wanting "$250,000 per year in cash flow income by 2035" is an okay goal. But wanting "$250,000 per year in cash flow by 2035 so I can take one international trip each year and help my parents retire" is better. One is specific and relevant, the other is not.

- You don't need to amass money for the sake of it. Look back at your values. If one of your values is to become a tycoon and be exceptionally rich, then go ahead and make a huge financial goal. For everyone else, I'd recommend you think carefully about what your values and expenses actually say about the amount of money you need. What amount of money will allow you to live in alignment with your values and support the lifestyle you want? My advice is to make that your goal, not trying to be wealthier than some family member or friend just because of ego or competitiveness. You may not hear this a lot on social media, but the majority of real estate investors I know maintain a small-to-modest-sized portfolio that supplements their income and helps secure a stable retirement; they aren't in it for super early retirement or to grow a massive business.

- Your expenses don't need to be super specific, but the more accurate, the better.

- Your goals can change in the future, but in order to create a good Portfolio Strategy today, you need a reasonable estimation of what you're trying to accomplish.

Because goal setting is so important, let's revisit our example from Chapter 12, Chloe, to see how she sets her goals. As a reminder, Chloe has a current monthly income of $5,100 and expenses of $3,638, leaving her with a current cash flow of $1,462.

After examining her current expenses and what she wants to add, Chloe has some concrete ideas of what she wants her portfolio to accomplish for her.

- Retire from W-2 job in fifteen years.
- Upgrade primary residence and get a nicer car.
- Buy a small lake house for herself and her future family.
- Increase her entertainment budget by 50 percent to enjoy the fruits of her labor.

- Increase her "misc." category to not have to worry about random expenses.
- Pay off her student debt.

After Chloe has completed this exercise, her cash flow goal spreadsheet looks like this:

CASH FLOW GOAL: CHLOE FRANKLIN
As of December 31, 2023

Time Horizon (Years)	15		
Income		**Expenses**	
	Estimated Value		Estimated Value
Transactional Income		Expenses	
Salary	$0	Mortgage	$2,800
Freelancing	$0	Second Home Mortgage	$2,000
		Car Payment	$600
		Student Loan Payment	$-
		Food & Groceries	$800
Transactional Income Total	$0	Entertainment	$750
		Gym	$90
		Gas	$100
		Medical Insurance	$500
		Misc.	$1,000
		Portfolio Reinvesment	$1,000
Monthly Cash Flow Goal	**$14,460**	**Total Expenses (current dollars)**	**$9,640**
Annual Cash Flow Goal	**$173,520**	**Annual Expenses (current dollars)**	**$115,680.00**
Total Monthy Income at Time Horizon	**$14,460**	**Estimated Expenses at Time Horizon**	**$14,460**
Personal Cash Flow			
		Monthly Cash Flow Goal	$14,460
		Annual Cash Flow Goal	$173,520
		Expected Return on Equity	5%
		Minimum Portfolio Value Goal	$3,470,400

Note the changes here from Chloe's financial audit from Chapter 12. She has gone through and made conscious decisions about what expenses she wants to change and by how much. She's also taken her salary down to zero. If Chloe wants to continue working after fifteen years, she can—she just won't have to. Also notice that Chloe doesn't want to withdraw 100 percent of her cash flow and has added an "expense" of $1,000 per month to represent reinvestment back into her portfolio.

When Chloe adds up all of her estimated expenses fifteen years from now , it comes out to $9,640 in today's dollars. Because her time horizon is fifteen years out, she adds 50 percent to her goal to account for inflation, and winds up with a cash flow goal of $14,460 per month at her time horizon.

When Chloe turns this numerical goal into a SMART goal, it is written as "Earn $14,460 in cash flow within fifteen years so I can quit my job, modestly expand my lifestyle, and buy a lakeside cabin." What a great goal—it's SMART and super motivating! Chloe isn't even a real person, and as I write this book, I find myself excited for her to go out and work toward this goal.

When you write out your cash flow goal, you should feel excited and motivated by it. Building a real estate portfolio is fun and rewarding, but there will be challenges along the way. To give yourself the best possible chance of success, make sure your cash flow goal is well aligned with what you want and reminds you why you want it.

> When your cash flow goal feels right and you've written it down on your *PREP*, it's time to move on to a related goal: your portfolio value.

PORTFOLIO VALUE GOAL

Your portfolio value is the number you get when you add up the equity in all of your real estate investments. Or, put another way, if you sold all of your real estate investments and paid off all of your liabilities, how much would you have left over? That's your portfolio value.

Your portfolio value, and how it's calculated, is very similar to net worth. The difference is that your net worth accounts for your investments and assets beyond your real estate investing portfolio. Because this book is about crafting a real estate investing portfolio, we're going to omit all non–real estate assets from this goal. Your 401k, stock portfolio, cars, or any other assets should be left out of your portfolio value calculations, even though they are most definitely a part of your net worth.

Calculating and setting a goal for your portfolio value is important for a few reasons: First, it's an important measurement of wealth and progress that investors should keep a close eye on. Having a portfolio value of $400,000 is solid, but it's a very different level of financial security than a portfolio value worth $4,000,000. The second reason you should care about portfolio value is as a hedge against risk. The equity value of your portfolio is what you could realistically invest into another asset class like stocks or bonds should you want to diversify out of real estate. Last, portfolio value is a great proxy for cash flow.

If you know your portfolio's equity value, it's fairly easy to extrapolate how much cash flow you could be earning. Simply divide your annual cash flow goal by your expected return on equity to figure out what your minimum portfolio value should be.

For example, imagine you have a cash flow goal of $150,000 and average a 7 percent return on equity across your portfolio. As such, your minimum portfolio value goal should be $2,142,857 (divide $150,000 by 0.07). Or, put another way, if you invest $2,142,857 at a 7 percent return on equity, you will hit your cash flow goal. This is important because, as we'll discuss later, you may not choose to prioritize cash flow in the short run. By tracking your portfolio value, you can choose to focus on building equity early in your investing career while ensuring you can still reach your cash flow goals over time.

Note that, so far, I've been saying this should be your minimum portfolio value goal. This calculation will yield you the approximate amount of equity you need invested, at the given rate of return, to meet your cash flow goal. For most people, this number is sufficient. After all, if you hit this number, in theory you will be able to achieve the lifestyle you want. Other people may want to pad this number a bit. Perhaps you want to ensure an inheritance for your children or donate a large sum to charity, or you have another goal.

If you want to, feel free to increase your goal beyond your minimum portfolio value. My only advice here is, again, to think through your goals now to avoid moving the goalposts later.

Take some time now to work through your net worth goal. It's just two simple steps.

1. Determine your minimum portfolio value by dividing your annual cash flow goal by your estimated return on equity.
2. Decide what padding, if any, you want to add. Remember to make sure that any additions are tied to something specific. Goals are powerful when you know WHY you are striving for them. Arbitrarily writing down $10,000,000 as your goal might sound cool, but it makes your goal less impactful. It's much better to have a lower goal, but with well-defined reasons why you have that specific goal.

Here are a few tips to help guide you.

- The return on equity figure you use is very important, but will be hard to estimate for any new investors. We'll talk about this more in the coming chapters, but I would recommend 4 to 5 percent for someone who considers themselves relatively risk averse, and 6 to 8 percent for someone who considers themselves comfortable with risk.

- Don't plan for everything to go right. Even the best-laid plans will have problems, and you should plan for those problems. I recommend doing that by estimating a conservative return on equity. I don't like plans where everything has to go right for the plan to succeed.
- Your minimum portfolio value has to have the same time horizon as your cash flow goal. You need equity to generate the cash flow.
- Your primary residence doesn't count because it's not a real estate investment in the traditional sense. It's still an asset and can earn you a modest return, but I would recommend omitting it from this calculation.

If we return quickly to Chloe, we can see how she calculates her minimum portfolio value using the cash flow goal she already set, and a conservative return on equity. Recall that Chloe's monthly cash flow goal was $14,460, which is $173,520 per year. Using a 5 percent return on equity, Chloe's minimum portfolio value should be $3,470,400.

Monthly Residual Income Goal	$14,460
Annual Residual Income Goal	$173,520
Expected Return on Equity	5%
Minimum Portfolio Value Goal	$3,470,400

Once you've determined your portfolio value goal, you're all set with your financial goals. Take a long, hard look at your cash flow and portfolio value goals and make sure they feel good to you. Once they do, make sure to write both your cash flow goal and your portfolio value goal in your PREP.

Unlike other parts of your Portfolio Strategy, your financial goals shouldn't ideally change very often. Remember, you don't want to move the goalposts, so think this through carefully! These goals should be exciting and motivating. This is what you're going to be working for over the course of many years, and it should be very meaningful to you. I should mention that it also may even be a little intimidating, but don't worry about that—by the end of this book you're going to have a detailed strategy to achieve those goals!

Chapter 15
VISION CONCLUSION

Building a real estate portfolio is exciting and fun, but success requires focus. Your Vision provides that. It gives you a clear articulation of what you want from your portfolio, and why you're doing this. It provides a goal to aim for and guardrails for what you will and will not commit to achieve that goal. Your Vision will keep you pointed in the right direction over the course of your investing career, through ups and downs alike.

Through the preceding chapters we've been crafting your Vision in a relatively linear fashion. We went from values to transactional income to resources to risk and finally to goals. But in reality, the crafting of a Vision and the ongoing maintenance of that Vision is iterative. You need to work through each component of your Vision, and then go back through to make sure they are all aligned with one another. For example, if your financial goals require you earning 20 percent per year in returns, but your risk capacity is moderate, something needs to give. Those two ideas are not aligned because any strategy that averages a 20 percent rate of return is inherently risky. So, take some time to read back through each component of your Vision before moving on. I encourage you to use the Excel calculators and tools I've provided for free alongside this book to check your assumptions. Spend a bit of time playing around with them, seeing how different assumptions and inputs change the potential trajectory of your portfolio.

You want to make sure your Vision both looks and feels really good. Remember, this Vision should feel inspiring to you. It should be motivating and exciting, and even a little bit scary. Do not hold back when articulating your values or your goals. Be honest about the time, skill, and capital you're willing to put into it. This is all about you, and the more honest you are about your Vision, the better your chance of your success. This is your opportunity to clearly state the financial life you want, so don't settle until you feel thoroughly inspired by what you've written on your PREP.

It takes a good amount of work and self-reflection to complete your Vision, so great job working through the exercises in the previous chapters! As you proceed through the remainder of this book, remember that your Vision is not a script. It's not turn-by-turn directions. It's meant to guide you toward the investing decisions that will get you closer to your financial goals. It's the lens through which you should view your other Portfolio Strategy choices.

The path you'll walk to pursue your Vision will not be a straight line. It will swerve and turn, and sometimes send you backward. That's life, and I won't pretend that your plans are always going to go perfectly well. Diversions from your plan can be frustrating, but to me that's all the more reason for you to have a clear Vision. As long as you know where you're trying to go, even when the path veers off course temporarily, you can still keep yourself pointed in the right direction.

With your Vision complete, you've established what you want from your portfolio and why you want it. Now that you know what you're working for, it's time to shift your focus to *how* you will realize your Vision. In Part 3, which focuses on Deal Design, we'll do just that.

PART 3
DEAL DESIGN

VISION

DEAL DESIGN

PORTFOLIO MANAGEMENT

In Part 2, you developed your unique Vision, which defines *where* you want to go, as well as *why* you're building your portfolio. This gives you a clear objective to aim for. Now, you can turn your attention to the *how* part of your portfolio. How will you use real estate to achieve your long-term goals? That's where Deal Design comes in. In Part 3, you will learn to create deals that are specifically designed around your Vision.

In real estate, when seeking a new deal, investors often talk about how to "find a deal." I get why people say this; the process of finding a property does involve some searching. But I don't think "finding deals" is an accurate way to describe how to identify deals for your portfolio. You don't just stumble across deals that are tailor-made for your portfolio. You need to proactively create deals that support your Vision. Great deals aren't found—they are designed. And designing deals is a very important, and fun, part of your Portfolio Strategy.

When people say they've "found" a great deal, they typically mean they have identified a property to buy. That is a critical step in landing a deal, but it's one of many steps. What about the financing? Who is going to manage the deal? How will you maximize value from the property? A real estate deal is more than just the property you invest in. It's a combination of several deal elements that can be strategically curated, combined, and customized to your Vision.

Real estate deals are extremely flexible. Some are capital intensive and high risk. Others are highly profitable, but time intensive. Other deals will look entirely different. Luckily, you get to design deals in whatever fashion is best for you. This reality—that you can design real estate deals to fit the specific needs of your portfolio—is one of the most empowering reasons to invest in real estate. You have a great deal of control over how your portfolio is composed and performs. The trick is to identify, of all the many ways to craft a deal, which ones are best aligned with your Vision.

To assist with this, I have created a Deal Design framework we're going to use throughout this book. This framework consists of eight deal elements, which you can think of as the raw ingredients for designing deals. Just like a chef combines different ingredients, flavors, and textures to create a great dish, you can combine these deal elements to design a great deal.

The elements are:

- Deal type
- Financing
- Ownership structure

- Operating plan
- Management plan
- Asset class
- Market
- Property class

Deal type is the high-level category of investment your deal falls into. In this book we'll talk about the following deal types: rental properties, short-term rentals, fix-and-flip, commercial real estate, development, and lending. Identifying what deal types align with your Vision is one of the most important decisions you'll make when developing your Portfolio Strategy. The deal types you choose will help guide what other elements within the Deal Design framework you can and should consider.

Financing is how you source the necessary capital to acquire and execute on your deals. In this book we'll discuss the various loans available to real estate investors and how they can be used. Financing decisions will play a big part in how quickly you can scale and how much risk you'll take on in that pursuit.

Ownership structure determines how and by whom a deal is owned. Will you own a property by yourself or with partners? Will you pool money with other investors in a syndication or fund? Determining your ownership structure will have big implications for how capital-, time-, and skill-intensive your deals are likely to be.

Operating plan is how you plan to get the most out of your investment. You can't just purchase a property and then wait to see what happens—you have to proactively pursue the outcome you want. There are many ways to maximize the performance of your deal, but in this book we'll cover some of the time-tested approaches like BRRRR, house hacking, value-add, and many more.

Management plan is determining who will manage the various responsibilities associated with your deal. Remember, each individual real estate investment is essentially a small business. Who is going to manage that business? Will you do it yourself or hire it out to someone else? Choosing a management plan will determine how much time you'll need to commit to each deal you do, or how much you'll pay to have someone do it for you.

Asset class is the type of structure you invest in, such as single-family homes, multifamily, retail, office, or self-storage. Many of the other components of your Deal Design will be heavily dependent on what asset class you choose. For example, certain loans are only available for residential properties and can't be used to buy an office building. In this book we'll focus on the asset classes most common among small-to-medium-sized real estate investors.

Market is the geographic area where your deal exists. Will you invest close to where you live or long-distance? The market in which you invest will impact the performance of your deal and the types of returns you're most likely to see (e.g., cash flow versus market appreciation). You will also want to select properties with the specific characteristics that are in demand in the markets where you invest.

Property class describes the condition of the property involved in your deal. Investors use designations such as Class A, Class B, and Class C to describe how desirable a property is relative to other properties. This allows investors to compare deals and risk profiles, and select an appropriate operating plan.

Each chapter in Part 3 will be dedicated to one of the eight deal elements. In each chapter I will explain the deal element and the strengths and benefits of some of the most common tactics. Your job is to identify which tactics are aligned with your Vision and which are not. Note that you won't actually be designing any deals in Part 3; that will come in Part 4 when you create a "Buy Box." Instead, think broadly about *all* of the possible tactics that will work for your future deals. You will likely find many tactics that will work for you, which is great! This is a "select all that apply" part of your strategy. The point here is just to filter out any tactics and deal designs that are not well aligned with your Vision.

For example, if your Vision favors low-risk investments over a lengthy time horizon, you should feel comfortable considering Deal Designs that include rental property, short-term rentals, or even commercial deals. But you'll likely want to omit flipping or developing from consideration because these deal types don't align well with your Vision

This is the process you'll repeat throughout Part 3: selecting tactics that are aligned with your Vision, and omitting those that are misaligned.

To demonstrate how your Deal Design should evolve, take a look at the current Deal Design on my PREP. Under each of the eight deal elements, I have listed the tactics that I will consider for future deals. These are the raw ingredients that I will bring together to add new deals to my portfolio in the future. I won't use *all* of them in any one deal—but I *could* use any of them. At the end of Part 3, you will have a completed PREP that looks something like this.

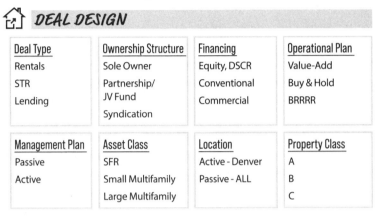

DEAL DESIGN

Deal Type	Ownership Structure	Financing	Operational Plan
Rentals	Sole Owner	Equity, DSCR	Value-Add
STR	Partnership/	Conventional	Buy & Hold
Lending	JV Fund	Commercial	BRRRR
	Syndication		

Management Plan	Asset Class	Location	Property Class
Passive	SFR	Active - Denver	A
Active	Small Multifamily	Passive - ALL	B
	Large Multifamily		C

Before we get started, a few notes about Part 3.

In each chapter I will discuss some of the most common trade-offs, risks, and benefits of each tactic. But note that my advice about each deal element is given in a vacuum. For example, if I say short-term rentals have great cash flow potential, that doesn't mean *all* STRs have great cash flow potential. My guidance is about the *average* deal under discussion. You can only truly evaluate the risk, reward, and resource intensity of a deal once your entire Deal Design is complete. To continue the example, only *after* you know that the deal is an STR owned by two partners, financed with responsible debt, operated with value-add, managed professionally, is a single-family residence in a popular vacation destination, and is a Class A property can you truly assess the risk reward and resource intensity of the deal. But we'll get to that later.

At the end of each chapter, you will find PREP work. In these sections, I will provide instructions for completing the PREP, questions that will help you narrow down which tactics you want to use, and a grading rubric. The rubrics will look like this and will provide a space for you to evaluate how each tactic aligns with your Vision. Remember, risk, reward, and resource allocation are all subjective, so it's up to you to decide how each option suits you.

	Resource Alignment			Risk/Reward Alignment	
	Time	Capital	Skill		Include in PREP?
Buy and Hold					
Value-Add					
BRRRR					
Operational Efficiency					
Rent by the Room					
Opportunistic					
Other:					

	Resource Alignment			Risk/Reward Alignment	
	Time	Capital	Skill		Include in PREP?
Rental Properties					
Short-Term Rentals					
Fix-and-Flip					
Commercial					
Development					
Lending					
Other:					

We will go through the deal elements in a specific order, but know that Deal Design is not a linear process. I have arranged the deal elements in an order that makes sense to me for educational purposes, but you can go about designing deals by prioritizing any individual element. For example, I'm discussing deal type first because it's the broadest element, and it's a common place for people to start their Deal Design process. However, it's also common for investors to start with a market in mind, or a management plan, and go from there.

As you read Part 3, think about which elements you want to prioritize and start with. Also remember that this book is not meant to teach you how to operate your deals. Each deal element and tactic is an important topic unto itself, so I can't possibly go into detail about how to execute on each one. Once you pick tactics to execute on, you should learn much more about how to be successful with the tactics you choose.

At the end of Part 3, you should have a completed Deal Design section of your PREP and a powerful tool at your disposal. This crucial part of your Portfolio Strategy will provide you with high-level guidelines for the types of deals you should consider for your portfolio. Of all the millions of possible deals out there, you'll be able to design deals specifically for your portfolio's goals. Let's get to it!

Chapter 16
DEAL TYPES

"Deal type" describes the sort of business you intend to operate for a given deal. Will you buy a rental property? A flip? A short-term rental? These are very different businesses, and your choice of deal type will determine much about your portfolio's performance. You may hear people refer to deal types as "strategies," which isn't wrong per se, but as I've said throughout this book, I think real estate "strategy" is much bigger than just what type of deal you do. In the Deal Design framework, we call them "deal types."

For many investors, choosing a deal type is the first decision made when considering a new deal because it helps frame other tactical decisions. Deal type determines the kind of income you generate, and the tax benefits you may or may not enjoy, and will play a huge role in the Risk/Reward Profile and resource intensity (how much capital/time/skill) of your deals. It will also make decisions about the other elements of deal strategy easier. As an example, if you start by deciding you want to pursue a short-term rental deal, it allows you to easily make other strategic decisions, like identifying locations, financing, and establishing management plans that work for short-term rentals. Alternatively, if you know you want to complete a flip, you will need a different type of financing, won't need a property manager, and may want to buy in an entirely different location. You don't have to start with deal type, but it's one of the most common places to start, and it's where we will begin our deep dive into Deal Design.

In this chapter I will provide a high-level overview of each deal type. I'll describe the basics, risk/reward profile, and resource intensity for the most common deal types. Remember, you don't need to pick just one deal type for your PREP. For now, just focus on familiarizing yourself with the various deal types available to you as a real estate investor and which ones you think could play a role in your portfolio.

If you're reading and start to wonder why some popular tactics like BRRRR or house hacking are not on the deal types list, it's because they are in a different element of the Deal Design framework, known as the "operating plan." We will discuss those in Chapter 19. This will all make sense soon, but just know that BRRRR and house hacking are really just operating plans within a rental property deal.

And if you're wondering why wholesaling is not on this list, it's because wholesaling is not an investment. Your portfolio is made up of deals you have an ownership stake in, but wholesaling entails no ownership stake or any investment of capital. If you're interested in wholesaling, it belongs in your Transactional Income Plan, not your Deal Design.

Over the course of this chapter, I'll walk you through the following deal types.

- Rental properties
- Short-term rentals
- Fix-and-flip
- Commercial real estate
- Development
- Lending

Pay attention to which deal types are of interest to you, as you will be adding the ones that align with your strategy to your PREP at the end of this chapter.

RENTAL PROPERTIES

Rental property investing is purchasing a property with the intention of leasing it out to tenants who use it as their residence. In other words, you provide housing to someone, and in exchange you earn stable residual income across several profit drivers. Rental property investing is a popular and proven type of real estate investing that offers long-term wealth creation with relatively low risk.

There are many benefits to rental property investing, but its popularity comes primarily from the stable income and utilization of all profit drivers: cash flow, appreciation, and tax benefits. To maximize these benefits, rental property investing is largely used as a long-term strategy. Typically, you need to hold a rental property for at least two to three years for it to break even, and longer to optimize your return.

Operating a single rental property is not particularly complicated or time-consuming, but it does require attention. When you provide housing for tenants, you have an obligation to provide safe, quality housing for those living in your rentals. You must take this responsibility seriously, and that means that you, or someone you hire, must provide high-quality property management. This includes finding, screening, and supporting tenants; overseeing repairs and maintenance; performing basic operations like bookkeeping and financial reporting; and handling many other tasks. Quality property management is critical to the success of a rental property.

One of the great advantages to rental property investing is its flexibility. Many Deal Designs work well with rental properties. As you'll see over the coming chapters, rental properties can be used with almost any operating plan and management plan. They work in most markets in the country and across different asset and property classes. There are many advantageous financing options for rental properties, including ones that allow you to put less than 20 percent down. Basically, rental properties are the Swiss Army knife of real estate investing because they can help you achieve almost any goal you have.

There are risks to rental property investing, however. As with all real estate, rentals are susceptible to short-term volatility in the housing markets. You are also exposed to income risk if you face vacancies or nonpayment of rent. That said, when a cash-flowing rental property is held for a long time, there is very little risk of principal loss.

Rental properties are good for investors who want a stable, solid investment. The risk is relatively low, but when held for an appropriately long period, the returns can be great. The flexibility offered by rentals is good for all investors, but it's particularly helpful for those just starting on their investing journey. There are many low-cost, low-risk ways to get into rental property investing. Really, anyone pursuing financial freedom and long-term wealth should seriously consider rental properties as part of their portfolio.

SHORT-TERM RENTALS

Short-term rental deal types involve buying a property with the intention of renting it out for a shorter period of time than a traditional rental property. This can be anywhere from a single night to several months.

Although the names are similar, short-term rentals (STRs) differ from rental properties in several significant ways. STRs are essentially small hospitality businesses. Unlike rental properties, which provide a tenant with a primary residence, STRs provide guests (not tenants) with clean, safe, furnished accommodation on a temporary basis. As such, the risks, rewards, and operations of an STR are unique.

The primary benefit of short-term rentals is the potential for strong cash flow. On a per-night basis, STRs typically offer higher revenue potential than traditional rentals. For example, if you had a property that could earn $2,000 per month as a rental property ($66 per night), but it could also earn $100 per night as an STR, your revenue potential is 50 percent higher as an STR ($3,000 as an STR versus $2,000 as a rental). A well-operated STR in a good area can produce cash-on-cash returns that exceed a traditional rental. For pure cash flow potential, STRs are one of the best deal types to consider.

You may be wondering, "What about medium-term rentals?" I group medium-term rentals (categorized as guest stays of thirty days or more) and short-term rentals into the same deal type. While a few tactics differ between short- and medium-term rentals (basically where and how you market your property), they are the same business at the core, aiming to provide a great, furnished place for someone to stay on a temporary basis. Both tactics offer excellent opportunities for cash flow alongside several other profit drivers like amortization, market appreciation, and tax benefits.

As with all things in real estate investing, there are trade-offs that come with the increased cash flow potential of STRs. First, there is more risk. Without long-term leases, STRs are more prone to vacancy from shifts in supply and demand. Demand can drop off due to economic cycles, weather, seasonality, and guest preferences. As STRs become more popular, supply can increase, and operators will need to be competitive to book guests. Additionally, regulations around STRs are becoming increasingly common, and in some cases can outlaw or severely limit the operations of an STR investor.

The second consideration for STRs is property management. Managing STRs requires considerably more work than a traditional rental property, even if you don't do that work yourself. Having guests come and go regularly means you need to be continuously marketing the property, communicating with guests, and scheduling cleanings, along with other high-touch property management tasks. STRs also tend to experience more "wear and tear" and require more frequent and expensive maintenance. Because STRs are furnished, you need to maintain not just the physical structure, but also linens, kitchen supplies, furniture, cleaning supplies, and more. Furnishing also increases the capital intensity of STRs. When you buy an STR, make sure you have enough capital to appropriately furnish your property.

STRs are a great investment type for investors who are looking for strong cash flow, amortization, and tax benefits. The return potential on an STR is great, but it requires more time and more skill to operate successfully. If you're able to commit the necessary resources, STRs are a great deal type for generating residual income and long-term wealth.

FIX-AND-FLIP

Fix-and-flip is the practice of buying a property, renovating it, and then selling it as quickly as possible. You may have heard this investment type called "house flipping" or just "flipping"—it's all the same thing. A fix-and-flip investor's aim is to buy an asset, add value, and then sell off the asset for more than it cost them to purchase and rehab the asset.

Because fix-and-flip deals are all about adding value, it's crucial to purchase a property that is undervalued, outdated, distressed, or has deferred maintenance. In other words, there has to be something wrong, or underutilized, with the property that you can improve in order to add value and build equity.

A simple example of a fix-and-flip might look something like this: You purchase a home built in the 1980s for $220,000. The home hasn't been renovated in twenty years, and it costs you $130,000 in renovation costs, putting your all-in costs at $350,000. Once the renovations are complete, the market value (known in the industry as the after-repair value (ARV)) of the property is $450,000. If you are all-in for $350,000 and sell the property post-rehab for $450,000, you would walk with approximately $100,000 in profit.

This is a gross oversimplification of the many fix-and-flip costs, but I think you get the point—profits on a fix-and-flip deal come from the difference between your all-in costs (purchase price + improvements) and the eventual sales price, minus transaction costs. That sounds simple, but it's not. Operating a successful flip is complex, cash intensive, and time-consuming. As a flipper, your profit is dependent on an accurate ARV estimation and the management of many moving parts, including different contractors, materials, budgets, and schedules.

If you can do that well, you can make tons of money. Flipping can be incredibly lucrative if you're good at it. It offers some of the highest—if not the highest—possible ROI of any real estate investing deal type.

But as you can probably guess, because the reward potential is so high, the risk potential is also high. (That's why flipping makes for great TV shows—it's often boom or bust!)

It's also important to know that flipping is not residual income. It is a labor- and time-intensive deal type, and therefore is very similar to a job. It also (usually) doesn't offer any tax benefits and is taxed as ordinary income. Despite being transactional income, flipping is still considered an investment (unlike wholesaling, which is also transactional income), because flipping requires an investor to a) invest capital into a deal and b) take ownership of the property.

One aspect of flipping that sets it apart from most other investment types is that it is designed for short-term holds. Most investment types do well or are even optimized for long hold periods; flips are the opposite. Due to holding costs and the lack of income during the renovation, the shorter a flip is held for, the better. This has its pros and cons. As we've discussed, short hold periods expose you to risk from market volatility. On the other hand, flips don't generally tie up your capital for very long and provide more liquidity than other types of deals.

Take a look at this example of an investor named Rosa who flips houses. Her current deal looks as follows:

Purchase Price	$250,000
Down Payment	$100,000
After-Repair Value	$400,000
Repair Costs	$75,000
Monthly Holding Costs	$2,000
Transaction Costs	$17,500

She is planning to spend four months renovating a home and then sell it. If she sells it quickly upon completion of her renovation, she'll maximize her profit and get a liquidity event in just four months. If it takes her longer than expected to sell her property, her profits and rate of return are going to decline with every subsequent month due to her holding costs.

MONTH	REPAIR COSTS	HOLDING COSTS	PROFIT	ROE
1	$18,750	$2,000		
2	$18,750	$2,000		
3	$18,750	$2,000		
4	$18,750	$2,000	$49,500	24.7%
5	$-	$2,000	$47,500	23.5%
6	$-	$2,000	$45,500	22.2%
7	$-	$2,000	$43,500	21.1%
8	$-	$2,000	$41,500	19.9%
9	$-	$2,000	$39,500	18.8%
10	$-	$2,000	$37,500	17.6%
11	$-	$2,000	$35,500	16.6%
12	$-	$2,000	$33,500	15.5%

Fix-and-flips are a great option for investors who want to earn transactional income. Flipping gives you the opportunity to make large chunks of capital all at once, which can then be reallocated into other deals quickly. That said, successful flipping takes a lot of time, money, and skill. Without the proper resources, flipping can go poorly in a hurry. But for those who have the right experience and resources, it can offer returns that exceed almost any other deal type.

COMMERCIAL REAL ESTATE

Commercial real estate (CRE) is a very broad category of deal type that spans many niches and asset classes, but always consists of properties that are used for business purposes such as retail space, office buildings, large multifamily properties (five or more units), self-storage facilities, industrial/warehouse space, and more. The descriptions below are broad generalizations about CRE, and if you're interested in commercial deals, you'll need to learn more about the specific asset class you intend to invest in.

Commercial real estate can be a very lucrative investment type for many reasons, but the primary benefit is scale. Commercial properties are typically bigger than residential properties, which means there are more tenants and more income. And bigger properties have more revenue opportunities. Similarly, expenses are often proportionally lower due to economies of scale; it can be far more efficient to spread expenses across more units and more tenants. When purchased and operated well, commercial properties can be very powerful cash flow and equity-building machines.

One of the primary differences between commercial and residential real estate is how they are valued. Unlike residential properties, which are typically valued based on comps (what similar properties in the area sold for), commercial properties are typically valued based on how much money they generate (usually measured by net operating income, NOI) and the capitalization rate (commonly known as "cap rate," which is a market-based measurement of how much investors are willing to pay for an asset). This makes the valuation of CRE more predictable, and in some ways more controllable. To increase the value of a commercial asset, you just need to focus on increasing your NOI. This is a whole topic unto itself that I am not going to get into in this book, but understand that the value of commercial properties is directly tied to the income they produce. You cannot control cap rates—they are set by broader investor sentiment and macroeconomic conditions—but if you can increase the NOI of a commercial property, you can positively influence the value of that property.

Given the scale of the deals, CRE tends to be capital intensive. The acquisition costs can be very high, and a larger team is usually needed to assist with the acquisition and management of the properties, which adds operational costs. Lastly, CRE debt is more expensive and often requires a larger down payment.

On top of being capital intensive, CRE is time and skill intensive. Commercial deals are big, sophisticated projects that typically require a relatively long hold period. To operate a large property well, the time requirement and the level of skill you (and your team) need are both significantly higher than for residential properties. This is probably obvious, but managing a large office building, retail complex, or mobile home park is just more complicated than managing a single-family home or small multifamily property.

Interestingly, despite CRE being time intensive, it's also one area of real estate where you can invest in an almost entirely passive way. If you want to invest in a fund or a syndication (which we'll talk about more in Chapter 17), CRE is the easiest place to do that. Because CRE is capital intensive and complex, it's difficult to do alone. As such, the industry has developed many efficient ways for investors to invest with experienced operators who pool together capital and have sophisticated and professional teams to manage the deals.

Although it can be tempting to "go big" and start investing in commercial real estate immediately, it's not the best place to learn. The deals are bigger, the loans are riskier, and the operations are more complex.

For these reasons many investors get into commercial deals later in their career, or not at all. If you do want to get into CRE at the outset, I highly recommend either partnering with an experienced commercial operator or investing passively in a syndication or fund, where an experienced operator manages the deal on your behalf.

Commercial deals are good for investors who have enough experience in the real estate industry and enough resources to pull off large-scale deals. They are also great for accredited investors who want to invest passively in syndications and funds. Because CRE spans many niches and asset classes, it can also be a useful diversification method. Generally, CRE is best for those a few years into their investing career and looking to scale.

DEVELOPMENT

Real estate development is the creation of real property for the purposes of generating a profit. In other words, development is building something from scratch. In a way, development is similar to flipping because the profit comes from value-add. But development takes value-add even further, and offers even more upside—and even more risk. On the spectrum of risk and reward, development is at the top for both.

The term "development" is not really one thing; instead, it's a broad category of activities that are required to turn land, or an underutilized property, into a functional building. That involves everything from land acquisition to permitting and entitlement, environmental studies, architecture, engineering, construction, sales, and more. If you pull it all off, the profits can be massive. But as you can imagine, there are plenty of places where things can go wrong.

The simplest form of development is the building of a single unit, like a single-family home or a small commercial building. But development can be scaled to almost any size. Some operators build large, mixed-use developments that include housing, office, and retail. Other developers buy acres of land and build entire subdivisions. A new and increasingly popular development tactic is known as "build-for-rent," where residential housing units are constructed with the specific purpose of turning them into rental properties. This vast spectrum obviously comes with a variety of time, capital, and skill requirements, but make no mistake about it—all development is complex.

One of the major challenges associated with development is timing. Again, development is similar to flipping, and recall that one key to flipping is to do it quickly. The same is generally true for development. But it can be difficult to build quickly. In development, you are often at the mercy of state and local governments, dozens of different contractors, material suppliers, and more. After you buy a property, by the time you've entitled it and received permits, the entire economic climate can have changed, and it may no longer be profitable to complete your intended development. Alternatively, if you time the market right, it can create windfall profits.

I am not trying to scare you away from development; it's a perfectly good strategy, but it's relatively uncommon for small-to-medium-sized investors. Unless you have a background in construction or development, it's a complex business to learn. For the average person who just wants to achieve financial freedom, the risks often outweigh the rewards. Due to its rarity among retail investors, we're not going to talk much about development in this book. But if it fits your Vision, add it to your Deal Design!

LENDING

When most people think about real estate investing, they think about buying physical assets. But there is another side of investing in real estate: lending. There are many ways to lend money and earn a return, but I will discuss two primary ways here.

The first option is known as note investing, which involves the buying and selling of debt. For instance, you can buy a mortgage from its current holder and collect payments from the homeowner or investors who took out the mortgage. You can invest in "performing" notes, where the borrower is paying as agreed, which is a relatively stable, low-risk investment. You can also buy and sell "nonperforming notes," where the borrower is not paying as agreed. These types of notes are sold at a discount and have much higher risk and reward (if you can rehabilitate the loan) than performing notes.

The other common form of lending that real estate investors partake in is direct lending to other investors (often known as private lending). Other investors look to private money for flexibility, faster closing periods, and obtaining debt on investments that banks don't like to lend on. In exchange for these benefits, borrowers tend to pay higher interest rates and fees to private lenders than they do to banks or credit unions. There are many different ways to lend money to other real estate investors, each of which can be a useful piece of your Portfolio Strategy.

Some common forms of lending are hard money lending, down payment loans, construction loans, and bridge lending.

While different loans have different risk/reward profiles, there are some commonalities between lending deal types. Generally speaking, the main reason people get into lending is for the predictability of the returns. When you lend money to someone, you know exactly what the borrower's obligation is to you. You sign an agreement that tells you precisely how much money you lent, when you'll get paid back, and at what interest rate. Of course, borrowers can fail to make payments or default (there is risk in every investment!), but unlike other types of investments, lending provides a very clear return profile for the investor before the investment even begins.

For real estate lending in particular, one main advantage is that the loans are "secured," meaning the loans come with collateral—usually the property itself. In the event a borrower defaults on a loan, you as the lender (should) have a means of recourse—you can foreclose or take ownership of the property as a means of recovering your principal. This is one way that investors who purchase nonperforming loans protect themselves against loss (and can turn a profit, even in the case of default).

The primary way investors make money from lending is cash flow. Borrowers have to pay back the principal and the interest on top. That interest is profit (cash flow) you generate. Depending on the loan, lenders can also make money from fees, value-add (rehabilitating a loan), repossession, and even some market appreciation.

Another advantage of lending is that it works well in high–interest rate environments. Rising interest rates are typically unwelcomed by real estate investors, as they increase operating costs for any property with debt and can put downward pressure on property prices. For a lender, however, rising interest rates can be a good thing. The higher the interest rate on a loan, the more profit the lender earns. Lending risk and reward doesn't always follow the same cyclical patterns as other deal types, and therefore can be a great way to diversify your portfolio.

The amount of time and skill needed to be a lender depends on the type of loan, but lending generally falls on the more passive end of the involvement spectrum. If you have a loan that is performing (being paid on time), there is not much to do. You can sit back and collect your payments every month. If a loan is in default or you are actively trying to rehabilitate a loan, more time and skill are needed.

Lending is a very different business than buying and selling physical real estate. As such, it tends to attract more experienced investors who are looking for balance in their portfolios rather than investors who are just starting out. There are also lending funds that accredited investors can participate in as a way to earn passive cash flow.

I'm not going to talk much more about lending in this book. Not because it's a bad investment (I invest in note funds!), but because the business is so different from buying physical property, it's beyond the scope I can address here. If you want to learn more about lending, I recommend two books: *Real Estate Note Investing* by Dave Van Horn and *Lend to Live* by Alexandra Breshears and Beth Pinkley Johnson.

PREP WORK
DEAL TYPES

STRATEGIC DECISION: Of the deal types explained in this chapter, which ones are aligned with your Vision and fit within your broader Portfolio Strategy? You don't need to make decisions now for your entire investing career—just select the deal types that fit your Vision for the next three years. Any deal types that fit your criteria should be written in your PREP. For additional guidance and a rubric that will help you test alignment, see more below.

Now that you understand the basics of the most common deal types, take some time to think through which deal types are aligned with your Vision. Feel free to select as many as you think you may realistically try in the next three years, but don't go overboard. You need to maintain your focus.

For all of Part 3, in the PREP Work at the end of each chapter, I will be providing two aids to help you determine what to write in your PREP. The first is a set of open-ended questions to get you thinking about how each tactic aligns with your Vision. The second is a rubric for you to score each tactic for yourself.

Below are the questions for deal types. Take some time now to think through them.

- What deal types work with the current resources that you have?
- How complex a business do you want to run?
- Given your risk profile, what deal types make the most sense?
- How do your values align with different deal types?
- Do you have the specific skills needed for the deal types you want to use? How easy would it be for you to acquire or source those skills externally?
- Do you need to prioritize residual income or transactional income?
- How important are tax benefits to you?
- What is the best way to learn so you can succeed in the long run?

Once you've considered the various deal types, feel free to use the rubric below to score how each deal type aligns with your Vision, and which ones should be included in your PREP. In the rubric, you can reference the descriptions above and determine which have the capital, time, and skill characteristics you're looking for. Do the same thing for risk and return. Finally, decide if each potential deal type belongs on your PREP.

	Resource Alignment			Risk/Reward Alignment	
	Time	Capital	Skill		Include in PREP?
Rental Properties					
Short-Term Rentals					
Fix-and-Flip					
Commercial					
Development					
Lending					
Other:					

For this first chapter in Part 3, I will show you how I fill out the deal type rubric at this point in my career. But these are just my subjective options based on my circumstances—you shouldn't be copying mine!

	Resource Alignment			Risk/Reward Alignment	
	Time	Capital	Skill		Include in PREP?
Rental Properties	Yes	Yes	Yes	Yes	Yes
Short-Term Rentals	Yes	Yes	Yes	Yes	Yes
Fix-and-Flip	No	Yes	No	No	No
Commercial	Passive Only	Yes	Passive Only	Yes	Yes
Development	No	Yes	No	No	No
Lending	Passive Only	Yes	Passive Only	Yes	Yes

I am an experienced investor with a solid portfolio. As such, I have the risk capacity and capital to take on any deal type. My time and skill, however, are limited. As such, I don't do any fix-and-flip deals because they're far too time-consuming, and while I'm interested in commercial deals and lending, they are also too time-consuming and are beyond my skill level to operate on my own from a different continent. I do consider those deal types in my Deal Design, but only as a passive investor in syndications and funds (which we'll discuss in the next chapter).

As an experienced investor, I am comfortable having four different deal types on my PREP. If you're just starting, it's okay to have fewer. In fact, as a newbie, it's often best to just have one. Focus can be a big advantage when you're learning and getting your first few deals. So don't feel pressure to do it all at once. If anything, I'd recommend you err on the side of fewer deal types.

Once you've considered each deal type and selected which ones could be beneficial to your portfolio in the coming years, write them down on your *PREP*. Knowing which deal types are of interest to you will be a big help as you move through the coming chapters and consider other strategic elements.

Chapter 17
OWNERSHIP STRUCTURE

Your portfolio is comprised of deals in which you have at least some ownership stake. But there are actually several different ways that you can own real estate. You can buy real estate on your own, or you can form a partnership with other investors and split the ownership between the partners. How you own a deal is known as the deal's "ownership structure." Recall from Chapter 6 that the word "equity" means a lot of things in real estate, but it always has to do with ownership. So when we talk about the ownership structure of a deal, we're also talking about the equity structure. In this chapter we'll review common ways that an investor can structure the ownership of their deals, and we'll break down the strategic implications of the various options.

Deciding what ownership structure to consider for your deals includes several variables. First, it depends on your resources. Many investors, especially when starting out, don't have the necessary resources to invest in a deal on their own. In these scenarios, taking on one or more partners is somewhat of a requirement to get started. But even if you have the ability to invest in a deal on your own, should you? It may seem like the obvious choice to own as much of your deals as possible, but that's not always the best option. As you'll see throughout this chapter, there are benefits and drawbacks to each type of ownership structure. The structure you choose will go a long way in informing how you allocate resources and finance your deals, and what management plans are available to you.

The ownership structures we'll be discussing in this chapter are:
- Sole ownership
- Partnerships
- Syndications/funds

As with every chapter in Part 3, there will be PREP work at the end of this chapter, where you will determine which ownership structures are aligned with your Vision and should be considered in your future Deal Designs.

SOLE OWNERSHIP

Sole ownership is the simplest of all ownership structures. As you can probably imagine, sole ownership means that a single person, or entity, owns 100 percent of the equity in a deal.

As an example, if an investor named Simon buys a rental property without any partners or other investors, he would be the sole owner of that rental property. It doesn't matter if Simon owns the property in his own name or in an LLC—if he is the only investor with an ownership stake, it is sole ownership. For the purposes of your strategy and Deal Design, if you own a property as a legally recognized couple, that is still sole ownership.

Sole ownership structures have several benefits. First and foremost, as the sole owner of a deal with 100 percent of the equity, you enjoy 100 percent of the upside in a deal! Any profits earned go to you. Second, sole owners get complete control of their deals. They can make decisions unilaterally without consulting any partners and have full freedom to operate their deals as they see fit. It also makes for relatively simply bookkeeping and tax preparation.

The flip side of freedom and ownership is responsibility and risk. If you are the sole owner of a deal, you take on 100 percent of the risk. If something goes wrong, it's entirely on you. Similarly, sole owners are 100 percent responsible for the operations. Sure, they can hire out property management and many other tasks, but at the end of the day, the success or failure of a deal falls squarely on the shoulders of the sole owner.

Given that sole owners are handling most elements of a deal themselves, this is the most time-, capital-, and skill-intensive ownership structure. If you want to own a property for yourself, you are responsible for contributing or sourcing all of the resources needed for the deal. You can still outsource operations, such as property management or repairs, to a third party, but you are ultimately responsible for the success or failure of your deals.

Sole ownership is a good option for investors who have sufficient time, capital, and skill to make a deal successful—and have the experience to confidently manage a deal on their own. It's also good for investors who enjoy simplified operations and recordkeeping, or who don't want to work with or consult with a partner.

PARTNERSHIPS

A partnership is an ownership structure in which two or more investors each own a portion of a deal's equity. A partnership in real estate is a very flexible ownership structure and can take on almost any format a group of partners can agree upon.

Partnerships are very common in real estate because they offer many advantages, primarily shared resources and responsibilities. Most investors I know partner on a significant portion of their deals, and some investors partner on every single deal they do! Investing with partners means there are multiple people who can contribute capital, time, and skill to the deal. You can draw from the experience, brainpower, and resources of a pool of people instead of relying solely on yourself. This is a powerful option for investors of all experience levels, but can be particularly helpful for those getting started.

The way in which resources are contributed and responsibilities are divided between partners is flexible. If you have two partners in the deal, it could be a 50/50 split of the equity, or it could be 90/10. Maybe one partner contributes just capital, while the other partner contributes time and skill. There are infinite ways to structure partnerships for real estate deals, but most partnerships fall into one of three broad categories: active, passive, or time/skill.

Active partners are coinvestors who contribute capital *and* other resources to the deal in the form of time and/or skill. Imagine an investor, Tamara, who needs $100,000 in equity to secure a loan and purchase a rental property for $400,000. Tamara has $100,000 in investable assets, but she wants to find a partner for her next deal because she doesn't like tenant management. So, she contributes $75,000 to the deal and brings on her friend Lewis to contribute the other $25,000 in equity financing needed to land the deal. In this example, Tamara will be contributing 75 percent of the equity and Lewis will contribute 25 percent.

If Lewis is to be an active partner, he will need to share in the management and operations of the deal. For example, perhaps Tamara handles repairs, maintenance, and bookkeeping, while Lewis is responsible for tenant management. This is just one option; how two (or more) active partners choose to divvy up responsibilities and ownership stake is entirely up to them.

Active partners are a great option for investors who have limited time to commit to deals, who want to learn from other investors, or who want to add outside expertise to their portfolio. Bringing on active partners can increase the overall skill and experience level in a deal, which can lower risk and improve upside. That said, active partners tend to be expensive, as they are contributing both capital and time to the deal. Typically, you have to give up a significant chunk of equity to bring on an active partner.

Passive partners are coinvestors who contribute capital but do not actively participate in the operations of the business. Going back to the example with Tamara, let's imagine that her friend Lewis is willing to commit $25,000 in capital, but he isn't interested in operating the business alongside her. In this case, Lewis can be a passive partner, while Tamara operates the business. Typically, in a passive partnership the active partner (Tamara, in our example) is compensated by the passive partner in some way for managing the business—extra ownership, more rights to cash flow, or any other arrangement the partners can agree on. For example, even though Tamara is contributing 75 percent of the capital for the deal, she may get an 80 percent share of the equity in exchange for being the active partner.

Passive partnerships are well suited for lead investors who want—and have the skill—to actively manage their deals on their own. Because passive partners bring capital to the deal but nothing else, the partnerships tend to be simpler and less expensive for the lead investor. As long as the terms of the partnership are being met and the deal is performing well, passive partners tend to be minimally involved. If you have capital but minimal time, being the passive partner in a deal is a great way to be involved in real estate.

Time/skill partners don't contribute any capital to a deal; instead, they contribute time and/or skill in exchange for equity (ownership). Let's go back to our example where Tamara contributes $75,000 and Lewis contributes $25,000, but this time neither of them is interested in tenant management. They have two options: 1) They can use some of their income to hire a property manager (which will eat up some cash flow) or 2) they can bring in a partner who will manage the property in exchange for equity (which will cost them some ownership percentage).

Bringing on a time/skill partner can be a good way to conserve cash flow in a deal. Rather than using some of the deal's income to pay cash for services like tenant management, the investor(s) can offer ownership. This will, of course, mean giving up some ownership (and some long-term upside), but it can make a deal more profitable in terms of cash flow.

If you're looking to get started and don't have a lot of capital to invest, being a time/skill partner is a great option. This is what I did! I traded my time to manage operations and did much of the repairs and maintenance myself to earn equity in my first deal.

Regardless of the structure, the commonality between all partnerships is that they divide the equity in a deal among several investors. Remember, equity means ownership! As you can see from the examples above, ownership doesn't always need to be bought with capital—it can be traded for time or skill. This is the Resource Triangle in action!

All partnerships come with risk. Differences can arise between partners, even between friends and family. Partners can, and often do, have differing opinions about how to manage their shared business—which can lead to trouble. I highly recommend you do your best to mitigate partnership risk by thorough vetting of potential partners and having strong, written, legally sound operating agreements in place.

Partnerships are good for almost all investors, but they are particularly good for those who don't have a lot of capital to get started, want to scale quickly, work well on a team, and want to leverage the experience and expertise of others. Almost all investors will use partnerships at some point or another in the course of their investing career—so perhaps the most pressing question is what type(s) of partnership would align with your Vision: active, passive, or time/skill?

SYNDICATIONS AND FUNDS

Syndications and funds are an ownership structure in which a group of investors pool their money together to execute large-scale deals. These are a form of partnership, but they have some particular characteristics that differentiate them from the simpler and more flexible types of partnerships discussed above. I am grouping syndications and funds together in this section because they share many commonalities. Before we get into those commonalities, let me quickly explain the differences.

Syndications are when investors pool their money to buy a specific asset, like a large multifamily complex, office building, etc. The benefit of a syndication is that when you invest in it, you know the specifics of the property you're putting money toward and can conduct due diligence on that specific asset. It's similar to buying a single property, but at a bigger scale and with a more complex ownership structure.

Funds are when investors pool their money to buy multiple assets. For example, there are single-family home funds that look to buy several single-family homes in a specific area. There are also lending funds and short-term rental funds. Funds can vary greatly in size and scope. They provide diversification for investors, but depending on your role in the fund, you may not be able to review and analyze each asset purchased.

While there are important differences between funds and syndications that you should thoroughly understand before pursuing one, there are many commonalities. First and foremost, they usually share a common structure. Within a syndication or fund, there are different classes of partner. Some will have multiple classes, but every syndication and fund has a general partner (GP) and a limited partner (LP). There can be many investors, or entire companies, at each level.

General partners are the active members of the deal. They are responsible for everything involved in the operations of the deal, including:

- Finding the deal
- Conducting due diligence
- Assembling the management team (or managing the asset themselves)
- Raising money
- Bookkeeping
- Investor relations
- Asset management
- And more

GPs typically have a lot of experience in real estate, work in the industry full-time, and have an in-house team capable of managing their deals. In exchange for this active work, GPs typically earn acquisition fees and management fees while also sharing in the deal's profits. When a deal goes well, the profits for a GP can be huge. Being a GP is great for experienced investors who are capable of managing complex deals, understand investor relations, and take the responsibility of managing other investors' capital very seriously.

Limited partners are passive partners in a syndication or fund. LPs contribute capital to a deal—and nothing else. An LP is essentially buying shares in the GP's investment(s). Being an LP is about as passive as it gets for real estate investors. As an LP, your work involves:

- Finding a great GP to work with
- Conducting your own due diligence and legal reviews on the specific deals you fund
- Contributing capital

That's about it. Once you sign the paperwork and contribute your money to the syndication or fund, control of the deal—and its success or failure—is out of your hands. This is an important consideration for anyone considering investing as an LP. You have little control or liquidity. Even if you have a cash crunch and need money, it's unlikely you'll be able to pull any money out of a syndication or fund. As such, it's incredibly important to manage your liquidity properly on a portfolio level, and to only work with experienced GPs who know what they're doing. As an LP you are buying the time and skill of the GP, and you have very few options for intervention once you contribute your capital. Make sure you only invest with qualified and reputable operators.

Being an LP is extremely low on the time and skill spectrum but can be very capital intensive. Most syndications have a minimum investment for LPs that starts around $25,000, but minimums can be $100,000 or more. Additionally, LPs usually need to be accredited investors due to the risk of investing in an unregulated security. Being an LP is a great option for accredited investors who want to diversify into new asset classes and deal types, or who have limited time to operate deals on their own.

PREP WORK
OWNERSHIP STRUCTURE

STRATEGIC DECISION: Of the ownership structures explained in this chapter, which ones are aligned with your Vision and fit within your broader Portfolio Strategy? Your ownership structure can change for each deal you do, so make sure to consider any ownership structure that may work for you in the coming years. Any ownership structures that fit your criteria should be written in your PREP. For additional guidance and a rubric that will help you test alignment, see more below.

Think through the contents of this chapter and determine which ownership structures belong on your PREP. Remember to include any structure that you think you could feasibly use in the coming three years. Below are some questions to help guide your thinking.

- Do you have sufficient capital to contribute to a deal? Or do you need to contribute time or skill to get started?
- Are you willing to assume all the risk from a deal?
- Would the performance of your deals benefit from the experience of a partner?

- Do you work well with others or work better alone?
- Are you an accredited investor?
- Do you have a high-quality professional network where you can find good partners?
- Are you comfortable giving up almost all control to a GP?
- Can you responsibly raise money from others, and will you be a good steward of their capital?

	Resource Alignment			Risk/Reward Alignment	
	Time	Capital	Skill		Include in PREP?
Sole Ownership					
Active Partnerships					
Passive Partnerships					
Time/Skill Partnerships					
Syndication Funds					

The ownership structures your write on your PREP should be based on your Vision, but I can share some observations about what most people do. Generally speaking, most investors favor sole ownership or partnership, particularly early in their career. Being a sole owner or a partner gives you direct control and experience with managing investments. Partnerships allow you to leverage the resources and experience of others. These are great ways to learn while building a professional network and more capital. Plus, most newer investors are not accredited and won't have access to many funds and syndication options.

As time goes on, some (but not all) investors start moving more toward passive investments by investing in funds and syndications as an LP. For investors who want to retire or reduce work hours, funds and syndications are attractive because they require some time up front, but almost no time for ongoing operations.

I see a lot of people attracted to the idea of being a GP, which can be great. But it's not advisable to start there. You're better off starting with your own project or working within a smaller partnership to learn the business before taking on the huge responsibility of managing the capital of many investors.

Once you've selected the ownership structures that are aligned with your Vision, write them down on your PREP. Now that you have an idea of how you want to own and control your investments, it's time to turn to a related and very important strategic decision: how to finance your investments.

Chapter 18
FINANCING YOUR DEALS

"Financing" is just another word for how you pay for your investments. As covered in Chapter 6, there are two broad options for financing: debt financing (a loan) and equity financing (owner's capital). You can finance a deal with 100 percent equity or 100 percent debt, but mostly debt and equity are used together. How you finance deals is not just a question of how much capital you have (although that is important!). It is a highly strategic decision that will impact the performance and Risk/Reward Profile of your deals. In this chapter I am going to walk through the key decision points in selecting financing and review some of the most common financing options used by real estate investors.

While this chapter, and all of Part 3 of this book, is designed to help you select tactics that align with your Vision, I am going to go a little deeper into financing than the other deal elements. With the other elements, it's mostly a matter of personal preference and alignment with your Vision. You can choose the tactics you want to use. With financing, it's a little different. Capital is the most common resource constraint, and financing is a common roadblock for new investors. Also, lending is a highly regulated industry, and not all loans are available to all investors, and for all deal types. As such, I think it's worth understanding some of the inner workings of financing so you can craft a long-term financing strategy to design your deals around.

EQUITY FINANCING

As a reminder, "equity financing" is capital supplied by the owner(s) of a deal—whether that's in the form of a sole owner, partnership, syndication, or fund. Although not very common, some deals are financed 100 percent through equity (also known as an "all-cash" deal). I am not going to go into too much detail about how to invest using all equity because we covered the benefits in Chapter 6, and the logistics are quite simple. The owner(s) provide 100 percent of the capital needed to purchase the deal, plus closing costs, cash reserves, and any repairs or value-add needed. As a reminder, the benefits of an all-cash deal are less risk, more flexibility, and higher cash flow.

Of course, most people cannot afford to invest in real estate using 100 percent equity financing, and even those who can often choose not to. Debt, when used properly, allows investors to use less capital, scale quickly, and retain ownership. Those benefits, however, come with the trade-offs of lower cash flow and higher risk. As such, the most common use of equity financing in real estate is in combination with debt—which is going to be the primary focus of this chapter.

DEBT FINANCING

"Debt financing" is just another term for using a loan. Debt is extremely common in real estate investing, given the capital intensity of buying property. Within the world of debt are many different types of loans, each of which have different strategic implications. Below I will explain how the two most common loan structures (term loans and lines of credit) work and the trade-offs with each. I will also dig into the three key variables in choosing the right debt for you: the loan-to-value ratio (LTV), fixed versus adjustable rate, and amortization schedule. This section gets a bit technical, but will help you select responsible financing options for your portfolio.

Term Loans

The most common form of debt financing, term loans, are structured around a specific length of time and have a set repayment schedule. Simply put, the borrower takes out money and agrees to pay it back by a certain date. Term loans are prevalent throughout the economy, not just in real estate. For example, most car loans and student loans are structured as term loans.

Within real estate, many types of term loans exist. A mortgage is a term loan, but even within the broad category of "mortgage" there are FHA loans, adjustable-rate mortgages, conventional loans, portfolio loans, and so on. No matter the specifics of the loan product, all term loans follow the same format: The borrower agrees to borrow **x** dollars, for **y** years, at **z** interest rate.

Later in this chapter, we will touch on some of the most common forms of term loans, but first we need to discuss the important variables to consider when picking a loan: LTV, fixed versus adjustable rates, and the amortization schedule.

Loan to Value

Loan to value (LTV) is a measure of what portion of a deal is financed using debt versus equity. (Remember, most real estate deals are financed using both debt and equity.)

Calculating LTV is straightforward: Take 100 percent and subtract the down payment percentage. If you are putting 25 percent down on a property, your LTV is 75 percent (100% − 25% = 75%). If you put 40 percent down, your LTV is 60 percent. Determining the right LTV is a question of the type of loan you want to use, and your overall strategy.

Different loan products have different LTV requirements. Most loans geared toward real estate investors require an LTV of 75 percent or less. Owner-occupied loans (for homeowners or house hackers) most commonly have an LTV of 80 percent, but they can have LTVs as high as 96.5 percent (meaning you put just 3.5 percent down!). Commercial loans tend to have lower LTVs—commonly between 50 and 70 percent.

The second consideration for LTV is strategic. A high LTV means you can put less money down, allowing you to use a minimal amount of equity to do deals. This can be great for investors with little capital to invest, and for investors looking to scale quickly. Of course, this comes with trade-offs. The higher the LTV, the more interest you will pay the bank, and the higher your debt service will be. This can hurt your cash flow and comes with a high risk of getting "underwater" on your loan (your property is worth less than your loan balance).

As an investor, you can choose to use high-LTV products that require minimal capital and allow for rapid scaling but come with risk. Or you can choose to use lower LTV debt that increases cash flow and reduces risk but requires more capital. As always, it's a question of resource allocation, risk, and reward.

Fixed Rate vs. Adjustable Rate

Most term loans offer a choice between a fixed and an adjustable interest rate. With a "fixed-rate loan," the interest rate is set at the time of origination (the beginning of the loan) and does not change for the duration of the loan. For example, an investor, Jamal, might purchase a house for $600,000, put down 25 percent ($150,000), and get a mortgage for the remaining $450,000 at a fixed 6 percent interest rate for thirty years. This type of loan structure comes with several benefits: First, Jamal knows exactly what his mortgage payments will be for the entirety of his loan. Second, even as his income and equity value (hopefully) increase, his debt service costs (which tend to be an investor's biggest expense) will stay the same, thus increasing his cash flow over time.

The primary downside of fixed-rate mortgages is that interest rates tend to be slightly higher on fixed-term loans because the fixed rate adds risk for the lender, and the lender needs to compensate for that risk with a higher profit margin. That said, most residential investors choose loans with fixed rates. It allows them to lock in a predictable payment over the lifetime of their loan. And if rates fall, they can always refinance (which does have fees associated with it).

An "adjustable-rate loan" (also known as an adjustable-rate mortgage, or ARM) has an interest rate that changes over the lifetime of the loan. When and how often the interest rate adjusts will depend on the terms of the loan. A 5/1 ARM, for example, means that the initial interest rate is locked in for five years, and then the rate is adjusted annually after that. The most common uses of adjustable-rate loans are for commercial properties, or when interest rates are high. Using an adjustable rate allows an investor to pay a lower initial interest rate, therefore improving cash flow. But there is uncertainty with adjustable-rate mortgages. If rates adjust downward, that's a benefit for the investor. If rates adjust upward, debt service goes up—which hurts cash flow. Unfortunately, no one knows which direction interest rates will go—and for investors uncertainty means risk. Therefore, adjustable-rate debt is considered riskier than fixed-rate debt.

Amortization Schedule

Recall from Chapter 6 that when a borrower pays off their loan, there are typically two parts of each payment. There is principal repayment, which is paying back the lender what was borrowed. There is also interest payment, which is the lender's profit. Principal repayment is good for an investor as it reduces the loan balance and is the source of the amortization profit driver. Paying off interest doesn't benefit the investor in any way. The proportion of principal paid versus interest paid changes for every debt payment and is dictated by the loan's amortization schedule. As an investor you will have options for different amortization schedules: fully amortized loans, partially amortized loans, or interest-only loans.

Fully Amortized Loans

With a fully amortized loan, the proportion of interest to principal paid declines consistently over the course of the loan. This is an important consideration for investors as it means that amortization increases as a profit driver over time. At the beginning of a loan, the benefits of amortization are minimal. But with every payment, the benefit of amortization grows.

FULLY AMORTIZED LOAN EXAMPLE

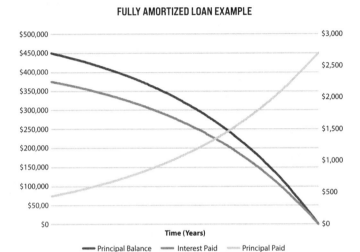

This can be a confusing topic, so let's return to our example of Jamal and his $450,000 loan. If he used a loan that is fully amortized over thirty years, at a fixed 6 percent interest rate, his payment would be approximately $2,698 per month. For thirty years he would pay the same amount every single month, but the portion of his payment that goes toward principal versus interest would change over time—and the benefits of amortization would increase.

Most common loans on residential properties are fully amortized. This includes conventional loans, FHA loans, VA loans, and more. Fully amortized loans can be a bit more expensive than partially amortized or interest-only loans, but they are widely considered less risky.

Partially Amortized Loans

One alternative to a fully amortized loan is known as a partially amortized or "balloon" loan. This type of loan is very common in commercial real estate. With a partially amortized loan, there are two key terms to know: "amortization period" and "maturity date." The amortization period is the length of time the amortization schedule is structured for. The maturity date is when the balloon payment is due. With a partially amortized loan, the amortization period and the maturity date are not the same. The repayment schedule starts the same as a fully amortized loan, but at some point (the maturity date) prior to the end of the amortization period, there is a lump sum (known as a balloon payment) due to pay off the remaining loan balance. If this is confusing, don't worry. An example will make this clear.

Let's assume Jamal takes out a partially amortized loan that has an amortization period of thirty years, with a maturity date of ten years. In this scenario Jamal is borrowing money for just ten years because he must pay back the loan balance at the maturity date of ten years. But his debt service is calculated as if he were paying back his loan over thirty years. In other words, Jamal's monthly payments are the same as the fully amortized schedule in the previous example for the ten years he makes payments ($2,698 per month). This is a big benefit to Jamal, as it increases his cash flow potential. Making payments as if he were borrowing for thirty years makes his payments lower than if he had actually borrowed for ten years. If he had taken out a ten-year fully amortized loan, his payment would be $4,996 per month. He's saving almost $2,300 per month by using a partially amortized loan.

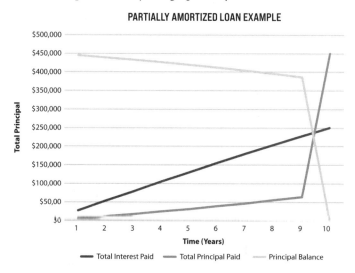

PARTIALLY AMORTIZED LOAN EXAMPLE

This loan structure can dramatically reduce debt service costs, and reduces the total interest paid by the borrower over the lifetime of the loan. Of course, partially amortized loans carry a major risk: being liable for a huge payment at the maturity date. Using the example of Jamal, he would owe a balloon payment of about $386,000 in the tenth year of his loan. That's a large amount of money, and if he cannot make that balloon payment, he could go into default, face foreclosure, or many other undesirable outcomes. Most investors simply seek to refinance their loan before the balloon payment comes due, which is usually possible but not guaranteed. If you pay the balloon payment through refinance or other means, you will be in trouble.

Partially amortized loans have both risks and benefits to investors, but are typically only used in commercial real estate. If you plan to invest in commercial deals, you should spend time learning about partially amortized loans. The debt on a commercial property can be a primary driver of the risk and reward associated with the deal, so make sure you fully understand it.

Interest-Only Loans

The last type of amortization schedule is to have no amortization schedule, by using an interest-only (IO) loan. With an interest-only loan, your payments are made up only of interest; there is no principal paid. Remember that an amortization schedule shows the proportion of interest versus principal paid by the borrower, but with an IO loan, the borrower doesn't pay any principal—hence no amortization schedule.

The benefit of IO loans is that debt service is lower than an amortized loan. For Jamal, using an IO loan at the same 6 percent interest rate would require him to pay just $2,250 per month, as opposed to $2,698 for the fully amortized option. This will help Jamal's cash flow, but it does remove the amortization profit driver. Remember, the benefit of amortization is that you use your investment's income to pay off your principal. Because IO loans don't pay down any principal, that benefit is lost. Some IO loans are interest-only for a few years and then convert to an amortized loan, which contains some of the benefits and downsides of amortization schedules.

IO loans can be beneficial to investors who want to focus primarily on cash flow by lowering debt service at the cost of building equity. They can also be beneficial to investors who are seeking a shorter hold period, because the benefits of the amortization profit driver take some time to ramp up.

Below is a brief overview of some of the more common types of term loans that real estate investors can use in their Deal Design.

Conventional Loans

Conventional loans are term loans offered by a bank, lender, or credit union, but are not insured by the government like an FHA loan (which we'll discuss next). Conventional loans are fully amortized (typically between fifteen and thirty years) and relatively flexible in terms of interest rates and LTVs. The most common LTV on a conventional mortgage is 25 percent for investors and 20 percent for any owner-occupied property.

Due to the well-established, regulated nature of conventional loans, they are relatively low risk. The underwriting standards and application processes for these types of loans have been iterated on for years to ensure lenders and borrowers are taking minimal risks.

Conventional loans are good for financing your personal home, traditional rentals, and short-term rentals. They can also be used to finance the purchase of a flip, but conventional mortgages cannot typically be used to finance the renovation costs of a flip or value-add project. It's important to know there is a ten-loan limit on conventional mortgages, which is something you may have to factor into your strategy if you approach that scale.

FHA Loans

The Federal Housing Authority (FHA) offers loans from federally approved financial institutions. FHA loans are designed to help borrowers with low income or poor credit qualify for competitive interest rates and loans. Generally speaking, FHA loans allow high LTVs. Some borrowers can put as little as 3.5 percent down. FHA loans are fully amortized and have options for both fixed and adjustable interest rates.

The downside of this program is that FHA loans come with additional fees on top of the principal and interest paid on other loans. Because FHA loans are higher risk for the lender, the program requires borrowers to pay mortgage insurance. The amount of mortgage insurance paid by the borrower varies, but it can substantially increase debt service costs and reduce cash flow potential—limiting upside and adding risk. Because mortgage insurance is a fee, it doesn't add any benefit to the investor in terms of amortization.

FHA loans are a great option for investors who have limited capital to invest, but they can only be used for owner-occupied properties. We'll talk about this more soon, but this means you must actually live in the property for a time if you're going to use an FHA loan. So, if you're interested in a house hack or live-in flip (two common owner-occupied tactics), FHA loans can work well for you. However, if you're looking to buy a traditional short-term rental, flip, or rental property, FHA loans are not an option.

VA Loans

Veterans Affairs loans (VA loans) are government-backed loan options available exclusively to current and former members of the U.S. military and their families. While only available for owner-occupied properties, VA loans offer significant benefits, including LTVs up to 100 percent (meaning you can put zero percent down), competitive interest rates, and none of the mortgage insurance that FHA loans require. VA loans are fully amortized and come with fixed-rate and adjustable-rate options.

Portfolio Loans

Portfolio loans are similar to conventional loans, but they are issued by a bank that keeps the loan in its portfolio for the lifetime of the loan. When you take out a conventional loan, the lender rarely holds onto the loan for the duration of the term. Instead, the bank will bundle your mortgage with others and sell them off to investors and other lenders. With a portfolio loan, the loan is not sold off—it is held by the issuing institution for the duration of the loan.

Because portfolio loans won't be sold on the secondary market (which has rigid rules about what can be sold), portfolio lenders have more flexible terms on the types of properties they will lend on, credit scores they will accept, and so on. Portfolio loans can be a great option for investors who have poor credit, want to purchase a property that is in poor condition (many investors love these places!), are self-employed, or don't qualify for a conventional mortgage for any other reason.

Of course, lenders don't loosen restrictions out of the goodness of their hearts. In exchange for flexibility on terms, they are going to charge a higher interest rate or charge higher fees for loan origination.

Hard Money Loans

Hard money is a term loan that's secured by real property, and terms are based on the value of the property being used as collateral—unlike a conventional mortgage, which uses the creditworthiness of the borrower. Real property is also often known as a "hard asset," hence the name "hard money."

Hard money loans are typically given out by private lenders or non-bank institutions. As such, hard money loans can have flexible terms, the application process can be simple, and the time to close is generally short. This is great for investors and deal types that don't typically qualify for conventional mortgages, but it also means more risk for the lender. And when a lender has more risk, they charge a higher interest rate and require a lower LTV. Interest rates on hard money loans can be double (or more) the interest rate on a conventional mortgage, and LTVs are often in the 50-to-70-percent range.

Because of the high price and low LTV, hard money loans are typically used for short time periods. Investors don't want to pay high interest rates for long-term holds or tie up a lot of equity. This makes hard money well suited for flipping deal types. It can be tricky to use a conventional loan to acquire a property in need of serious repair, and because flippers don't intend to hold properties for a long time, they are willing to deal with the high interest rates over the rehab period. Hard money can also work well as a short-term option for value-add operating plans like BRRRR before being refinanced into a loan better suited for a long-term hold. Hard money is not a good option for a deal intended to be held for a long time.

Private Loans

Private loans encompass many different term loans that are made by private individuals. Private loans could be issued by a friend or family member, another investor, or just someone you know in your community.

Because private loans are agreements between two individuals or two private entities, they are very flexible. They can have fixed or adjustable rates, any LTV, and, feasibly, any amortization schedule. These loans can be used for an acquisition, closing costs, rehab costs, operational expenses, or anything else. They can close quickly, and the application process theoretically can be very simple. In short, private loans can be whatever the lender and the borrower agree upon. Flexibility is a great part of private loans, but it also makes them difficult to discuss generally in the context of this book.

If you do decide to use a private loan, it's important to make sure there is a proper contract in place that details all the terms of the loan. Even if—or especially if—the loan comes from friends or family, you need clear terms that are legally documented. Having an informal loan agreement is a huge risk to the lender and borrower alike.

Seller Financing

Seller financing is a form of private loan where the seller of a property is also the lender. Similar to other private loans, seller financing is very flexible on terms, and can take on almost any form depending on the seller's personal situation, the condition of the property, the seller's existing debt, and any other variable you can think of.

Not all sellers want to offer seller financing (in fact, very few do), but it can be an attractive idea to certain sellers, as they earn interest as a lender over time, and can sometimes command a higher price for their property than they might otherwise. Because banks are not involved, this is great for investors and properties that face challenges qualifying for bank loans .

Subject-To

Subject-to is not actually a loan type, but an increasingly popular financing tactic that uses debt. As such, it's worth a brief explanation. Subject-to (often called "sub-to") is where an investor takes over the seller's existing loan upon purchase. The new owner then makes payments on the original owner's loan.

There are several benefits to subject-to deals: First, the buyer does not need to apply for a loan or deal with any lenders. Second, subject-to deals can have small or even no down payments. Third, the buyer can take over loans further into their amortization schedule (increasing that profit driver!). Finally, subject-to deals can also allow the buyer to get a mortgage rate for a lower interest rate. For example, as of this writing, the average mortgage rate is about 7 percent—but if you use a subject-to deal, you can perhaps find a deal with a lower interest rate around 3 to 4 percent.

There are risks associated with subject-to deals, such as the "due on sale" clause, getting insurance, maintaining a relationship with the loan holder, and the original seller filing for bankruptcy, to name a few. Just like with all financing options, there are trade-offs with the subject-to. If you're interested in learning more, you can check out the book *Wealth without Cash* by Pace Morby.

Remember, though, if you use subject-to, you still need to understand the loan on which you're going to be taking over payments. As such, you need to make sure the loan you take over is appropriate for your Vision and overall deal strategy. Just because you can take over a loan doesn't mean you should. You should only take over loans that are right for your portfolio.

Debt Service Coverage Ratio Loans

A debt service coverage ratio (DSCR) loan is a residential loan type that mimics commercial underwriting. Like a commercial loan, a DSCR loan is underwritten based on the fundamentals of the deal, not the strength of the individual investor's credit profile.

The term "debt service coverage ratio" references a simple formula that compares a property's income to the cost of the debt. It is calculated by dividing a property's net operating income (NOI) by the total debt service. A DSCR of 1 means the property will break even after debts are paid; anything above 1 means the property will be cash flow positive; and anything under 1 indicates a property that will be cash flow negative.

For example, if you have a property with an NOI of $50,000 and debt service of $30,000 annually, the DSCR would be 1.67, which is high! The higher the DSCR, the lower the risk for the lender, and the easier it will be for an investor to find financing. Lenders want to see the highest possible DSCR, because higher DSCR means more cash flow with which the investor can service their debt. The DSCR that a lender will accept is dependent on the individual lender and the macroeconomic environment.

DSCR loans are great options for investors who cannot qualify for loans based on their personal creditworthiness or who have reached a point of scale in their portfolio where they can't get any additional debt in their name. They can work well for rental properties and short-term rentals, but are not typically used for flips. Generally speaking, DSCR loans have higher interest rates than conventional mortgages. DSCR loans can come in many forms: fixed or variable interest rates, any amortization schedule, and a variety of LTVs.

Commercial Loans

Commercial loans are term loans specifically designed for commercial properties: office, retail, industrial, multifamily, or any of the many other commercial asset classes. Commercial properties tend to carry more risk than residential properties, and therefore commercial loans often look very different than the residential loan options I've mentioned.

The biggest difference with commercial loans is that many of them are partially amortized, and therefore have balloon payments. Some commercial loans are fully amortized, or interest only, but partially amortized loans are the most common amortization schedule for commercial properties.

The capital intensity also differentiates commercial from residential loan situations. The LTV for commercial loans is typically lower, and it's fairly standard to see a 30-to-50-percent down payment required on commercial loans.

Commercial loans do have benefits, primary among them that they are underwritten based on the strength of the deal, not the creditworthiness or debt of the individual borrower (just like a DSCR loan). Commercial lenders look at the quality and experience of the operator and financial projections of the deal—not how many mortgages the lead investor has. This is a great benefit to investors as they scale. With some residential mortgages, the total number of properties financed and the amount borrowed can be limited by the individual borrower's existing debt. That issue doesn't exist for commercial loans since financing is tied to deal quality, not to personal financials.

If you're pursuing a commercial deal, you're going to need a commercial loan. The way I am describing commercial loans here, however, is overly simplistic. Getting a loan for a commercial deal—and more importantly, getting one that will help the performance of your deal—is a complex topic. Any investor considering commercial debt should do serious research into the topic before selecting a debt product.

As you can now see, there are many different types of term loans available to real estate investors, each of which offers unique benefits and trade-offs. But before you write down the loan types you're interested in, we need to discuss the other major debt option available to investors: lines of credit.

LINES OF CREDIT

Lines of credit (LOC) differ from term loans in that they are more of an open-ended agreement between a lender and borrower, whereas a term loan has a specific end date. As a borrower, when you are granted a line of credit, the lender is providing you with money that can be tapped at any time—up to a certain limit. The borrower can then withdraw money as they see fit, and then make payments on the money withdrawn. This is known as a "revolving" line of credit and works similarly to a credit card.

Lines of credit are attractive options because they provide the borrower with a lot of flexibility and can provide liquidity. Being able to take out money as needed, and in whatever increments you like, is a great benefit. You always know the money is available to you, but you aren't required to make payments on the loan until you need and use the funds. In the real estate investing world, LOCs are commonly used to finance flips, fund rehab projects, or even to make down payments for rental properties.

As an example, let's imagine Jamal has a good deal of equity built up in his personal residence and decides to apply for a home equity line of credit (HELOC). After reviewing his application, Jamal's lender grants him a $100,000 line of credit. Jamal now has permission to borrow $100,000 whenever he sees fit. He doesn't have to borrow anything right away, and therefore isn't paying anything to have his HELOC just yet.

Let's imagine that a few months after Jamal gets his HELOC, he decides to renovate one of his existing rentals, which will cost him $30,000. Jamal withdraws $30,000 from his line of credit and starts making payments on that $30,000. Even though he has a limit of $100,000, Jamal only pays on the $30,000 he is using. A few months later, if Jamal needs another $25,000 to contribute as a down payment on his next deal, he can tap his HELOC again and start making payments on the $55,000 he's borrowed. Jamal's LOC provides him with a good deal of liquidity and flexibility that he can deploy as he sees fit.

The terms for a line of credit can vary, but most are fully amortized adjustable-rate loans. The concept of LTV is a little different for LOCs than it is for term loans. Most lines of credit don't have a down payment because they are secured by collateral (like your primary residence or a rental property). Therefore, the lender will underwrite your LOC and determine your borrowing limit based on the equity value of your collateral, not as a percentage of the asset's value. That said, there are also unsecured LOCs that come with higher interest rates.

There are many types of lines of credit, but below are a few of the more common types used by real estate investors.

Home Equity Line of Credit

A home equity line of credit (HELOC) is a very common tool for real estate investors. As the name suggests, HELOCs use the equity you have in a property to secure a line of credit. If Jamal's personal residence is worth $450,000 and he has $100,000 of equity in the property, he can use that $100,000 as collateral to secure a line of credit. Note that you can only borrow against the equity value of the property, not the "estimated value of the property."

HELOCs are a great option for investors because the interest rates tend to be low, particularly when you use the equity in your primary residence as collateral. Lenders see lending against your primary residence as relatively low risk, and therefore offer low rates for this type of HELOC; the rate can be similar to that of a thirty-year fixed-rate mortgage. Getting a HELOC against an investment property is possible, but interest rates tend to be higher, and they are harder to come by. Not all lenders offer HELOCs on investment properties, and the qualification process tends to be more difficult.

The risks associated with a HELOC are similar to a conventional mortgage. If you fail to make payments on your HELOC as agreed, the bank can foreclose on your property.

Business Line of Credit

A business line of credit is a loan that is secured by the cash flow and track record of a business. It can be used to fund operations, invest in new equipment, hire new people, or anything else a business needs. Business lines of credit are not typically granted to new businesses because they don't have a track record or cash flow to be used as collateral. These loans are best used by existing, successful businesses looking for financing options to expand.

Personal Line of Credit

Unlike a HELOC or business line of credit, a personal line of credit is a loan that is not secured with collateral. With a personal line of credit, the lender underwrites the loan based on the borrower's credit score and payment history. Because these loans aren't secured, they carry significant risk to the lender, and therefore come with interest rates that are much higher than other credit line options. They are also difficult to qualify for.

Personal lines of credit have a time and place for those who can qualify. But given the relatively high interest rates, they are generally best used for short-term financing needs and not for long-term investments, like the down payment on an investment property.

PREP WORK
FINANCING YOUR DEALS

STRATEGIC DECISION: Of the financing options explained in this chapter, which ones are aligned with your Vision and fit within your broader Portfolio Strategy? Select any financing options that could work well for you and try to be as specific as possible. Will you use term loans, lines of credit, or both? What amortization schedules, LTVs, and interest rate structure will you pursue? Any financing options that fit your criteria should be written in your PREP. For additional guidance and a rubric that will help you test alignment, see more below.

We covered a lot in this chapter, but you don't need to figure out every financing detail right now. Instead, focus on the big-picture questions and the major variables that will impact your Deal Design in the coming years.

- Do you (and any potential partners) have sufficient capital to purchase a property using equity financing alone? If so, do you want to do that, or would taking on debt provide positive leverage (boost your returns)?
- Are you considering an owner-occupied operating plan like house hacking or a live-in flip? Owner-occupied deals can often get favorable financing.
- What type of risk are you willing to take on? The higher your LTV, the less capital you need, but the more risk you take.
- Do you have equity in your home, or in a business, that you can use to secure a line of credit?
- What types of loans are possible on the type of asset you intend to buy?
- Are you close to hitting your limit on conventional mortgages?
- What is your intended hold period? Different loans should be considered depending on how long you intend to hold a deal.
- What is the current interest rate environment?

	Resource Alignment			Risk/Reward Alignment	
	Time	Capital	Skill		Include in PREP?
Equity (All Cash)					
Conventional Loan					
FHA Loan					
VA Loan					
Portfolio Loan					
Hard Money Loan					
Private Loan					
Seller Financing					
Subject-To					
DSCR Loan					
Commercial Loan					
Line of Credit					

Once you've thought about the above questions, identify a few financing options that work well to support your Vision. Write those down in your *PREP*. Remember, before you actually use any of these financing options, you should learn more about them and fully understand the terms. Talking to lenders is a free and very informative way to understand what loans you can qualify for, and what terms may look like.

Next, we'll turn to operating plans, where you'll consider the various ways to run your business in order to maximize returns.

Chapter 19
OPERATING PLANS

When you invest in a real estate deal, you need a plan for how you're going to operate it. Knowing the deal type is great, but it doesn't tell you enough about how you're going to manage your business and achieve your desired performance. For example, you may know you want to buy a rental property, but there are tons of ways to operate a rental property. You could use an owner-occupied strategy, known as a house hack. You could do a major renovation and then refinance it, known as the BRRRR method. Or you could buy a stabilized asset (a property in already good condition). Even within a single deal type there can be many operational plans for you to consider.

An operating plan is your intended approach for generating maximum value from your deal. It's not set in stone, and it can always change, but when designing a deal, you should have a clear intention for how you plan to operate that deal. There are many different operational plans—far too many for me to name here, but I will cover the following common ones:

- Buy and hold
- Value-add
- BRRRR
- Operational efficiency
- Owner occupancy
- Rent by the room
- Creative opportunities

Although I will describe each of these operating plans one at a time, operating plans can be, and often are, combined with one another. For example, you can buy a commercial property as a buy and hold, but also seek to improve operational efficiency. Or you can buy a distressed property, complete a value-add project, and then rent it by the room. Operating plans are not mutually exclusive.

The idea here is not for you to chart the precise course for your next deal—it's to understand some of the operating plans you *can* use to design a deal.

BUY AND HOLD

Buy and hold is a simple, proven operating plan. If you're looking for a sexy investment, this isn't it. Buy and hold is as plain and predictable as it comes. The idea is to buy a property and then hold it indefinitely. Given the high potential for cash flow, appreciation, amortization, and tax benefits that many deal types offer over a long hold period, this can be an excellent way to build long-term wealth and achieve financial freedom.

The term "buy and hold" is often used only to describe rental properties, but it can be used with other deal types too. You can buy and hold a short-term rental, commercial properties, and even loans. If you buy an asset with the plan to hold on to it for a long time, it's buy and hold.

Buy and hold's popularity is due to relatively low risk and complexity combined with solid returns. Recall our earlier discussion of risk: Holding real estate for a long time is one of the best ways to mitigate risk and optimize returns. If you buy and then hold for a long time, it greatly reduces risk. But remember, to enable a long hold and further reduce risk, your deals need to cash-flow. This is why I recommend that in all but a few unusual circumstances, all buy and hold deals should provide at least a bit of cash flow.

The trade-off with buy and hold deals is that it can take a relatively long time to generate strong returns. This is probably evident from the name, but due to high transaction costs, buy and hold deals need to be held for at least a few years to reach the point of maximum return potential. This operating plan doesn't come with a lot of liquidity or opportunities to reallocate resources.

In terms of resources, buy and hold is quite flexible. There are many ways to design a buy and hold deal using relatively little capital, time, and skill—at least compared to other operating plans. This flexibility, combined with a beneficial Risk/Reward Profile, makes buy and hold an excellent option for any investor with a time horizon that allows a longer hold.

VALUE-ADD

We discussed value-add earlier in the book as a profit driver that builds equity. But value-add is also an operating plan (which some people call "forced appreciation"—it's the same thing). Unlike the other ways of building equity, which are byproducts of the normal operations of your business, value-add is something you can plan out and execute deliberately, making it an operating plan.

Value-add is taking an asset that is performing below its full potential and improving the quality of the asset to drive up the value and "stabilize" it. The key is to increase the value of the asset more than the cost of making the improvements. As a very simplified example, if you purchase a single-family home for $200,000, renovate it for $50,000 and drive up the value to $300,000, you've made a $50,000 profit.

Many investors love value-add because it is relatively predictable, and it's fast—when you're good at it. If you are good at estimating rehab costs and understand how much you can increase the value of a deal, you can build a lot of equity in a relatively short period of time using the value-add operating plan.

The intensity of value-add deals can vary greatly. On one end of the spectrum, there are cosmetic rehabs where the investor does minor improvements like painting, upgrading finishes, or improving landscaping. Regardless of the deal type, these projects tend to be fairly low risk/reward and not require a huge amount of time, skill, or capital. On the other end of the value-add spectrum are full-gut rehabs. This is where a property is almost entirely rebuilt. Of course, these types of projects are complex, capital intensive, time-consuming, and risky, but they offer great return potential.

In between these two extremes of the spectrum are many other opportunities for value-add: adding bedrooms, renovating kitchens, finishing basements, improving bathrooms, and pretty much anything else you can imagine—as long as it improves the value of the property by more than it costs.

You probably recognize by now that the entire premise of house flipping is value-add. The fix-and-flip deal type requires a value-add operating plan. But pretty much every other deal type has the option for value-add. You can increase the value of a rental property, a short-term rental, or a commercial property!

So far, my examples have shown how value-add can build equity, but value-add can also help drive cash flow. By improving the quality and value of a property, you make your space more desirable to tenants, which, in turn, can improve your rental income and cash flow. Plus, increasing your rental income doesn't just improve your cash flow—it can also help improve the resale value of your property. Higher cash flow can help command a higher price from other investors.

Commonly, investors choose to add value shortly after they acquire a project. This is the obvious course for flips, but since value-add can help boost cash flow, it makes sense for rentals, STRs, and commercial properties as well. That said, value-add can come at any point in your hold period. Sometimes, depending on market conditions, wear-and-tear, labor and material pricing, or many other variables, it makes sense to add value later into a hold. Keep your mind open!

Value-add is a great option for almost all investors. For beginners, I'd recommend starting with smaller value-add plans and working your way up to larger projects as you gain skill.

BRRRR

BRRRR stands for "buy, rehab, rent, refinance, repeat" and has become an incredibly popular operating plan. The power of BRRRR comes from its use of a value-add operating plan combined with a cash-out refinance.

The idea is that with a standard value-add operating plan, investors can build significant equity, but a lot of capital gets locked into that deal (the down payment, closing costs, cash reserves, rehab costs, and built equity), unless it is sold as a flip. BRRRR solves this with the cash-out refinance. The investor does a normal value-add project, but once they have built sufficient equity to qualify, they complete a cash-out refinance. This allows the investor to hold onto the property long-term while also gaining liquidity for use in other investments.

The BRRRR operating plan was popularized with rental properties, but the same idea (value-add plus a cash-out refinance) can be used in short-term rentals (which I've recently heard called an AirBRRRRnb) or in commercial properties. This operating plan works across multiple deal types and offers the same benefits: Build equity through value-add and hold onto the deal without locking up excessive capital for a long period.

The risk, rewards, and resources that go into BRRRR are very similar to value-add. As with value-add, the scope of renovation will determine the profile of the deal. If the renovation is large, the time, capital, and skill intensity will be high—as will the risk and the reward. If it's a small, mostly cosmetic renovation, the risks and required resources will be relatively lower.

One additional consideration with a BRRRR operating plan is the risk of refinancing. If you plan to refinance a BRRRR deal, there are no assurances that you'll be able to complete the refinance or what the terms of your new loan will be. If your project goes as planned, you build a lot of equity, and market conditions remain strong, completing a cash-out refinance shouldn't be very hard. BRRRR tends to work well in a growing housing market with stable interest rates. However, if the market shifts, interest rates rise, or your project builds less equity than anticipated, you may not be able to refinance. This can mean you have to keep more money in a deal than you like, which can add to the risk of underperformance and reduce liquidity.

When BRRRR goes well, it can be a powerful force in portfolio development. Due to the cash-out refinance portion of the BRRRR operating plan, it means you can hold a property while gaining liquidity and having relatively frequent opportunities to reallocate capital into new deals. Consider a deal that you buy for $300,000 ($75,000 equity down payment and $225,000 debt) and invest another $75,000 into value-add renovations. Let's imagine that this property is now worth $440,000 and generates positive cash flow. If you refinance, keeping 25 percent down in the new loan ($110,000) and paying the bank back the $225,000 from the first loan, you could cash out approximately $105,000 ($440,000 – $110,000 – $225,000) minus transaction costs. You are keeping a cash-flowing asset and still have a big chunk of principal to invest elsewhere. Of course, this is a very simple example of a deal that went well, but hopefully you can see why BRRRR is such a popular operating plan. BRRRR is a great option for investors who are confident with value-add projects and are looking to scale quickly.

If you want to learn more about the BRRRR method, check out David Greene's book by the same title at www.biggerpockets.com/brrrrbook.

OPERATIONAL EFFICIENCY

Operational efficiency is an operating plan that improves the performance of an asset through operational changes. It's similar to a value-add deal, but rather than improving the asset physically, you're improving the business practices used to manage the asset.

Imagine a twelve-unit multifamily property that is owned by an older couple who have owned the asset for decades. When they first bought it, they were running a tight ship, but over the years they've grown a little complacent. Rents haven't kept up with market rates, the tenant experience has slipped and turnover is high, expenses have ballooned in an unexplained way, and bookkeeping is poor. This would make a great opportunity to boost the performance of the deal through operational efficiency. If you invested in this property, you could bring rents up to fair market rate, improve the tenant experience, and reassess and reallocate expenses to make sure the business is running smoothly. And just like that, you've improved cash flow and the value of the asset.

Operational efficiency is a great business model because it doesn't always require a large amount of capital. If you are good at operating a real estate investment business, you can often use just your skills and your time to increase operational efficiency and the performance of your deal. Of course, if you're wiping the slate clean, installing new technology, hiring expensive contractors, or making any other large-scale changes, it could cost a good deal of money, but it doesn't have to. Operational efficiency is about using business acumen to increase performance. As such, it's relatively low risk and requires low capital intensity, but usually takes a good deal of time and skill to do.

Given the nature of the operational efficiency operating model, it tends to work best for experienced investors who have developed the "operations" skill and have a strong professional network they can rely on. New investors shouldn't assume they can walk into a business they have no experience with and improve efficiency. This operating plan also works particularly well with commercial assets, where incremental efficiencies applied across many units can yield big results.

OWNER OCCUPANCY

Owner occupancy is when investors live in the residential property (four units or less) they invest in. This comes with many advantages and is relatively low risk, making it an excellent option for beginners.

The benefits of owner occupancy come from rules by the government and by lenders that favor homeowners over investors. For example, if you sell a property that you've lived in for two out of the last five years, you pay zero capital gains on your equity growth. That's amazing! In terms of lending, owner occupants can typically qualify for a broader range of loan products, many of which allow the buyer to put less money down (as little as 3.5 percent down with an FHA loan), qualify for government grants, and get lower interest rates than investors do.

House hacking is the most common form of owner occupancy and refers to an owner-occupied rental property. This typically takes on one of two forms: The investor either 1) buys a single-family home, lives in one bedroom, and leases out the other(s) to roommates, or 2) buys a duplex, triplex, or fourplex, lives in one unit, and leases out the other(s) (anything over four units qualifies as a commercial property and cannot be owner occupied). House hacking is an extremely popular way to build your portfolio because you can significantly reduce your living expenses, potentially generate positive cash flow, and learn on the job. Living in your property and doing much of the management yourself is a crash course in real estate investing and property management. I did this myself and can attest that house hacking is a great place to start.

A *live-in short-term rental* is similar to a house hack, but with a short-term rental. For example, if an investor buys a duplex, they can live in one unit and use the other unit as a short-term rental. Similarly, the investor could buy a single-family home, live in one bedroom, and rent out other bedrooms to guests. This owner-occupied strategy is also a great opportunity to learn and offers the potential for great returns. As short-term rental regulations increase, live-in short-term rentals are a way to enjoy the higher returns of short-term leases that often comply with local rules.

A *live-in flip* is an owner-occupied operating plan for flipping in which investors purchase a home to live in and renovate the property over time. While you may not love the idea of living in a construction zone, this is the only flipping niche (that I know of) that offers great tax benefits. As of this writing, if you live in a property for two out of five years, you don't have to pay any tax on your gains when sold, meaning you can essentially do a flip tax-free.

Due to the nature of owner occupancy, it is an approach with lower resource intensity. You can put relatively little money into these deals, and living on-site makes managing your tenants or rehab a bit easier than it would be otherwise.

The biggest issue with owner occupancy is scalability. You can only live in one property at a time! This limits how much you can use owner occupancy to build your portfolio over time, though it can be done. Some investors I know move from one owner-occupied house to another while buying other non-owner-occupied deals at the same time. For example, my friend Mindy Jensen, cohost of the *BiggerPockets Money* podcast, has been doing live-in flips with her family for years! She completes a flip, gets her tax-free profit, and moves into a new one and does it all over again. You can also move out of a house hack and keep the property as a rental before moving into another house hack—you just need to refinance the original property into a non-owner-occupied loan.

Blending your primary residence with an investment through an owner-occupied operating plan is a powerful way to invest. I strongly believe in house hacking and highly recommend it for new investors. Owner occupancy is a proven, low-risk way to get into real estate investing and learn the ropes.

RENT BY THE ROOM

Rent by the room is an operating plan where, rather than renting a property to a single household (an individual or couple, a family, or even roommates who know one another), the investor rents each room within a property to individual tenants. For example, in a three-bedroom house, the property manager will find three different tenants and sign three unique leases for the property. This approach often yields higher income per square foot of the property, and thereby can boost cash flow.

This strategy is most common in rental property investing, as in the example above, but also works for other deal types. For short-term rentals, it's possible for an investor to rent out just a single room in their property, or to lease out individual rooms to multiple guests who share some common space. Within commercial real estate, there is a similar concept for office space, typically called "coworking." The particulars of how to implement a rent-by-the-room operating plan will depend on the deal type, but the idea is always the same: maximizing revenue by subdividing space in your property.

Rent by the room can sometimes require more capital than a traditional rental to subdivide the space practically, but the primary consideration is management. Having multiple tenants in a single space adds management complexity to the business. Rent by the room means you'll have more work to do to find, screen, and maintain relationships with tenants. You also may need to mitigate issues between tenants! This complexity adds risk. With multiple tenants, there is more risk of turnover and vacancy, both of which cost money. There are some property management companies that specialize in rent by the room, but investors considering this approach should make sure the extra revenue is worth the additional complexity.

CREATIVE OPPORTUNITIES

There are some opportunities that real estate investors encounter that defy definition, all of which I group into the "creative opportunities" category. A creative operating plan is an investment with a unique approach that is designed around the specific property being purchased.

For example, I know someone who bought an old church and subdivided it into a very unique aparthotel. I've seen motels repurposed into office suites. I've known investors who have purchased single-family homes that don't cash-flow but have favorable zoning to add an accessory dwelling unit (ADU) that *will* cash-flow. These creative opportunities are hard to plan for at scale, but they can be lucrative (and fun!) when they come along.

One type of creative opportunity deal is speculation. Before you get up in arms, know that 99 percent of the time (or ever, for new investors) I wouldn't recommend speculating. But are there times it could be a good play? I think so. Perhaps you learn through legal means that a tech company is planning a new distribution center in your town, and you have the opportunity to buy land adjacent to the new building for a cheap price before the building is completed. That's speculation for sure, but there is logic behind the investment. For an investor with some extra cash, a long time horizon, and a high risk tolerance, it could make sense.

Due to the nature of creative opportunities, I cannot say how risky each is, or what resources are required—each one is different! As such, I advise against anyone specifically counting on "creative opportunities" as an operating plan in their Portfolio Strategy. Creative deals are best for experienced investors who are willing to put in the time to figure out a custom operating plan for a new deal. That said, keep your eyes open! If you are creative and resourceful, you might just be able to find a great deal that others don't see.

PREP WORK
OPERATING PLANS

STRATEGIC DECISION: Determine which operating plans are aligned with your Vision and fit within your broader Portfolio Strategy. Remember that operating plans can be combined together and are not mutually exclusive. Any operating plans that fit your criteria should be written in your PREP. For additional guidance and a rubric that will help you test alignment, see more below.

The above list of operating plans represents only the most common approaches. There are plenty of other plans worth exploring: distressed properties, medium-term rentals, and "wholetailing," to name a few. But if you're just getting started or want to stick to the most proven approaches, this list is a good place to begin.

Use the rubric below to list which approaches you want to consider in your future Deal Design. As you do, recall two key points from this chapter: First, operating plans are not mutually exclusive; they can and will be used together. Second, your operating plan can change over the course of a hold period. When you go out to do a deal, you should have an operating plan in mind, but if conditions on the ground change, you can change your plans. The idea is simply to have an idea of how you plan to extract the most value from your future deals and then adjust if necessary.

Now, as you prepare to write down potential operating plans in your PREP, consider the following questions.

- How experienced are you as an investor? Certain operating plans favor newer investors (like owner occupancy), while others are better for experienced investors.
- What skills do you have? Operating plans are one of the most skill-dependent considerations in your Deal Design, and you should select plans that you can confidently execute on.
- Are you willing to owner occupy? If so, it's a great way to get started (and is not nearly as awkward as many believe it to be).
- How can you combine multiple operating plans to achieve the maximum value of your deals?
- Which operating plans will work well together across your portfolio to achieve the right balance of risk, reward, and liquidity?

	Resource Alignment			Risk/Reward Alignment	
	Time	Capital	Skill		Include in PREP?
Buy and Hold					
Value-Add					
BRRRR					
Operational Efficiency					
Rent by the Room					
Opportunistic					
Other:					

Once you've decided which operating plans belong in your Deal Design tool kit, write them down in your *PREP*. Next we'll talk about who will be responsible for your deal's performance in the Management Plans chapter.

Chapter 20
MANAGEMENT PLANS

Every real estate deal you do is a business, and no business is entirely passive. Who is going to operate your business? Will you operate your deals yourself? Or will you hire out some of your management to third parties? Managing your own deals is generally the most profitable option, but it will cost you time and skill resources. Outsourcing your management is time efficient but will cost you money. As always, there are trade-offs.

When we talk about managing your investments, there are two different categories of responsibilities: First, there is the obvious piece, the day-to-day management of your business—also called "operational management." What is involved in operational management depends largely on the deal type and the operating plan. Operational management is mostly property management: working with tenants, managing maintenance and repairs, and doing your basic bookkeeping, reporting, and everything else. For a flip, operational management is overseeing the renovation. Every deal, regardless of its type, needs operational management.

The other component of management is known as "asset management," which concerns the long-term planning and strategy of a particular investment. The asset manager makes decisions like which capital improvements to make, whether to convert deals from one type to another (e.g., long-term to short-term rental), whether to refinance, when to sell, and so on. The asset manager is responsible for ensuring the long term success of an investment

When determining a management plan, you need to consider both operational and asset management responsibilities. As an investor, you will need to decide what role, if any, you want to play in the management of your businesses.

ACTIVE MANAGEMENT

Active management means you are doing both asset and operational management and is therefore the most involved you can be in your investments. You are responsible for both the day-to-day operations of the deal and the high-level strategic decision-making. You can still hire contractors and delegate as needed, but you are the point person for every decision.

Active management takes the most time of all the management plans and often requires the manager to have a broad set of skills. As a successful active manager, you need to have a baseline understanding of most elements of running a real estate business. For example, you don't need to know how to fix a refrigerator when it breaks, but you do need to have a good sense of how to find and vet appliance technicians to ensure you're getting high-quality work at a fair price. The same goes for hiring a bookkeeper, CPA, or any other person. You also need to be adept at asset management—knowing how to continually optimize the performance of your deals over the long run. You need to know a bit of everything to be a good active manager.

The breadth of knowledge needed to be an active manager may sound intimidating, and maybe this is controversial, but I think it's okay to start as a mediocre active manager. I often recommend that new investors actively manage because you learn so much. You will figure out what skills you pick up easily, as well as which ones you hate and want to outsource—thereby setting you up for long-term success. I'm not saying you should go into active management blindly and without preparation, but everyone starts somewhere. You may make a few mistakes, but if you stick with it, you will get better. This is how I started —and I have a long list of silly decisions to prove it.

The specific requirements of active management depend heavily on the deal type. For rental properties and short-term rentals, active management requires skills in tenant management, partner management, and repairs and maintenance on the operational side. On the asset management side, you'll have to manage capital expenditures, financing options, and liquidity. For a flip, operational management entails overseeing contractors, buying materials, permitting, etc., while the asset management requires decision-making on a high level like financing, budgeting, and sale strategy. For a commercial property, there is usually a general partner who is typically responsible for both operational and asset management.

Active management is a great way to get started and will increase your income potential because you're not paying any third parties for management. But regardless of deal type, active management is time-consuming. It is possible to be an active manager while having a full-time job, but there are limits. With rentals and short-term rentals, it's possible to actively manage a modest portfolio while working full-time (I think up to about ten units). For a flip or commercial deal, it can be a challenge to actively manage multiple deals while working full-time, unless you have hired a team in-house.

If you want to prioritize hands-on learning and limit what you pay third parties, active management could be a great option for you. However, if your values indicate you want to maximize free time, active management may not be the best choice. Instead, use some of your capital resources to purchase the expertise of someone else in either a hybrid or passive management plan.

HYBRID MANAGEMENT

Hybrid management is an approach in which an investor outsources some elements of managing their business while doing others in-house. There are many ways to construct a hybrid management plan, but the most common is the lead investor doing the asset management but hiring out some or all of the day-to-day operations. This is a proven way to scale.

It's relatively easy to hire out operational management. There are many good contractors and property management companies out there. On the other hand, it's difficult to hire out asset management. As an investor, it's no small feat to find someone who can make long-term decisions about your deals on your behalf. Since asset management is closely aligned with your Portfolio Strategy, you'll usually be the best person for that job. And while asset management is generally less time-consuming than operational management, it does take time. And as you scale, asset management will likely take more and more of your time.

Within hybrid management, there is a vast spectrum of involvement. As a rental property owner, you can hire a property manager but still do tenant screening yourself. (I still do this for a few of my properties, even while living in Europe!) As a short-term rental owner, you can hire a full-service property manager, or you can hire a cleaner and handle some of the other operations yourself. For flips, an owner will often hire out a general contractor but do the asset management themselves.

Even rental properties that market themselves as "turnkey" (buying a rental from a company with all repairs done, tenants and property management team in place, etc.) are a form of hybrid management because you are still the asset manager. It's your responsibility to oversee the property management team, decide when to buy or sell, and make many other high-level decisions.

Hybrid management is a good management plan for almost every type of investor because it's so flexible. A good hybrid management plan allows you to use the skills that you have and hire out the tasks you can't (or won't) do. Of course, hiring out some pieces of your management will require that you devote capital resources, but it will free up time that you can use to focus on asset management and Portfolio Strategy.

PASSIVE MANAGEMENT

Passive management is, unsurprisingly, the opposite of active management: It's where you hire out both operational and asset management. Passive management is the least involved you can be with your investments. It allows you to commit very little time and skill to your portfolio; instead, you leverage the time, skills, and experience of other real estate professionals.

Passive management is highly scalable because it requires so little of your time. As we've discussed, time is the only finite resource, and passive management allows you to maximize it. Passive management does cost money, as you are buying the time and skill of a property manager and an asset manager. This means that on paper, all other things being equal, your deals will earn a lower return.

Fully passive management is relatively uncommon in rentals, flips, and short-term rentals because of the difficulty of outsourcing asset management for residential real estate. This is why I say that these strategies are not really passive—the majority of these deals require you to do the asset management yourself. Unless you hire an in-house team, it's very difficult to find someone you trust to do the asset management of a residential portfolio on your behalf.

The most common form of passive management is as an LP in either a fund or a syndication. As discussed in a previous chapter, as an LP you still have to do some work upfront, mostly in the form of vetting operators and selecting deals. But you outsource both the operational management and the asset management to the GP. You do not choose the tenants or oversee any repairs. You don't decide what improvements to make or when to sell. Once you make your investment as an LP, you do pretty much nothing except monitor results. This is as passive as it gets in the world of real estate investing, which is great for those who qualify as accredited investors and are looking for deals with a low level of time commitment.

PREP WORK
MANAGEMENT PLANS

STRATEGIC DECISION: Which management plans best support your Vision? Determine which management plans work with your current resources and write them in your PREP. For additional guidance and a rubric that will help you test alignment, see more below.

Of all the Deal Design elements, your management plan will have the largest impact on your time resources. Buying and selling deals is often the most fun and glamorous part of investing in real estate, but in terms of time spent on your portfolio, it's relatively small. Instead, most of the time your portfolio demands is managing your operations and assets. Think carefully about how you want to align your management plans with your portfolio Vision.

- How much experience do you have? Active management is a great way to learn the business.
- How much time are you committing to your portfolio? Are you working full-time?
- Do you have any real estate skills that you can efficiently contribute to managing your portfolio?
- What skills are you better off buying or trading for than contributing yourself?
- Do you want to invest passively? Are you willing to pay third parties for both operational and asset management?
- Do you qualify as an accredited investor, and can you get access to truly passive deals?

As you implement your Vision for your portfolio, you can and likely will use different management plans for different deals. I started actively managing all of my deals, but now exclusively do hybrid or passive deals. Even within a single deal, you can change and adjust your management plan over time. I still own a few deals that I used to actively manage but have now outsourced the operational management for them (hybrid). That said, it's helpful to think about what management plans are currently aligned with your portfolio Vision so you can select deals accordingly.

	Resource Alignment			Risk/Reward Alignment	
	Time	Capital	Skill		Include in PREP?
Active Management					
Hybrid Management					
Passive Management					

Chapter 21
ASSET CLASSES

There are many different types of properties you can invest in: single-family homes, shopping centers, multifamily, and more. In our Deal Design framework, we call these different types of properties "asset classes."

Although you may associate certain asset classes with certain deal types (e.g., all short-term rentals are in single-family homes), that's not the case. Asset classes work across deal types and operating plans and are an important element of Deal Design. For example, you may know you want to invest in rental properties, but will you buy a condo, a single-family home, or a large multifamily building? Most people flip single-family homes, but you can flip a duplex or even commercial properties! There are pros and cons to each asset class, and you need to be strategic in your choice. The asset class you choose plays a big role in the capital intensity and Risk/Reward Profile of your deals.

Real estate asset classes are broken down into two major buckets: residential and commercial. Residential includes common housing types like condos, single-family homes, and small multifamily buildings. Commercial is a broad category that includes everything from large multifamily buildings to self-storage facilities, medical offices, and more.

In this chapter I will review the key differentiations between residential and commercial asset classes, and then provide information about the benefits, risks, and resource intensity of some of the most common asset classes.

RESIDENTIAL ASSETS

Residential assets consist of properties that have four or fewer units designed to provide shelter to tenants or guests. As such, these types of assets are popular among investors and homebuyers alike, and the market for residential assets is largely dictated by homebuyers. When you bid on a residential property, you are primarily competing against owner-occupant homeowners, not other investors. Although the share of residential properties being purchased by investors has risen over recent years, about 80 percent of residential purchases are still made by homeowners as of this writing, according to Redfin.[3] Given this, residential properties are typically valued the way homeowners would value a property—based on comparable properties that have sold recently (comps). It also means there are more emotional buyers in the residential asset market than the more calculating and sophisticated buyers you'll find in the commercial space. Homebuyers are buying a home, not a business.

Residential properties are very popular among small- and medium-sized investors because they are abundant, are relatively low risk, are eligible for favorable loan products, and require less time and money to purchase. Within residential real estate, there are three distinct assets, each of which offers pros and cons of their own.

- Detached single-family residence
- Attached single-family residence
- Small multifamily property

Detached Single-Family Residence

A detached single-family residence (DSFR) is what most of us think of when we think of a "house"; it's a single housing unit on a single plot of land. When you buy a DSFR, you are buying both the structure and the land the structure sits on. DSFRs are the most common real estate asset class in the United States, making up roughly 82 million of the 144 million housing units (57 percent) in the country as of this writing.[4] For investors, DSFRs are the most common asset class for rental properties, flipping, and short-term rentals .

---

3 Lily Katz and Sheharyar Bokhari, "Investor Home Purchases Fell a Record 49% Year over Year in the First Quarter," Redfin Real Estate News, May 30, 2023, https://www.redfin.com/news/investor-home-purchases-q1-2023/.

4 Michael Neal, Laurie Goodman, and Caitlin Young, *Housing Supply Chartbook*, Urban Institute, January 2020, https:www.urban.org/sites/default/files/publication/101553/housing_supply_chartbook_1.pdf.

The primary strength of DSFRs as an asset class is demand. Most Americans (roughly 80 percent) want to live in a single-family residence.[5] Whether it's freedom from neighbors, HOAs, co-op boards, or the traditional depiction of the "American Dream," for one reason or another, Americans want DSFRs .

With strong demand comes a consistent pool of buyers. Because DSFRs are in demand among homeowners, house flippers, short-term rental investors, and rental property investors, there tend to be more buyers for single-family homes than any other asset class. This demand can put upward pressure on asset values and provide more exit strategies than any other asset class.

Another benefit of strong demand is that DSFRs tend to generate higher revenue per square foot. If you compare two rental properties that are comparable in every way except that one is a DSFR and the other is a condo, the DSFR will typically generate more revenue. The same goes for short-term rentals. Americans, on average, just value space in a DSFR over the same space in an "attached" unit.

Although DSFRs are a very stable asset class, they do come with trade-offs. First, DSFRs typically have only a single tenant (unless the rent-by-the-room operating plan is being used). In some respects, this is a benefit, as it reduces the time involved in finding, screening, and managing tenants. But it also leaves DSFRs susceptible to turnover and vacancy risks. If you have just one tenant in a rental property and that tenant fails to pay rent for a month, you lose 100 percent of your revenue. The same goes for vacancy. In other larger asset classes, you spread your income risk across multiple units.

Another trade-off with DSFRs is that they are one of the hardest asset classes to scale. If you're buying one unit at a time, it can take a long time to build up a significant cash flow. A portfolio of DSFRs can also be difficult to manage. As a general rule of thumb, it is more efficient to manage a single triplex than it is to manage three DSFRs. With DSFRs there are three roofs, three HVAC systems, three foundations, three yards, and so on. DSFRs do earn more revenue per square foot, but they also tend to require higher maintenance costs per square foot in exchange. That said, DSFRs are a reliable asset class that almost any type of investor can consider.

5   Charlotte O'Malley, "80 Percent of Americans Prefer Single-Family Homeownership," *Builder*, Auugst 13, 2013, https://www.builderonline.com/money/economics/80-percent-of-americans-prefer-single-family-homeownership_o.

Attached Single-Family Residence (Townhome/Co-op/Condo/Etc.)

Attached single-family residences (ASFRs) refer to a conglomeration of residential asset classes: condos, co-ops, townhomes, row homes, and more. Each of these asset classes is unique, but for our purposes they share many of the same benefits and drawbacks, so I am lumping them all together.

While similar to DSFRs, ASFRs involve the sharing of some aspects of the property with neighbors or other shareholders. The specifics of what is shared are unique to each asset class.

- In a **condo**, the property owner owns the unit but not the land. Condo owners share ownership of common areas and facilities with other condo owners on the same property.
- A **co-op** or **"cooperative housing"** is an arrangement where the occupants buy into a business that owns the property.
- **Townhomes** are attached units where certain walls have joint ownership between neighbors, but the land underneath belongs to the individual unit owners.

In the most general sense, ASFRs share several commonalities. First, ASFRs tend to be less expensive than DSFRs, making them an attractive asset class for newer investors. One reason ASFRs tend to be less expensive than their detached counterparts is due to efficiencies of scale. ASFRs are more efficient to build and maintain than DSFRs because the costs of building and maintenance are spread across more units.

The other reason ASFRs typically have lower prices is due to lower demand. Although some markets have ASFRs in high demand (mostly high-priced urban areas, where DSFRs are scarce), typically people prefer "detached" housing. This smaller demand compared to DSFRs can limit appreciation potential, your buyer pool, and thereby your exit strategies.

The reasons fewer homeowners want to buy an ASFR are often the same for investors. You have less control over your property with an ASFR than with its detached counterpart. Co-ops or condos have a governing entity (like an HOA or board of directors) and many (often strict) rules about what you can and cannot do with your property. Townhouses have more control, but you will still have a party-wall agreement that dictates how certain situations and expenses will be handled.

ASFR owners often jointly own, and are therefore jointly liable for, the maintenance of shared spaces such as the exterior, roof, and foundation of a building. If any of those shared spaces needs repair or replacement (as determined by the board of directors) that costs more than the property has in reserves, the owner can be billed for a "special assessment," which is an additional burden on top of normal maintenance fees. My mom lives in a co-op, and due to a structural problem with the building's patios that originated before she moved in, there was a $2 million special assessment she had to contribute to. This is an extreme example, but it can happen. If you buy an ASFR, it's important to thoroughly vet the board of directors, the bylaws, and the financial statements of the building. You don't want to be buying into a bad situation.

> All types of residential assets (not just "attached" units) have the potential to be governed by a homeowners association (HOA) or similar organization like a condo or co-op board. HOAs come in all shapes and sizes, but generally speaking, they create and enforce rules about how properties within a given community can operate. If you choose to invest in a property that is governed by an HOA, you should understand what, if any, restrictions will be placed on your property. You will also want to thoroughly vet the HOA. Learn who is on the board, examine the organization's finances, and understand what sort of fees and special assessments have been levied in the past. HOAs reduce your control as an investor, which is a risk that needs to be mitigated.

Each ASFR is different, but overall, the more control of your investment you cede to outside parties, the greater the risk. Almost every person I know (investor or homeowner) who owns a property in a co-op, townhome, or condo has faced some disagreement with the property's governing body. That doesn't mean those disagreements lead to poor performance, but it's an additional variable to consider.

The management structure of an ASFR tends to come with both upside and risk. Large ASFRs like condos and co-ops typically have a professional management company handling day-to-day operations. For investors who want to be passive, this is great! But it also comes with a cost, in the form of monthly maintenance or HOA fees. If the company running operations is good, that could be well worth the cost. But you won't have much (or any) say in what company is hired, so you're giving up control over a big expense in your business.

Overall, ASFRs are a low-cost option for investors to get into real estate investing, but they offer less of the upside of a DSFR. That said, ASFRs are good options for new investors who have less capital to put down, plan to invest in a market with few DSFRs where an ASFR asset is in high demand (such as an urban center or a short-term rental in a vacation town), or are seeking an ASFR as a well-balanced portfolio.

Small Multifamily

A small multifamily building is any residential property with two, three, or four units. You may also hear small multifamily units called by their specific unit count, like duplex, triplex, or quadplex. If the distinction of four units feels arbitrary, it not; it's actually important and comes from lending practices. Properties that have four units or fewer qualify for residential loans; anything that's five units or larger goes into commercial territory.

Small multifamily properties tend to be a sweet spot for small-to-medium-sized real estate investors. Think about it—most homeowners don't want to own a multi-unit property. On the other hand, large institutional investors tend to buy large commercial properties because this is a more efficient way to deploy their vast capital resources. This leaves small multifamily as a great target for many retail investors like you and me.

Small multifamily assets benefit from the economies of scale that come with multiple units, but without the operational complexity of large commercial buildings. For example, a quadplex earns you four units' worth of income but only costs you one roof, one foundation, one HVAC system, etc. And because the property is relatively small, the complexity of managing a small multifamily is not much greater than managing an SFR. You can get significantly more income without a proportionate increase in operational complexity.

The second major benefit of small multifamily assets (over commercial multifamily) is residential financing. Residential loans are generally more favorable than commercial loans because they often require less money down, can be fixed rate for longer periods of time, and can have better interest rates. Better financing terms will reduce the risk of your investment and potentially increase your cash flow over your hold period.

Small multifamily is an excellent option for rental property investors and can also be used for short-term rentals. You can even do a combination of both deal types within a single property. I know loads of investors who buy a duplex to long-term rent one side for the stable income, and then short-term rent the other side for cash flow upside.

One of the most powerful applications of small multifamily properties is combining it with an owner-occupied, house-hacking operational plan. Let's say you buy a triplex, live in one unit, and rent out the other two units. This approach allows you to put as little as 3.5 percent down (because owner-occupied properties can often put down very little) and own three units. Imagine that. If this triplex costs $600,000, you could put as little as $21,000 down and own three income-producing units. There's a reason we call it "house hacking"—because it almost feels like a cheat code.

The trade-offs with small multifamily are lower demand, lower rents per square foot, a smaller buyer pool, and a higher capital intensity. As mentioned above, DSFRs tend to attract the highest revenue per square foot, with small multifamily rents lagging (only slightly) behind due to lower demand among renters for attached units. This relatively lower demand means it can be more difficult to find tenants. And while less competition from other buyers is a sweet spot for retail investors when purchasing, that can turn into a detriment when selling your property to that limited buyer pool. However, with the increasing popularity of rental property investing, this isn't a significant issue in most locations.

With regard to capital intensity, small multifamily units are more expensive than single-family residences because you're buying more units, although it's worth noting that the cost per unit is lower when you buy small multifamily properties (it's typically significantly less expensive to purchase a duplex than it is to purchase two single-family residences).

As an asset class, small multifamily properties are an excellent option for investors of all types and experience levels. They provide strong upside with relatively low risk and can help investors scale their unit count faster than buying single-family homes.

COMMERCIAL ASSETS

When we discussed deal types in Chapter 16, I explained that commercial real estate is different from residential real estate in several unique ways. To name a few, commercial deals are larger, more capital intensive, valued differently than residential properties, and eligible for different loan products. Each asset class within commercial real estate is fairly distinct and has different risks, rewards, and operating models. Below I'll provide a high-level overview of the most common commercial asset classes used by retail investors.

- Large multifamily
- Mobile home parks

- Self-storage
- Retail/office/industrial

Large Multifamily

For most people reading this book, the most intriguing and common commercial real estate asset class is large multifamily, which is defined as a building with five or more housing units. This is a popular commercial asset class for retail investors because it offers many of the same benefits of small multifamily, but at scale. Additionally, the deal analysis and business operations for a large multifamily property are relatively similar to those of residential properties. Although large multifamily is more complex, with several important differences from residential asset classes, at the end of the day they are all businesses that provide housing to renters on either a short- or long-term basis. Many of the skills needed to manage a large multifamily property are the same as managing a residential building—just at a larger scale.

The benefits of large multifamily are probably obvious to you at this point. Large multifamily buildings allow investors to scale their revenue and unit counts quickly and can be managed cost-effectively due to efficiencies of scale. As with small multifamily properties, large multifamily deals carry lower risk of catastrophic income loss from vacancies or nonpayment, as both income and expenses are spread across a large pool of tenants. And because large multifamily assets almost always fall under a rental deal type, they are relatively stable, predictable businesses that take advantage of every profit driver. There's a lot to like about large multifamily assets!

Of course, there are also some very considerable trade-offs. First, larger buildings are more expensive and require more capital upfront. Second, financing is more expensive. As I mentioned, the cutoff between small and large multifamily properties comes from lending practices, and properties with five or more units require commercial loans. This may not seem like a big deal, but it can be. As we've discussed, commercial loans are quite different than residential loans: They have lower LTVs, more complex terms, and carry greater risk. Last, the scale of large multifamily properties requires more sophisticated operational and asset management.

As with most commercial deals, large multifamily assets are most often valued based on cap rates (NOI ÷ cap rate = price) instead of comps. Unlike residential assets, large multifamily assets are usually owned by sophisticated investors, making the market for these assets very efficient—meaning large multifamily assets are usually priced accurately along the risk/reward continuum. If you see a property selling at a cap rate considerably higher than that of comparable properties, it's unlikely you've found a steal; instead, you're probably missing a risk that other investors see.

For all of the reasons above, a popular way to invest in large multifamily assets is with a syndication/fund. These ownership structures work well for large assets because they allow investors to pool their money, which reduces the capital intensity for each individual investor and spreads the risk among all of the individuals in the group.

There are several niches within large multifamily, such as apartment buildings, student housing, senior/assisted living, and more. Regardless of the specific niche, large multifamily deals are a profitable and efficient way to scale a portfolio, but be prepared to deal with sophisticated players, efficient markets, and more complexity all around. It can be difficult to get into large multifamily deals when you're starting out, but that's okay. Most investors learn the industry in smaller residential assets and work their way toward commercial deals like multifamily properties if it's aligned with their Vision and as their resources and risk capacity grow.

Mobile Home Parks

Mobile home parks are properties that provide land and services for multiple mobile homes. There are two primary models for mobile home park investing. The simplest model is to purchase the land and then rent out "pads" to residents who live on the pad in mobile homes they own. This is a relatively low-risk model with low capital and time intensity. When you don't own the mobile homes, you're not responsible for maintenance or repairs. Instead, you're responsible for managing tenants, maintaining the grounds and shared amenities, and handling the other operations needed for any real estate business like bookkeeping and tax preparation.

A second model of mobile home park ownership is to purchase the land and own some or all of the mobile homes on the pads. This model has a higher potential for profit, since you earn rent for both the pad and the home itself, but it also comes with more maintenance and higher capital requirements.

Mobile home investing has several key advantages to consider: First, unit costs are much lower in mobile home parks than in other asset classes, making it relatively inexpensive to scale. Mobile home units also tend to be affordable for tenants, and affordable housing is in short supply in the U.S. This means you can provide a high-quality, safe, and affordable place to live while experiencing consistent demand and low vacancy. This, coupled with low costs, offers great cash flow potential.

The biggest obstacle for mobile home parks is that they can be more challenging to finance, as many banks don't offer loan products for this asset class. Rent delinquencies are also higher, requiring more diligent property management. And last, mobile home parks lack some of the efficiencies of scale that other multifamily asset classes have.

Self-Storage

Self-storage is a unique commercial asset class that involves renting out storage facilities to individuals or businesses. There are many macroeconomic trends that have led to increased demand for self-storage facilities, particularly urbanization and consumerism. When bought and operated properly, self-storage can generate excellent cash flow.

Unlike assets that provide housing, office, or retail space, a self-storage facility has relatively low physical requirements. It needs to be safe and secure, but it doesn't require costly investments like plumbing or appliances. While some facilities are temperature controlled, generally speaking, the cost to build and maintain self-storage facilities is very low compared to other asset classes.

Operationally, the business of self-storage is different from many other asset classes. Because most clients care about convenience and price (over comfort, style, or amenities), self-storage is a marketing-intensive business, especially in urban areas where there is a good deal of competition. You need to be adept at marketing and able to handle seasonal cash flow changes to succeed in this business.

For successful operators who can rent their units, the potential benefit is large. Self-storage facilities can collect a lot of revenue relative to their maintenance expenses, and if they can market and operate efficiently, the cash flow potential is huge. Because of this, however, the market is highly competitive, with many large, publicly traded companies in the space.

Retail/Office/Industrial

I am going to lump together several commercial asset classes: retail, office, and industrial assets. These are relatively uncommon asset classes for the type of investors this book is written for, and if you are considering an investment in any of them, you'll need to learn much more about these asset classes than I can discuss in this book.

Retail real estate is space used to sell goods and services. This can be anything from a restaurant to an entire shopping center. Retail can be very lucrative on a per-square-foot basis but is also a volatile industry.

Office real estate is space where individuals or businesses conduct their work. This can be as small as a single-person office or as large as a massive skyscraper.

Industrial real estate is any property designed to house industrial activities such as warehousing, manufacturing, production, storage, and distribution. Industrial spaces can be attractive due to long lease terms and relatively low overhead.

I'm lumping these asset classes together because they often (though not always) share a common lease structure known as a triple-net (NNN) lease.

NNN is a lease type in which the tenant is responsible for paying all of the property-related expenses in addition to rent. This includes property taxes, insurance, maintenance, and repairs. Because tenants are responsible for their own maintenance and expenses, NNN provides the owner with a simplified management process and more predictable and stable streams of rental income. Additionally, NNN leases tend to be very long (sometimes up to ten or twenty years!), which means investors who find good tenants have less vacancy, fewer turnovers, and a reliable source of income.

The downside of NNN leases is that your income depends on the success of someone else's business, and working with businesses has trade-offs. First, finding and signing new tenants can be a long and costly process; businesses can be deliberate about their property search and take months to sign leases. Second, NNN leases often come with large upfront renovation expenses known as "tenant improvements." For example, the owner of a restaurant space may agree to add new countertops, fire mitigation systems, or fancy cooking equipment to attract high-quality tenants. While the tenant will pay for upkeep, the property owner takes on these upfront expenses. Finally, the reality is that your tenant's business can fail—and lots of them do. Because turnover costs are so high, you're making a big bet on the businesses you sign leases with. If the tenant business fails, your income is at risk. As with residential tenants, it's crucial to screen likely tenants thoroughly to understand their likelihood to pay as agreed.

Investing in NNN asset classes like retail, office, and industrial can provide a very stable and predictable source of income with relatively low management intensity—but it is capital intensive and comes with risk. These types of deals are best for investors with a solid existing portfolio who are looking to diversify and have experience with commercial tenants.

OTHER ASSET CLASSES

The residential and commercial asset classes listed above are some of the most common and popular asset classes, particularly for retail investors. But there are dozens of asset classes and niches, many of which I can't get into in this book. Some other common asset classes are land, hotels, and mixed-use assets. These asset classes are best for experienced investors, but if you're interested in them, there are good online resources for you to explore and determine if they're right for your portfolio.

PREP WORK
ASSET CLASSES

STRATEGIC DECISION: Which asset classes are best aligned with your Vision and fit within your broader strategy? The most important decision is whether you'll focus only on residential assets or on commercial assets or will be open to a combination of the two. When you've decided which asset classes are aligned with your strategy, write them in your PREP. For additional guidance and a rubric that will help you test alignment, see more below.

Consider the various asset class options above and determine which asset classes could be a part of your Deal Design. Asset class selection plays a big role in the complexity, risk profile, and resource intensity of your deals. Will you stick to residential assets (like most small-to-medium-sized investors do) or are you interested in commercial assets as well?

I want to make it clear that you don't need to rush into commercial assets or get into them at all. Many investors achieve all of their goals without ever touching a commercial property. Don't feel like you have to go big right away; residential properties alone can make an excellent portfolio. It took me nine years to invest in my first commercial deal, and I only did so because I moved abroad and wanted to start investing passively in syndications and funds.

To help you think through which asset classes belong on your PREP, consider the following questions.

- How much capital do you have to invest? The capital requirements differ greatly between asset classes.
- What are you prioritizing at this point in your investing career? Rapid scaling? Risk mitigation? Solid, predictable returns?

- Are you willing to buy a property with an HOA or other governing body?
- How sophisticated is your management plan? The bigger the asset, the more complex the operations. Make sure you're prepared.
- Can you qualify for residential financing? If you can, it can help reduce risk and lower costs.
- Do you want to focus on providing shelter, or are you interested in working with retail and office tenants?
- Do you want to consider an owner-occupied deal type like house hacking or a live-in flip? These options are only possible for residential assets.
- How can you invest in different asset classes to create diversification in your portfolio?

	Resource Alignment			Risk/Reward Alignment	
	Time	Capital	Skill		Include in PREP?
Residential					
Detatched SFR					
Attached SFR					
Small Multifamily					
Commercial					
Large Multifamily					
Self-Storage					
Mobile Homes					
Office/Retail/ Industrial					

Once you've determined which asset classes belong in your Deal Design, write them down on your *PREP*.

Chapter 22
PICKING A MARKET

There's an old saying that real estate comes down to just three things: location, location, and location. And while the existence of this book demonstrates there is more to real estate strategy than just where you buy, location is extremely important. Location matters because there is no such thing as "the housing market." Instead, there are thousands of individual housing markets across the United States, each with its own price points, supply-and-demand dynamics, regulatory environment, and other unique attributes. Yes, analysts like me often aggregate the country's housing activity into broad statistics to help explain nation-wide trends, but the reality is that each individual market is unique. Housing markets are entirely local. Even within a given metro area or city, each neighborhood, zip code, and even each block is different. The market you invest in plays a huge role in the types of income you can earn, the deal types and operating plans that work, and the overall risk/ return profile of your investments.

In real estate, the word "market" means the high-level area where you invest. Often, this is a metro area, city, or town. A "submarket" is a more refined location within the market. For example, Dallas, Texas, is a market. Within Dallas, there are many submarkets, such as the Kessler neighborhood or the zip code 75208. In this chapter we'll discuss how to select markets and submarkets for your portfolio, and I'll provide some tips for finding and analyzing data about different markets.

WHY MARKETS MATTER
Before we get into how to select markets for your portfolio, we first need to discuss the key variables that differentiate markets. If you understand the trade-offs between markets, you can better pick the markets and

submarkets that are right for you. The key variables are price point, performance, and cash flow versus appreciation.

Price Point

Different housing markets across the U.S. offer vastly different price points, even for the same type of property. As an example, as of this writing, the median home price in Los Angeles is about $800,000, while the median home price in Philadelphia is $240,000. That is an enormous difference in affordability! The price point in a given market will dictate what type of assets you can buy and how quickly you can scale. You need to pick markets that have a price that aligns with your overall strategy.

Performance

Every market has a different potential for performance. Like everything in a market economy, prices are determined by supply and demand. And when it comes to real estate, supply-and-demand dynamics are local.

In areas with strong demand, or areas with low supply, prices tend to appreciate—both in terms of property values and rents. In areas with weak demand, or excessive supply, prices can remain flat or fall. In each market, what is in demand, and what there is supply of, is very different.

For example, I invest in Denver. As of this writing in mid-2023, Denver has a very low supply of single-family homes, with decent demand. As such, prices for single-family homes are rising, even though interest rates have risen. On the other hand, Denver has seen a massive construction boom in the multifamily space, and there is an oversupply of apartment units. As such, rents for multifamily buildings are falling. In other markets, there is a shortage of multifamily units, and prices are rising. In some markets there is demand for small, affordable houses, and in others there is more demand for luxury properties.

Each market has different supply-and-demand dynamics, and those dynamics dictate prices as well as what strategies deliver the best performance. You need to pick markets that have supply-and-demand dynamics that support the specific deal types and operating plans you are using.

Cash Flow vs. Appreciation

Different markets offer different profit drivers. The most prominent example of this is the historical relationship between markets that cash-flow well and markets that have strong market appreciation. I know that on the heels of the pandemic housing boom this may be hard to fathom, but historically not all local housing markets appreciate in the same way. In normal times, some markets offer better cash flow, while other markets offer better appreciation potential.

When you look at the relationship between cash flow and appreciation (during pre-pandemic years), there is a trade-off. The markets that offered the best cash flow offered the worst appreciation. Likewise, the markets that offered the best appreciation offered the worst cash flow.

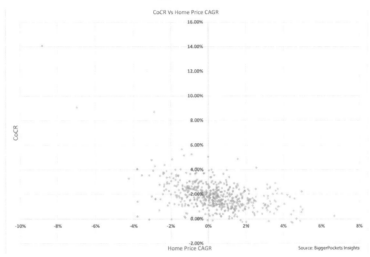

This scatterplot shows a few important things (and deliberately omits the anomalous data from 2020–2023): First, the majority of markets offer average returns—somewhere around 1–2 percent price growth and a 2 percent CoCR for the average property in that market. Of course, as an investor you should be seeking returns above average for your market, regardless of what market you choose! But the other, perhaps more telling story from this chart comes from the outliers. As you can see, I've highlighted three markets as outliers for exceptional cash flow: Flint, Michigan; Detroit, Michigan; and Youngstown, Ohio. Each of these offers a CoCR of above 8 percent, which is well above most other markets. However, note that these markets are also outliers in another respect: negative home price growth. The same is true in reverse. The markets that have excellent appreciation (think markets like Seattle, Denver, and Salt Lake City) are far below average for cash flow potential.

The lesson here is clear: If you want high potential for market appreciation, you usually have to give up some cash flow. If you want amazing cash flow, you probably have to give up some market appreciation upside.

And if you want average cash flow and average appreciation potential, there are plenty of places where you can get that.

It's worth mentioning again that this traditional relationship got upended from 2020–2022. During that time, asset prices went wild all over the country in a way that defied traditional patterns. It's unclear if market-based performance will return to a more traditional historical pattern, but my guess is that it will.

As shown above, what market you pick is very important to how you scale, the performance of your deals, and the types of returns you can generate. Some markets are great for medium-term rentals, while others are better for short-term rentals. Some markets don't work well for flips, while others excel at it. When it comes to Deal Design, your market and tactics have to go hand in hand. Now, let's discuss how to select markets for your portfolio.

MARKET RESEARCH

The first step in selecting markets for yourself is to do some market research. This isn't hard; you just need to understand some key metrics that can help you evaluate a market's strengths and weaknesses. If you're new to this type of analysis, I recommend you look up this data for your local area first—even if you're planning to invest somewhere else. It can be helpful to get comfortable with the data using a market you already know. From there, you can start looking at areas across the U.S. to see how different markets compare to one another.

If you don't know where to start, I have resources that can help you. I publish a lot of blog posts on BiggerPockets.com and videos on BiggerPockets' YouTube channel comparing and contrasting different markets. These reports are not definitive, but they can help point you in the direction of markets that might align well with your portfolio.

When you look at these metrics, there are a few things to pay special attention to.

1. **Current state.** What is happening in the market right now with this metric?
2. **Historical performance.** How has the metric changed over time in this market?
3. **Growth rate.** How quickly does this metric grow, on average, in the market?

4. Recession performance. What happened with this metric during previous recessions?

5. Volatility. Does the metric move in one direction consistently or are there lots of peaks and valleys?

UNDERSTANDING DATA POINTS

Looking at data is not something everyone has experience or is comfortable with. Luckily, the data we need to examine for portfolio management are relatively easy. There are a few simple things you want to look for. To help explain the basics here, I'll use the median sales price of a single-family home in Dallas.

1. **Current value.** This one is the easiest—just check out the most recent data point for Dallas. As of this writing, it's around $383,000.

2. **Trend.** Use the eyeball test to see if the metric is trending upward or downward over time. See how trends may have changed recently.

3. **Month-over-month.** Look at how prices have changed from one month to the next. As of this writing, the median sales price in Dallas fell by 0.1 percent from the previous month to the current month.

4. **Year-over-year.** Looking at the same month of data over several years is very helpful when examining data that is seasonal (like home prices and rent). For example, when I look at the median home price in Dallas for March 2023 compared to March 2022, I see home prices actually went up 0.1 percent.

Looking at data points in these ways is not hard and gives you a thorough understanding of what's happening with each indicator. Most of the websites and sources I've listed in the book—like the FRED and Redfin websites—make it easy to look at data in all these ways.

Remember that historical performance does not ensure future performance, but looking at historical data can teach us a lot about a market and give a fairly good idea of what might happen in the coming years.

There are many free sources available online to find this information, but here are a few of my favorites.

- **Redfin Data Center** (www.redfin.com/news/data center). Provides great market-level data for housing prices
- **FRED** (https://fred.stlouisfed.org): An economic data aggregator
- **Google:** You know what this is!

Home Prices

The first metric most people look at when considering a new market for investment is home prices in the area. Of course, this is helpful for determining the capital intensity of a market given that average property prices vary wildly. One of the first considerations you should make when selecting a market is if you can afford to buy there!

The second thing to look at is the historical growth rate of property prices in the area. In other words, do prices tend to go up in this area, and if so, by how much? This data is very easy to come by (websites like Zillow, Redfin, and Realtor.com all have this for free). Remember, some markets tend to see property prices appreciate far more than others. If you're investing primarily to maximize cash flow, price appreciation potential might not be your primary concern (and most experienced investors don't plan for appreciation), but most investors don't want to buy in places where prices might decline. At the very least, you should understand what you're getting into. The average growth rates can tell you a lot, but not everything, about the risk in a given market. You should also look at volatility.

Recall that market volatility is a risk and can lead to principal loss. Even if a market has grown quickly in the past, you should check to see if it has also experienced large declines. Some markets are prone to boom-and-bust cycles. One way to examine volatility is to look at how prices have been impacted by previous corrections, like the Great Recession. From 2008–2012, housing prices fell around 20 percent on a national level from peak to trough, but, of course, each market fared differently. If a market only fell 8 percent during that time, it likely has low volatility, and lower volatility means lower risk. If the market fell 40 percent during the Great Recession, it's likely a riskier market that is more prone to price declines.

As you look at this data, I want to again caution you against the home (and rent) price data from 2020–2022. The price appreciation seen over those years was immense, and you should not count on those growth rates happening again, possibly ever. Instead, I would look at the historical appreciation rates from 2008–2019 to get a sense of what type of price growth is typical in the markets you consider.

Rent Prices

Similar to home prices, looking at the average rent price and rent growth rates in a market is essential for all investors. If you're thinking about investing in short-term or medium-term rentals, you should be looking at the average daily rate (ADR) and occupancy. For rent prices, BiggerPockets has a free rent estimator you can use,[6] or you can get aggregated data from sites like Zillow. For short-term rentals, I've used AirDNA and found it a solid data source.

Again, similar to home prices, you don't just want to look at the current income potential for a deal. You should also be looking at the historical growth rate of rents in the area to get a sense of whether rent has grown, stayed flat, or declined over time. Examining the market for income volatility and performance during recessions can also be helpful.

Understanding current rent and rent growth is important for any cash-flow-centric deal, but it's of particular importance for deals with long hold periods. With any deal, your expenses (like labor and repair costs) will go up over time. Ideally, you want to identify markets where your income is likely to keep pace with or exceed your expense increases to ensure you maintain or grow your cash flows.

Rent-to-Price Ratio

The rent-to-price (RTP) ratio is another simple but useful metric to use when estimating the cash flow potential of a given market. To calculate RTP, simply divide the median monthly rent in an area by the median home price. For Charlotte, North Carolina, we'd divide $1,600 ÷ $375,000 to get an RTP of 0.43 percent. An RTP of 0.43 percent is low and means that cash flow will be relatively hard (but not impossible!) to find in Charlotte.

RTP is a relatively crude proxy for cash flow because it doesn't consider expenses like maintenance, taxes, insurance, or others. But it can be helpful for comparing markets against one another. According to my research, if you see a market with an RTP above 0.7 percent, there is a chance the average deal will cash-flow. Any market where the RTP is above 0.85 percent is going to offer good cash flow potential relative to the market as of this writing (2023).

When using RTP to screen markets, it's important to remember that this ratio is measuring the *average* deal. Even if the RTP of a city is 0.6 percent, there are individual deals with higher and lower RTPs. While RTP is a useful screening tool, you should look at some individual deals to see what the cash flow prospects of an area really are. After all, as an

---

6 BiggerPockets, "Real Estate Rent Estimator," www.biggerpockets.com/insights/property-searches/new.

investor, you're hopefully investing in deals that are far better than the average deal in your market.

Economic Climate

The economic situation in a market plays a huge role in the performance of your deals. When a city is booming, property prices tend to go up, as does rent. Tenants typically pay on time, and opportunities abound. If a city faces difficult economic circumstances, property values and rent can decline while vacancies and nonpayment of rent can rise.

There are many different ways to measure the economic strength of a market, but here are a few of my personal favorites.

- **Gross Domestic Product (GDP):** GDP is a measurement of the total economic output of a market. The higher the growth rate of GDP in an area, the better.
- **Unemployment Rate:** Low unemployment helps boost GDP, increases demand for housing, and makes for a strong and thriving community.
- **Employment Diversity:** Markets that have strong jobs in multiple industries tend to be less volatile than markets that rely on a single industry. For example, a city like Tampa, Florida—which has strong financial services, healthcare, tech, and other high-paying industries—is likely more insulated from market downturns than a market like Las Vegas, which is highly dependent on the tourism industry.
- **Wage Growth:** The more income growth in a market, the better. Higher wages drive GDP growth, increase tax revenues that can be reinvested into public amenities, and help support income and property price growth over the long run.
- **Population Growth:** Supply and demand determine the price of an asset, and population growth in an area is a great way to measure and forecast overall demand.
- **Household Formation:** In my opinion, this metric is the best way to measure the overall demand for housing (rentals and owner-oc-cupants combined). A "household" is simply a distinct group of people living together, regardless of relationship (e.g., family, friends, roommates). Therefore, the total number of households in a market and the rate of change are critical to understanding demand.

You don't need to measure every single one of these metrics, but it's helpful to keep an eye on the economic climate in any market where you intend to invest. Most of this data is tracked by the government and is available for free on the FRED website. You can even set up free dashboards with the metrics you want to watch that will be automatically updated.

Property Taxes

The tax advantages I've discussed as a profit driver refer to the income tax you pay on your profits, not on property taxes. There is no way to get around paying property taxes. Property taxes vary considerably from state to state and city to city, and they will impact your profits. For example, Louisiana taxes property at just 0.51 percent of the property value per year—one of the lowest in the country. In Texas, however, property is taxed at 1.6 percent—three times higher!

Luckily, this information is easy to find. You can run a simple Google search or check the local government's website and find out the property tax rates. Additionally, taxes on an individual property are public record. If you are looking at a deal on the MLS, it will likely tell you what the most recent tax assessment was for the target property.

Regulatory Environment

The regulatory climate of a market isn't exactly a metric because it's not quantifiable. However, it's information you should collect about any market you're considering. State and local governments enact all sorts of laws that impact real estate investors, such as taxes, incentives for development and investment, eviction rules, and rent control. As an investor, you need to understand the regulatory climate of the places you invest so that you can 1) decide if the regulatory climate supports your Portfolio Strategy and 2) comply with all the laws.

There is no centralized place I know of that aggregates regulatory information pertinent to real estate investors. Instead, I recommend looking on local government websites, as well as talking to experienced real estate agents and fellow investors in the area to get a sense of the regulations that may impact you.

Zoning

I think zoning is one of the most underappreciated and underutilized real estate metrics. If you're unfamiliar with the concept, "zoning" is a blanket term for the laws that cities and local governments use to determine what can be built where and how different properties can be used. For example, many suburbs have single-family zoning, meaning the homes in this zone are limited to single-family residences; a developer cannot come in and build a high-rise in the middle of this zone. On the other hand, downtown areas are often zoned for retail, office space, and other commercial applications.

As an investor, there is great opportunity in understanding zoning, particularly when a property isn't being used to its full potential. One strategy I like to use is to find deals that work well currently but have favorable zoning upside. For example, imagine a run-down single-family home that needs a full-gut rehab to be occupied. If that property is zoned only for single-family homes, the investor doesn't have many options; they have to rehab the home as is or scrap it and build a new SFR. However, if that property is zoned for a triplex, the investor could choose to change the use of the property and build three units—increasing the value of the property, driving up the cash flow potential of the property, and providing more housing units to the community.

Finding a good deal that has upside zoning potential gives you great options as an investor. Zoning can give you strategic flexibility—a great way to mitigate risk.

Schools

Schools are a major driver of demand for housing. For most families with young children, living somewhere within proximity of a school, and ideally a good school, is important. Investing in markets that have good schools will typically increase demand from prospective tenants and future homebuyers. For example, according to a 2003 study from the National Bureau of Economic Research, for every $1 spent on public schools, home values increased $20.[7] Data about school rankings can be easily found on sites like www.niche.com or www.greatschools.org.

Crime Rates

The relative amount of crime in a given area is likely to impact demand for a property, both in terms of property price and revenue potential. There is a good deal of scholarly evidence that crime rates impact

---

7   Linda Gorman, "School Spending Raises Property Values," *The Digest* 1 (January 2003), National Bureau of Economic Research, www.nber.org/digest/jan03/school-spending-raises-property-values.

housing prices,[8] but the specific impact is difficult to measure. From the articles I've read, the theme seems to be that violent crime in particular has a negative impact on home values. Property crime, on the other hand, has a less obvious connection to property values, but does impact the cost of insurance in a given market and is an obvious risk to investors in terms of expenses. I've sold properties because the amount of nuisance and petty property crime in the area became too much of a headache. Most local governments have data about a market's crime rates that you can access for free.

Amenities and Proximity

Demand is highest for properties that have easy access to amenities. Renters and homeowners, generally speaking, want to easily get to the places they go most: their office, grocery stores, pharmacies, restaurants, cultural sites, etc. A property that is a quick drive from an area's top destinations will have more demand than a market that requires sitting in traffic to get anywhere.

Sometimes there are easy metrics to measure this (like a Walk Score), and other times you need to drive around or use a tool like Google Maps to get a sense of the types of amenities in a market and how easily accessible they are. Assessing the quality and proximity of amenities is difficult to quantify, but doing it well can give you an edge as an investor.

X Factors

There are many (hundreds!) of other variables to consider about a particular market or submarket—everything from average lot size to local infrastructure. I've given you some of the metrics I look at for every deal, but when it comes to selecting a market, sometimes there are important variables that don't easily fit into the components above. I call these variables the "X factors."

X factors are the deal elements that defy categorization; they are unique to your specific deal and portfolio Vision. Not every deal has an X factor, but sometimes small details can make all the difference. Normally, it takes intimate knowledge of your market to uncover the X factors that can boost the potential of your deals.

As an example, I don't always care about the bedroom count of a

---

8   Martin Maximino, "The Impact of Crime on Property Values: Research Roundup," The Journalist's Resource, March 12, 2014, https://journalistsresource.org/economics/the-impact-of-crime-on-property-values-research-roundup/#:~:text=Some%20studies%20have%20found%20that,on%20transactions%20to%20estimate%20prices.

rental property. But when I was buying a short-term rental in a ski area, my research showed revenue dramatically increased for properties that had four or more bedrooms, while the price of such properties didn't go up proportionately. I therefore only targeted properties with four or more bedrooms because I knew that X factor would boost my returns.

Other examples of X factors are:

- Garages or carports in markets where the weather is rough
- Having a pool, outdoor kitchen, tennis court, or other premium amenities for a short-term rental
- Close to public transportation in a market where traffic is particularly bad

While many X factors include property features like a garage or pool, notice that they are driven by the market. Using my example, having four or more bedrooms isn't an advantage in all markets—it was just an advantage in the particular market I was investing in. Having a carport may not make a big difference in San Diego, but is super important in Colorado (where it hails a lot!).

The nature of X factors is you can't just look them up. You have to uncover X factors by knowing your market really well. Ideally you can do this yourself, but a good real estate agent or property manager should also be able to help. They see a lot of deals, and they know what homeowners and tenants are looking for in the area. Study the specifics of supply and demand to uncover variables that can drive profits that homeowners or other investors won't see.

PREP WORK
CHOOSING MARKETS

STRATEGIC DECISION: Select at least one market to include on your PREP. This could be your local market or somewhere "long-distance" (for help with that decision, see below). If you're new to investing, try to choose up to five markets to focus on. If you're experienced, you can select as many markets as is practical. Once you have chosen your target markets, write them in your PREP. For additional guidance and a rubric that will help you test alignment, see more below.

There are hundreds of metropolitan areas in the country, and many thousands of submarkets—but choosing a market doesn't need to be difficult. It is, however, where a lot of investors get stuck. As such, I am going to provide a little extra guidance on how to narrow down a list of markets to include in your PREP.

Local vs. Long-Distance Investing

The first consideration in picking a market is deciding whether you'll invest locally or long-distance (or a combination of the two). I recommend making this decision first because if you decide to invest locally, your search is over—just write your local market on your PREP. If you decide to invest long-distance, there are more considerations.

Local investing is when you participate in a deal within a reasonable distance from your permanent residence. Think of "reasonable" as any distance within which you would regularly visit your property. That could be two hours from your home or only twenty minutes, depending on your lifestyle. Anything beyond the range you would regularly visit is long-distance investing, because it means you'll be relying heavily on third parties.

The primary advantage of local investing is that you can invest in an area you know well and can be close to your deals. This gives you more opportunities to scale and provides flexibility in your management plan. The downside to local investing is that your local market may not have the characteristics you're looking for. It's ideal to be close to your deals, but if you're looking for cash flow and your local market doesn't offer any, being close to your deal won't really matter.

Take some time now to look at the market conditions in your local market. Does it provide a price point that works for you? Are the market conditions conducive to your overall strategy? Are the profit drivers aligned with your Vision? Consider how well your local market supports your Portfolio Strategy. Depending on where you live, you may not find what you're looking for in your local area in terms of price point, performance, and profit drivers. If that describes you, you should consider investing long-distance.

The primary benefit of long-distance investing is that you can select any market in the country. You're not limited to what market conditions are available nearby and can choose the markets that are best aligned with your strategy. The downside of long-distance investing is that you're highly reliant on your team to assist with management. At BiggerPockets, we often refer to the team you need in any market as your "core four," referring to your real estate agent, property manager, contractor, and lender. Before you invest in any market long-distance, you need to find a reputable person or company to serve each of these core four roles. This book isn't going to get into advice on finding a great team, but there are plenty of free resources you can use on BiggerPockets.com or elsewhere on the internet that can help you with this.

Take some time now to analyze a few long-distance markets and see how they compare to your local markets. Do they offer better cash flow? Appreciation? What option is better for your Portfolio Strategy as a whole? If you need help picking some markets to analyze, you can find plenty of articles and YouTube videos I've posted on BiggerPockets for free.

If you're on the fence and unsure if you want to invest locally or long-distance, here are a few considerations you should think through.

- Does your local area support the deal types and deal tactics you're interested in? For example, if you're set on investing in short-term rentals, does your local area have good demand for STRs and an accommodating regulatory climate?
- Can you afford to buy locally? Does the price point in your local market support your goals? Will you be able to scale faster locally or long-distance?
- Does your local market offer the return profile you're looking for? Some markets are better for cash flow and others are better for appreciation.
- Are the types of assets you want to buy available in your area? Are there mobile home parks for sale near you? What about small multifamily buildings? Different markets have different zoning laws and different housing supply. Check to make sure your desired market has the types of assets you want to invest in.
- Are you interested in owner occupancy? This low-money-down operating plan option obviously requires local investing.
- How well do you know the local market? There is an advantage to investing in a market you understand deeply. But if you're new to an area, the market knowledge advantage you get from investing locally is minimal.
- Investing long-distance requires that you build a great team. Are you comfortable managing a team remotely?

If you're going to invest locally, great—write down the name of the local area(s) you want to consider for your portfolio on your PREP.

If you prefer to invest long-distance (or want to consider long-distance in addition to local investing), you'll need to come up with a short list of markets to consider. I think the best course of action is to identify about five markets you believe are aligned with your Vision. To build out a short list, consider the following questions.

- Which markets have an abundance of the deal types you are looking for?
- Which markets have the profit potential you need right now?
- Are there certain areas of the country with a price point that is attractive to you?
- Which markets have the best macroeconomic conditions that support (but don't guarantee!) future growth?
- How are local housing market conditions in the markets you are considering?

I know at this point it can be tempting to scrutinize what the "perfect" market is for you. I'll save you the effort—there is no such thing. I know analysts like me post lists of "the best" markets, but those are just meant to point you in the right direction. The reality is there are probably dozens of markets that will work well in supporting your Vision. Again, my recommendation is to narrow down your list to about five markets that will work well and then write them down on your PREP. You don't need to find one perfect market.

	Resource Alignment			Risk/Reward Alignment	Include in PREP?
	Time	Capital	Skill		
Market 1:					
Market 2:					
Market 3:					
Market 4:					
Market 5:					

Remember, you can choose to invest locally *and* long-distance. Or you may choose to invest in several long-distance markets. Remember, market is only fixed for an individual deal. At a portfolio level, you can operate a variety of local and long-distance deals. So, keep your options open right now and write down a few markets that are interesting to you. Once you have this list, write it down on your *PREP.*

Chapter 23
PROPERTY CLASSES

There are many variables that factor into a property's condition, demand, and performance potential. For example, the age of the building, amenities, quality of finishes, maintenance record, landscaping, and others all play a role. Since there are so many variables that go into evaluating quality, investors often use an aggregated metric known as "property class" to describe the condition of a property.

Property class is a subjective measurement of the quality of a real estate asset and is designated by letter, with Class A being the highest-quality class and Class D being the lowest. Property classes are intended to act as relative metrics to compare properties in the same market or region against one another. Knowing the class of a property is helpful for you to understand what you should pay, the risk/reward profile of an asset, and what operating plans could work for your investment. Property classes are a great example of the balance between risk and reward for investments. The higher the property class, the less risk and the lower the reward potential. The lower the property class, the higher the opportunity for profit and the higher the risk.

It's important to know there are no fixed criteria to determine a property's class, and different investors use different variables. In fact, I don't think I've ever met two investors who think about property class in exactly the same way. That said, I am going to use some common variables in our discussion of property class.

- Building age and construction quality
- Property features and amenities
- Tenant profile and rental income
- Growth and appreciation potential
- Overall risk versus return profile
- Location within a market

Note that the location used in property class is only within a market. As we learned in the previous chapter, deciding what markets and sub-markets to invest in is an entirely different calculation.

Property classes are not just subjective to the investor but are also relative to one another. For example, a Class A property in Miami may look different from a Class A property in Duluth, Minnesota. Classes are also relative to the type of asset classes being considered. For example, there are Classes A, B, and C for office space, multifamily, and even self-storage facilities, but it's not useful to compare a Class A multifamily asset to a Class A office building. For property classes to be useful to your strategy, you need to compare properties that are in the same asset class and in a similar market.

Although the evaluation of a given deal's property class is subjective, there are some commonly agreed upon definitions of property classes that are useful for your strategy. Below I will provide descriptions of each property class and how they can be used in the context of your Deal Design. As you read, take note of the classes that will best support your Vision and future deals.

CLASS A: **BEST-IN-CLASS PROPERTIES**

Class A properties are the highest tier of property within their asset class. These are premium buildings that generate premium income. Class A properties are usually in, or close to, the central business districts in densely populated urban areas. They are close to amenities that make the property more desirable to tenants. Class A properties tend to be newer (built within the last fifteen years or have had major renovations) and managed by high-quality, professional management companies.

The key distinction of a Class A property is that the tenant experience is excellent, which creates strong demand. Class A properties strive to attract tenants who are creditworthy, have high incomes, and are very likely to pay as agreed. As such, they tend to have low vacancy rates. Class A properties need to be considered the best possible option by the tenant pool so the property can command higher revenue, which is then used to maintain the excellent tenant experience.

Class A properties will require sufficient repair budgets to ensure the property stays in great shape, but they have little to no deferred maintenance issues. As an investor, if you're buying a Class A property, it should have great construction quality; systems and appliances that are in good repair; and very little immediate need for capital improvements.

This means the time intensity required to manage a Class A property is low, relative to other property classes.

Class A properties are a relatively low-risk proposition for investors. With little to no deferred maintenance, high demand, and low vacancy, Class A is the lowest-risk property class there is. As such, Class A properties are also the most expensive property class to buy. Class A is almost always used with a buy and hold business plan. Given the high quality of the asset in its current state, there is generally little to no room for value-add. Sometimes you can improve operational efficiencies, but it's not very easy to increase the NOI of a Class A property from operations alone. Due to the low risk and high costs, deals with Class A properties tend to have lower margins. When you pay up to have a top-tier property that is stabilized and has little risk, the returns will be on the low side.

Class A properties are great for investors who have a low risk profile, don't want to commit a lot of time to their investments, or value stability and predictability above top-tier returns. I think of Class A properties sort of like a U.S. Treasury bill. They don't produce the best returns, but they can serve the important purpose of providing stable, low-risk returns in the context of a broader portfolio.

CLASS B: AVERAGE PROPERTIES

Class B properties are a tier down from Class A both in terms of the building quality and the income they can generate. They are generally average buildings with average income potential. Really, when it comes to Class B, "average" is probably the best word to describe most things.

Locations for Class B properties are typically a bit outside of the "prime" areas within a market, but it's not always the case. Older buildings in top-notch locations may also be considered Class B. The designation of a Class B property, like all property classes, is subjective, but generally speaking, Class B properties offer fewer amenities and perks than Class A properties. They're not the most exciting offering on the market in terms of tenant demand, but are still desirable.

Management of Class B properties generally entails (you guessed it!) average costs and an average time commitment. Because these assets tend to be older, there can be deferred maintenance issues (something to vet very carefully when analyzing a deal), and the time required to manage a Class B property is higher than it is for Class A. That said, Class B properties are not held to the same standard as Class A, and material costs are often lower. As a small example, if a refrigerator breaks in a Class B property, the management team will likely replace it with a quality, functioning, reliable replacement, but not with an expensive, state-of-the-art appliance.

Class B properties work with a wide variety of operating plans. Because they are older, but still solid buildings, investors can choose to buy and hold a Class B property, use the BRRRR method, flip the property, or consider some other type of value-add. Class B properties also tend to be managed by a second-tier management firm, meaning there is often room to improve operational efficiency. One of the great strengths of Class B properties is the flexibility they offer investors.

Due to the average quality, Class B properties have average income potential. There tends to be good demand for Class B properties among tenants, but they cannot command top-dollar rents or top-tier tenants. As such, Class B properties trade for lower prices than Class A. Commercial assets that are considered Class B trade for higher cap rates (less expensive) than Class A properties in the same asset class.

Class B properties are solid options that offer a strong balance between risk and reward. These properties are average in terms of time and capital intensity, and they can be used with a wide variety of deal types and operating plans. Class B can be useful in almost any portfolio.

CLASS C: **BELOW-AVERAGE PROPERTIES**

Class C properties are generally low quality and generate lower rents. They tend to be older properties and lack the modern amenities and facilities of a Class A or Class B building. In addition to being older and dated, Class C properties tend to have deferred maintenance and require investments into expensive repairs like a new roof, HVAC system, foundation, or other infrastructure. Class C properties are often in locations with lower demand—typically on the outskirts of a city center, with low proximity to key amenities.

Class C properties are not always managed by a high-quality property management company (often the source of the deferred maintenance), which can lead to high "loss-to-lease" (renting units for under market value) on Class C properties. Due to the relatively low quality of the buildings and the propensity for poor management, Class C properties have lower rental rates and higher vacancy rates than either Class A or Class B properties.

Class C properties are generally a high-risk/high-reward proposition for investors. The deferred maintenance and poor management mean the properties carry significant risk, and therefore trade for lower prices, making the initial capital intensity low. But most investors who buy Class C properties don't use a buy and hold strategy. What makes Class C attractive to investors is the opportunity to implement a value-add and/or operational efficiency operating plan. Value-add can work very well in Class C properties, as a high-quality renovation can restore the property to its highest and best use, which in turn drives higher rents and higher value for the property. In the case where a Class C property is poorly managed, implementing quality property management can help improve rents, improve tenant satisfaction and retention, and lower vacancy, all leading to higher incomes. Of course, large-scale renovations and operational changes require investments of time, money, and skill, and come with inherent risks.

Class C properties are best suited for investors who have a lot of time, have strong management skills, and are comfortable with risk. Class C is often the sweet spot for investors who favor strategies that include value-add, like flipping or BRRRR.

CLASS D: **UNINHABITABLE PROPERTIES**

Class D properties are uninhabitable properties that do not collect any current income. These are properties that are not safe for renters, have been condemned, or have other significant issues preventing them from being rented out.

Some investors loop these types of buildings into Class C (and don't have a Class D at all), but I like to separate out Class D buildings because they have a different risk profile and less operational plan flexibility than Class C.

Class D properties are, of course, the least expensive property class. Because they need large-scale improvements and generate no income, they are inherently very risky. This risk drives down demand and means that prices are lower. For investors, Class D is the ultimate high-risk/high-reward approach. Unlike Class C, where you can feasibly use a buy and hold strategy, and can often collect income while adding value, Class D is a one-trick pony—it has to include a renovation. This makes Class D popular among house flippers, but you don't necessarily need to flip a Class D property. You can use a value-add operating plan and then rent it out once improved, and you can certainly use a BRRRR operating plan. But you cannot avoid a renovation with a Class D property.

This makes Class D properties the highest possible risk of any property class, but due to their very low entry costs, they can generate large profits. Class D properties are best for investors who want to build equity through value-add, are good at managing renovations, and are comfortable with risk.

PREP WORK
PROPERTY CLASSES

STRATEGIC DECISION: Select which property classes are aligned with your Vision and overall strategy. Write down all that apply on your PREP. For assistance in this decision and a rubric that will help you test alignment, see below.

How will property class factor into your Deal Design? Will you prioritize deals that offer huge upside, but come with higher risk and more commitment of time? Or will you look for more stable assets that produce stable but modest returns? Think through the different classes and determine which ones could be useful to your portfolio in the coming years.

Remember that you don't need to pick just one single property class to invest in. In fact, property classes are a great way to diversify your portfolio. For example, a common approach would be to buy Class A and Class B rental properties to deliver strong, predictable, tax-advantaged returns, while gaining upside from renovating Class C and Class D properties.

To help you think through what property classes to include in your PREP, here are some questions.

- What property classes work best with your intended deal types? Some property classes are better suited for specific deal types than others.
- How do the operating plans you are considering align with various property classes? For example, if you want to do a BRRRR, buying Class A won't work. You'll need to invest in a property class with room for value-add.
- Which class best represents your preferred Risk/Reward Profile?
- Do you have the skills needed to manage major renovations and more difficult tenant management circumstances?
- Do you want your investment to cash-flow from day one or are you willing to stabilize the asset yourself?
- Given your time preferences, which property class would be best for you?

Once you've thought through which property classes could serve your portfolio, write them down on your *PREP*.

	Resource Alignment			Risk/Reward Alignment	
	Time	Capital	Skill	Return	Include in PREP?
Class A					
Class B					
Class C					
Class D					

You should now have filled out every element on the Deal Design section of your PREP. Great work!

Chapter 24
DEAL DESIGN CONCLUSION

Learning the eight elements of Deal Design allows you to strategically identify real estate tactics that support your Vision. It is a filtering process that lets you concentrate on a limited set of investing options and omit everything else. Through Deal Design, you have built up a tool kit of investing tactics that you can strategically deploy as you move forward to build your portfolio.

The key to good Deal Design is to strike the right balance between focus and flexibility. You don't want to be overwhelmed with too many options. This can lead to indecision. But at the same time, you don't want to limit yourself to only a few tactics. This can lead to underperformance. I think the best way to achieve this balance is to be rigid with the deal elements that are most important to you, and flexible with everything else.

Of all eight deal elements, which are most important to your Vision? For some it might be deal type, for others it could be market. Think about which elements are the most crucial for achieving your Vision and design your deals around them. For example, if cash flow is most important to you, build your deals accordingly by selecting deal types, markets, and management plans that are cash flow–oriented. Or, if time is important to you, select management plans that allow you to spend little time on your portfolio. Once you have nailed down the elements you want to prioritize, it's usually beneficial to be flexible on the other elements to keep yourself open to opportunity.

At the outset of my investing journey, deal type and ownership structure were very important to me. I definitely wanted a rental property and needed equity partners to get started—as such, I was inflexible on those elements of Deal Design. Meanwhile, I was flexible on asset class, property class, financing, and management plan. I was just trying to get into the game, and I shaped my Deal Design accordingly. I had a focused list of tactics and options I could employ based on market conditions and my evolving portfolio.

 DEAL DESIGN 2010

Deal Type	Ownership Structure	Financing	Operational Plan
Rentals	Partnership/JV	Conventional FHA	Value-Add Buy & Hold BRRRR

Management Plan	Asset Class	Market	Property Class
Active	SFR Small Multifamily	Denver Metro Area	A B C

Fast-forward to today, where I start my Deal Design with my management plan. While I live abroad, I can only consider passive or hybrid management plans. I am willing to asset-manage, but operational management is off the table for me. From there, I can design deals that support more passive management.

 DEAL DESIGN 2023

Deal Type	Ownership Structure	Financing	Operational Plan
Rentals, Short-Term Rentals, Commercial Lending	Sole Ownership Partnership/JV Syndications/Funds	Any	Value-Add Buy & Hold BRRRR

Management Plan	Asset Class	Location	Property Class
Hybrid Passive	SFR Small Multifamily Large Multifamily	Any	A B C

Notice that in my Deal Design from 2010, I had fewer options listed. This is common and recommended for newer investors. I had fewer resources back then, particularly in terms of capital and skill. As such, I took a narrower, more risk-averse approach, but left myself open to as many options as I reasonably could. Today, I have more capital and skill resources, which have added more options to my Deal Design. These days, I consider a far wider range of potential deals, as my risk capacity and resources have grown, and I focus on scale and diversification. My strategy is now much broader.

I recommend you take some time now to go back through your Deal Design to make sure that you are achieving a good balance of focus and flexibility. Consider what deal elements are essential to achieving your Vision, and then work backward from there. As you review your Deal Design, remember a few things.

- Deal Design is not where you select the specific deal you're going to do next (that comes in Part 4). Select any tactics that are aligned with your Vision and resources.
- Your Deal Design can and will change—as mine has. Think about the next three years.
- Make sure that all of your choices are aligned with one another. For example, if you're dead set on using a value-add operational plan, then you should omit Class A properties—they just don't work together. Make sure your tactics work well together.

Do you feel excited and confident about your Deal Design? As with everything you write in your PREP, your decisions should motivate you. If something feels uncomfortable or off, eliminate it! If you feel something is missing, add it back in! You need the right tools to build your portfolio.

Once you're confident in your Deal Design, your strategy is starting to take shape. I hope you're excited about where you're heading! You have a clear Vision that tells you where you want to go and why. You have built a tool kit of tactics to use in your future Deal Designs. The last step of developing your strategy is Portfolio Management. This is where things get specific and actionable. In Part 4 you'll further refine your Deal Designs into a "Buy Box" that suits your current resources and market conditions. You'll learn how to optimize your existing deals, create liquidity, and plan several deals into the future. As we work through this final phase of your strategy development, recall your Deal Design often. It will help you pick what deals to do next, how to get the most from your existing portfolio, and how to scale for the future.

At the end of Part 4, you'll have a clear list of action steps, a complete Personal Real Estate Portfolio, and you'll be ready to start executing on your strategy!

PART 4
PORTFOLIO MANAGEMENT

VISION

DEAL DESIGN

PORTFOLIO MANAGEMENT

Portfolio Management is the art and science of selecting and overseeing a group of investments that are aligned with your Vision. In other words, Portfolio Management is the action part of your Portfolio Strategy. This is where you decide what deals to pursue, how to manage your existing portfolio, and how to scale up and reach your goals. After spending the first three parts of this book gaining foundational knowledge, setting a Vision, and learning Deal Design, this is the final component of your strategy. It's time to put everything you've learned and decided into action with Portfolio Management.

The process of Portfolio Management contains two broad activity sets. The first is research and analysis. This is where you study your existing portfolio and current market conditions to inform your decision-making. I'm sure you're eager to make investments, but of all the Deal Designs you could pursue, which deals work best in your local market, with your current resource levels, at this specific point in time? Who should you be networking with? What about your current deals? Should you hold on to them? Sell them? Refinance? You'll encounter many questions while managing your portfolio, and thoroughly understanding your current portfolio's performance and keeping tabs on current market conditions will help you derive informed answers.

The second activity set is translating your research into action. Once you've analyzed your portfolio and understand your potential options, you need to commit to a set of activities to move forward. This starts by summarizing your priorities, preferences, and intentions into an Investment Thesis. From there, you define specific tactics and a Buy Box that you are going to execute on in the near future.

Combined, these two activity sets will give you the tools to build and manage your portfolio and bring your entire strategy to fruition. Portfolio Management is both "an art and a science" because some aspects of Portfolio Management can be tracked and measured objectively, while others are subjective decisions based on your Vision and intuition. While there are no "right" answers in Portfolio Management, by learning the concepts and activities in Part 4 of this book, you'll be able to make well-informed Portfolio Management decisions that have a high probability of success.

A few years ago, a partner of mine needed liquidity and wanted to exit a deal we held together. We had a strong relationship and partnership agreement, and I had the choice to buy him out or we could sell. But which one was better for my portfolio? If I sold, what would I do with the money? Would I buy a similar deal or diversify into new Deal

Designs? If I bought him out, would my portfolio performance suffer or improve? I had a few good options, but an abundance of choice can be overwhelming.

Luckily, over my investing career I have honed and refined my Portfolio Management skills into a process to follow when making big decisions. So, I followed my process. I reviewed my portfolio's performance, studied current market conditions, and considered how my resources were allocated. From there, I decided the best path forward and put together an action plan. This process didn't tell me exactly what to do, but it gave me a clear understanding of my options and allowed me to make informed, high-probability decisions. Ultimately, I decided to sell, complete a 1031 exchange, and used my Deal Design decisions to diversify my portfolio. I was informed and therefore could act with confidence. It worked out great.

The following chapters will give you the tools to manage and grow your portfolio over time. We will start with the basics of how to monitor the performance of your portfolio. If you're going to make good Portfolio Management decisions, you need to know where you stand today (even if you're new). Next, we'll step outside your own investments and examine how current market conditions—both macroeconomically and in your local area—may impact your current portfolio and future opportunities. In Chapter 28 we'll talk about resource allocation and how to ensure you're using your resources to their maximum potential. In Chapter 29 I'll share some common growth paths used by successful real estate investors. And finally, in Chapter 31 we'll put everything you've learned thus far in the book into a detailed investment thesis, action plan, and Buy Box for you to execute on.

The concepts and skills you'll learn in Part 4 are likely the ones you will use most frequently over the course of your investing career. While your Vision and Deal Designs will change over time, those change over years. Portfolio Management, on the other hand, is continuously evolving. As such, you may want to revisit this part of the book and this part of your PREP frequently. You don't need to review your Vision or Deal Design more than once a year, but I recommend revisiting the Portfolio Management portion of your PREP every three months.

While there are some solid Portfolio Management tools out there, I've never found one I love, and the best ones can be expensive. As such, I created my own tool in Excel to help you with your Portfolio Management. The tool is called the Portfolio Tracker and is designed specifically for readers of this book. It contains all of the concepts in this book and uses the same naming conventions and ideas we've talked about so far. I encourage you to use it as you read through Part 4, and in the future as you grow your portfolio. It's free for anyone who is reading this book and can be found at www.biggerpockets.com/strategybook.

Portfolio Management is where you move from the learning and decision-making you did in Parts 1, 2, and 3 into action. No matter your Vision, no matter your Deal Designs, there are things you can do, starting today, to move closer to your financial goals. In Part 4 you will chart that path. No more indecision, no more hesitation, no more overwhelming optionality—it's time to focus on your next big moves. Let's turn your Vision into reality.

Chapter 25
PORTFOLIO TRACKING

The first step in effective Portfolio Management is understanding your portfolio's current contents and performance. If you are coaching a sports team and have to decide which play to run next, you probably want to know what the score is, how much time is on the clock, and what the other team has been up to. It's the same idea with Portfolio Management—you need to look at what's going on in your portfolio right now before you decide what to do next. In this chapter we're going to discuss how to track and evaluate your portfolio's performance.

Given that your portfolio is a collection of individual investments, tracking your portfolio is basically an exercise in tracking your individual deals and then summarizing the results. That said, I find that visualizing the current contents and performance of your portfolio adds more value than the sum of its parts. Seeing all of your individual deals compared against one another unlocks important insights and serves as the basis for future decisions about your portfolio. The idea here is to look at your current collection of deals, decide if they are the right collection, and determine the best opportunities for future action.

Because deal analysis is a huge topic (I wrote an entire book about it![9]), and because this book is focused on portfolio-level considerations, I will only briefly cover the basics of deal analysis and concentrate mostly on how to holistically examine your portfolio. The Portfolio Tracker tool that accompanies this book (www.biggerpockets.com/strategybook) can help you calculate the financial metrics that are discussed in this chapter. This should allow you to track your portfolio easily, even if you don't know every formula by heart.

---

9 Dave Meyer and J Scott, *Real Estate by the Numbers* (Denver, CO: BiggerPockets, 2022), www.biggerpockets.com/bythenumbers.

If you're brand new to real estate investing, this chapter won't require a lot of action on your part, but it will still be valuable to you. Even before you join the game, you need to know the rules and how to keep score. Tracking your portfolio is a skill you'll need for the entirety of your investing career, and you have to be able to do it well and often. Make sure you learn these skills! They offer you a way of thinking about your portfolio that is useful regardless of your portfolio's current size.

When you analyze your current portfolio, you're not just looking at financial performance. Ensuring alignment with your Vision, maintaining portfolio balance, allocating resources properly, and identifying opportunities for improvement are all important considerations.

THREE ELEMENTS OF PORTFOLIO TRACKING

Tracking and analyzing your current portfolio breaks down into three key steps.

1. **Deal Design:** Listing out and visualizing the design of each of your current deals helps you understand your portfolio balance, risk level, and potential for return.

2. **Financial Performance:** You need to know the returns your deals are generating. The metrics we'll use in this section are cash flow, equity value, return on equity (ROE), annualized ROI, and compound annual growth rate (CAGR). This isn't a comprehensive list of performance metrics but is sufficient to understand how your deals are performing on a portfolio level. Advanced or commercial real estate investors should consider adding other metrics, like internal rate of return (IRR). If you need a refresher, we defined these metrics back in Chapter 3.

3. **Resources and Risk:** How are your resources spread across your portfolio and how efficiently are these resources being used? You'll want to see how much capital, time, and skill is invested into each deal, how resource intensive each deal is, and the risk level.

To demonstrate how these elements paint a portfolio-level picture, let's look at an example of an investor, Justin, who has been steadily building a portfolio over the last several years. Justin is in his early thirties and works full-time. His primary goal for real estate investing is to move up his retirement date to his early fifties. As such, he is looking to create $200,000 in cash flow per year within twenty years . Given his goals and time horizon, Justin wants steady, moderate-risk deals. His PREP, so far, looks as follows:

VISION

Personal Values
What do you value most in life? What can you not live without?
1. Accountability
2. Competence
3. Freedom
4. Learning
5. Balance

Resource Audit
Money:
- Net Worth: $165,000
- Personal Cash Flow: $1,300/month
- Investable Assets: $45,000
- Cash Reserves

Time: 20 hours

Current Skills: Tenant management, deal analysis, partner

Risk Profile
Time Horizon: 20 years
Risk Tolerance: 3
Risk Capacity: 3
Current Risk Profile: 3

Transactional Income Plan
Stay at current job. Fulfilling + resources.

Financial Goals
Reinvestment Rate: 100%
Residual Income Goal: $200,000
Portfolio Value Goal: $2,500,000

DEAL DESIGN

Deal Type	Ownership Structure	Financing	Operational Plan
Rentals	Sole Owner	Equity	Owner Occupied
STR	Partnership/JV	Conventional	Value-Add
Commercial	Syndication	Commercial	Buy & Hold
			BRRRR

Management Plan	Asset Class	Location	Property Class
Hybrid	SFR	Charlotte, NC	A
Passive	Small Multifamily	Joshua Tree, CA	B
	Large Multifamily		C

Current Deals

In pursuit of his goals, Justin has acquired three properties with the following Deal Designs over the last five years:

DEAL TACTICS	DEAL 1	DEAL 2	DEAL 3
Deal Type	Rental Property	Rental Property	Short-Term Rental
Financing	Conventional	Conventional	Conventional
Ownership Struture	Sole Owner	Partnership	Partnership
Operating Plan(s)	House Hacking	Value-Add	Buy and Hold
Management Plan	Active Management	Active Management	Hybrid
Asset Class	Duplex	Triplex	DSFR
Market	Charlotte, NC	Charlotte, NC	Joshua Tree, CA
Property Class	B	B	A

As you can see, Justin has used the tactics from his Deal Design and acquired deals that are well aligned with his Vision and his Deal Design guidelines. Rental properties and short-term rentals are good for long-term cash flow, and he has selected asset classes, property classes, and financing that are all relatively low risk. He has employed solid tactics that allow him to limit his risk while opening himself up to sufficient upside.

Looking at his Deal Designs is helpful, but this alone is not enough to evaluate Justin's portfolio for future opportunities. For that, we need to add in the next layer: financial performance.

Financial Performance

PERSONAL FINANCIAL PERFORMANCE	DEAL 1	DEAL 2	DEAL 3
Cash Flow	$6,350	$4,200	$6,750
Equity Value	$85,115	$92,798	$79,290
Estimated Proceeds if Sold Today	$72,172	$82,273	$67,115

PERFORMANCE METRICS	DEAL 1	DEAL 2	DEAL 3
Property Value CAGR	1.6%	7.0%	2.6%
Equity CAGR	5.7%	12.9%	8.7%
Cash Flow CAGR	5.9%	4.4%	15.4%
Return on Equity	7.5%	4.5%	8.5%

Adding in some simple financial performance metrics gives Justin a deeper look at his portfolio. Now he can see that all of his deals are producing cash flow and have strong equity values—which is great. Next, when Justin looks at the efficiency and growth metrics, he can start to see how his deals are performing relative to one another. Here are a few key insights from Justin's Portfolio Tracker.

1. Deal 1 has the lowest property value growth but has still averaged 5.3 percent equity growth over the hold period due to amortization. Cash flow growth is excellent at 5.5 percent, and the ROE is good at 7.5 percent.

2. Deal 2 has experienced excellent equity growth, which makes sense because it used a value-add operating plan. The cash flow growth rate is strong at 4.0 percent, but due to the rapid increase in equity value, the ROE is relatively low at 4.5 percent (the denominator is growing faster than the numerator).

3. Deal 3 is offering great returns all around. Equity growth is strong, cash flow growth is outstanding, and the ROE is the best in the portfolio.

An analysis of Financial Performance reveals a lot about a portfolio's overall performance, but for Justin to make actionable decisions, he needs to layer in the last component: resources and risk.

Resources and Risk

CURRENT RESOURCE INPUTS	DEAL 1	DEAL 2	DEAL 3
Capital Invested (Estimated Equity Value)	$85,115	$92,798	$79,290
Subjective Risk Assessment (1-5)	1	2	4
Monthly Time Invested (Hours)	5	9	3
Skills	Tenant management, repairs, operations		

Resource Allocation			
Current Resource Inputs	Deal 1	Deal 2	Deal 3
Estimated Equity Value	$85,115	$185,595	$158,579
Subjective Risk Assessment (1-5)	1	2	4
Monthly Time Invested (Hours)	5	9	3
Skills	Tenant management, repairs, operations	Tenant management, repairs, operations	Portfolio Management
% of Portfolio Equity Value	33.1%	36.1%	30.8%
% of Portfolio Cash Flow	36.7%	24.3%	39.0%

This final step unlocks many additional insights that will guide Justin's future investment decisions. First, we can see how much capital he has locked into his deals. Note that the equity value is the initial principal invested, plus any equity growth (or minus any losses). This number represents the value of the property to Justin should he sell it.

Justin has also added his subjective risk assessment for each deal, the average time he spends on each deal per month, and the skills he is *currently* using to run his business.

DEAL TACTICS	DEAL 1	DEAL 2	DEAL 3
Deal Type	Rental Property	Rental Property	Short-Term Rental
Financing	Conventional	Conventional	Conventional
Ownership Struture	Sole Owner	Partnership	Partnership
Operating Plan(s)	House Hacking	Value-Add	Buy and Hold
Management Plan	Active Management	Active Management	Hybrid
Asset Class	Duplex	Triplex	DSFR
Market	Charlotte, NC	Charlotte, NC	Joshua Tree, CA
Property Class	B	B	A
Financial Performance			
Personal Financial Performance	**Deal 1**	**Deal 2**	**Deal 3**
Cash Flow	$6,350	$4,200	$6,750
Equity Value	$85,115	$92,798	$79,290
Estimated Proceeds if Sold Today	$72,172	$82,273	$67,115
Performance Metrics	**Deal 1**	**Deal 2**	**Deal 3**
Property Value CAGR	1.6%	7.0%	2.6%
Equity CAGR	5.7%	12.9%	8.7%
Cash Flow CAGR	5.9%	4.4%	15.4%
Return on Equity	7.5%	4.5%	8.5%
Resource Allocation			
Current Resource Inputs	**Deal 1**	**Deal 2**	**Deal 3**
Estimated Equity Value	$85,115	$92,798	$79,290
Subjective Risk Assessment (1-5)	1	2	4
Monthly Time Invested (Hours)	5	9	3
Skills	Tenant management, repairs, operations	Tenant management, repairs, operations	Portfolio Management
% of Portfolio Equity Value	33.1%	36.1%	30.8%
% of Portfolio Cash Flow	36.7%	24.3%	39.0%

When we look at all of this together, there is so much to learn! There are more insights than I can write out here, but there a few key observations in particular that can help Justin.

- Justin has balanced his equity very well, as each of his three deals contains roughly one-third of his total equity value. This is solid risk management.
- Deal 1 is offering very good returns for Justin, given the very low perceived risk and time commitment. Remember, returns need to be evaluated relative to their risk and invested resources!
- Deal 2 is requiring nine hours per month, more than Justin's other two deals combined. Yet the deal has the lowest ROE, and only accounts for 24 percent of his portfolio's total cash flow. This deal may be an inefficient use of Justin's time.
- Deal 2 saw huge gains in equity value due to the value-add strategy. However, Justin has completed his renovations and is not currently using his construction and capital improvement skills at all. Perhaps this is a missed opportunity.
- Deal 3 is the riskiest asset Justin holds, but given the very high performance and low time commitment, it's currently the strongest deal in Justin's portfolio.

With the details of each of his deals laid out, Justin can now clearly summarize and visualize how his portfolio's overall performance is tracking against his long-term goals.

PORTFOLIO SUMMARY	CURRENT	GOAL	PROGRESS TO GOAL
Equity Value	$257,202	$2,000,000	13%
Annual Cash Flow	$17,300	$200,000	9%
Portfolio ROE	6.7%	8%	84%
Portfolio Outstanding Debt	$711,319		

RESOURCE ASSESSMENT	CURRENT	GOAL	PROGRESS TO GOAL
Current Investable Assets	$45,000	$80,000	56%
Portfolio-Level Risk Assessment	2.30	3	Under Risked
Time Investment (Hours)	17	20	Within Range

He can also compare each individual deal against one another, and the average of his portfolio:

PORTFOLIO BENCHMARKS	DEAL 1	DEAL 2	DEAL 3
Remaining Estimated Hold Period (Years)	1.83	3.15	1.64
% of Portfolio Equity Value	33.1%	36.1%	30.8%
% of Portfolio Cash Flow	36.7%	24.3%	39.0%
ROE Performance Against Portfolio	On Target	Off Target	On Target
ROE Performance Against Market Deals	On Target	Off Target	On Target
Estimated Annual Cash Flow Benefit (if traded for benchmark)	$(1,298)	$1,559	$(2,052)

Look how helpful this is! From this simple summary, Justin can see tons of valuable information about his portfolio's current performance. From here, Justin's path forward becomes clearer.

- Justin is five years into his twenty-five-year time horizon (20 percent), but he is only 9 percent of the way to his cash flow goal. While this isn't ideal, it's actually not that bad. Remember, compounding returns means Justin's ability to generate cash flow should accelerate over the remainder of his time horizon. That said, Justin may want to prioritize opportunities to improve his cash flow.
- Justin is targeting a moderate risk profile for his portfolio (3 on the 1–5 scale). However, Justin's current portfolio has an average risk profile of 2.3. While not far out of range, Justin does have the capacity to take on more risk in the pursuit of higher returns as he scales.
- Justin's goal is to spend no more than twenty hours per month on his portfolio and is currently at seventeen hours. This means there is room for Justin to commit more time, but not much more—something he'll need to think through when he decides what to do next.
- Justin has $45,000 in investable assets, which is not enough to put 20 percent down on another property in his typical price range at the moment. That doesn't mean Justin can't do deals, but it means he'll either want to favor low-capital-intensity Deal Designs for his next deal or wait to accumulate more capital.

This portfolio analysis empowers Justin to track progress toward his goals, compare his deals against one another, and gain portfolio-level insights that will help him determine what to do next. He can evaluate any future opportunities against his current performance and resource allocation. Portfolio tracking is a powerful tool, and investors of all experience levels should track their portfolios diligently for the lifetime of their investing career.

PREP WORK
TRACKING YOUR PORTFOLIO

STRATEGIC ACTIVITY: Track your current portfolio's composition and performance, if you have one. Write down the following key metrics in your PREP: total equity, total cash flow, average ROE, average risk, and monthly time commitment. If you're new to investing and haven't yet participated in a deal, you can skip this section of your PREP. For more information about how to track your portfolio, and the significance of your findings, see below.

Tracking your portfolio requires a bit more work than other parts of your PREP, but it's not difficult. The easiest way to track your portfolio is to use the Portfolio Tracker Excel file that accompanies this book. It's designed around the contents of this book, so the concepts and nomenclature should be familiar to you. I've done all of the difficult calculations for you, and it's easy to use! That said, if you want to create your own portfolio tracking tool, you're more than welcome to. I advise you to do it digitally—your portfolio will change over time, and updates are easier on a computer. (Plus, computers don't make computational errors, so you have more assurance that your metrics are correct.) If you make your own, just be sure you calculate all of the relevant metrics that go on your PREP (total equity, cash flow, and average ROE, at a bare minimum).

In this section I am not going to provide detailed instructions for how to fill out the Excel Portfolio Tracker, as I have included thorough written instructions and links to video instructions in the actual file (find it at www.biggerpockets.com/strategybook). But we will review the concepts in the Portfolio Tracker tool in detail, so you fully understand how to track your portfolio and interpret the results. The key concepts include those discussed above—Deal Design, financial performance, and resource allocation—but also require some additional information from your Vision and your deals' purchase conditions to make all the calculations work.

Vision: Your portfolio performance is relative to what you want to achieve. You should always be comparing your current portfolio's performance against the Vision you've created: your financial goals, risk profile, time commitments, and values. Given that you're reading this book right now, you likely have the details of your Vision ready to put into the Portfolio Summary section of your Portfolio Tracker. But if you need to, revisit your Resource Audit, financial goals, and Risk Profile to remind yourself of the Vision you've laid out.

Purchase Conditions: Purchase conditions are the details of your individual deals at the time of purchase, like the date of purchase, purchase price, etc. These metrics should be relatively easy to track and put into your snapshot because they are objective, and they don't change. These are the purchase conditions I track.

- Purchase Date
- Current Hold Period (Years)
- Estimated Hold Period (Years)
- Purchase Price
- Down Payment (%)
- Down Payment
- Initial Loan Amount
- Interest Rate
- Loan Length (Years)
- Closing Costs
- Cash Reserves at Purchase
- Rehab Costs
- Total Principal Invested
- After-Repair Value
- Annual Cash Flow at Purchase
- Loan Period Remaining (Years)
- Date of Next Interest Rate Adjustment

While this may look like a long list, it's easy to track these metrics. As you go through the process of investing in any deal, you will know the value for each of these inputs. You can probably even pull these metrics from any deal analysis calculator you use. I recommend that whenever you buy a new deal, you *update your tracker right away*. Your purchase conditions will still be top of mind, and it will only take you a few minutes to fill this out.

Deal Design

Next comes the more dynamic part of your portfolio snapshot. Write out the Deal Design for each deal in your portfolio. This should be easy, since you're writing down decisions you've already made. I recommend you input your Deal Design any time you purchase a new deal, as it will be fresh in your mind. But unlike purchase conditions, your Deal Design can change. You may change your management plan (e.g., active to hybrid), operating plan (e.g., house hack to buy and hold rental), or the class of your property (e.g., through value-add). As your design changes, it's important to update your portfolio snapshot accordingly.

Financial Performance

Measuring the financial performance of your deals is a topic unto itself, but for portfolio tracking, the following metrics are sufficient: cash flow, equity value, return on equity (ROE), annualized ROI, and compound annual growth rate (CAGR).

Although this list of metrics may seem long, it doesn't require many inputs. Financial analysis uses some of the purchase conditions you already input into your snapshot, with only a few metrics to incorporate your current conditions: hold period, annual cash flow, loan balance, estimated property value, and estimated equity value. Basic financial analysis and bookkeeping will easily produce these numbers, with the exception of the estimated property value.

ACCURATELY UPDATING PROPERTY VALUE: *You simply cannot know the value of a property until it is sold. For this analysis, you need to continuously estimate and update your property's value. The best ways to estimate your property's value are through comping, an agent, or an automated valuation model (AVM), like a Zestimate.*

As of this writing, the most accurate way I've found is with using comps. Comps (short for "comparables") is the relatively tried-and-true practice of looking at recently sold comparable properties and estimating the value of your property based on them. Comping is both an art and a science that takes time to master, but it's a very worthwhile skill! There are many good resources online to learn how to comp well. If you don't want to learn or haven't yet mastered comping, you can ask a high-quality real estate agent to do it for you.

As a last resort (or as a sanity check), you can use an AVM. The truth is, although I love data science, I've found that AVMs haven't yet proven to be as reliable as quality comping by an experienced real estate professional.

Once you have all of your financial inputs, type them into the Portfolio Tracker Excel file, and all of your performance metrics will be calculated for you.

Resources and Risk

The last things to track are the resources and risks involved in each deal. Again, this should be relatively simple given the work you've already done.

First, your resources. Start by writing down the capital in each deal. This should be easy at this point—it is equal to your estimated equity value, as we discussed in the example with Justin above. This figure is what you would walk away with should you sell the deal. Next, write down the amount of time you're committing to each of your deals by estimating your average monthly commitment over the last several months. Then, write down the skills you're currently contributing to your deal.

Make sure to track your risk score in addition to your resources. Remember, risk is always a subjective measurement, which is why I recommend quantifying your level of risk for each deal. (I prefer the simple 1–5 scale, from lowest to highest risk). This will allow you to easily calculate the average risk across your portfolio and compare it to your stated risk target.

Evaluating Your Portfolio

Once you've input your deal metrics and the calculations are made, you can analyze where you stand today. Remember, the point of this exercise is to see progress toward your goals, compare your deals against one another, and identify potential opportunities.

The first thing to examine in your tracker is how you're performing against your Vision. If you're like me, you'll probably want to check out the financial metrics first and see how your total cash flow and equity value are pacing against your long-term goals. Watching your cash flow and portfolio equity value climb over time should serve as motivation on your journey toward financial freedom! Who doesn't like watching their financial situation improve?

Next, take a look at your resources and risk. Are you spending an appropriate amount of time on your portfolio, and is your risk acceptable? Take some time to think through how your portfolio-level metrics compare to your Vision. Finally, look at your individual deals to see how they compare to one another, and look for opportunities to improve. Go through your financial metrics, your deal tactics, and your resources and risk to get a holistic sense of your portfolio composition.

As you review your portfolio snapshot, here are some considerations to think through.

- **Are your deals offering similar financial performance?** Which deals offer the best cash flow? What about ROE or equity growth? Try to identify which deals are doing the best for you and which are lagging. Have any deals run their course and are starting to see performance decline?
- **How balanced is your portfolio in terms of deal tactics?** Are you all in on a single deal type, asset class, or location? If so, are you comfortable with that or would you prefer to diversify your portfolio in the future? Compare your deal tactics to your financial performance to see what tactics are yielding you the best (and worst) results.
- **How much capital do you have invested?** Could you add more? Is one of your deals hogging all of your capital or is it evenly spread? Do you think you could deploy some of your capital in a better way to optimize your portfolio?
- **Is your committed time aligned with your Vision?** Are you spending too much time on your portfolio? If so, what deals are taking up the most of your time? Could you reduce your involvement? Perhaps consider selling off a time-consuming deal or altering your management plan. Are you spending too little time on your portfolio? If you have more time to give, consider learning a new skill, using your time to find new deals, or taking on more active management to improve your returns.
- **Are you properly utilizing your skills?** If you're contributing skills you haven't mastered, that could be an inefficiency. Consider hiring out those skills and reallocating your time to contributing a skill you're great at. Alternatively, are there skills you could be using that you're not? For example, are you great

at value-add, but all of your deals are stabilized? Look for areas where you can better leverage the skills you have.

- **What are the risk levels of each of your deals?** Do your deals have a similar risk profile, or do you want to balance your portfolio with a combination of low-risk and high-risk deals? Has the risk level changed for any of your deals? For example, if you bought a deal for value-add and have completed the renovation, there is probably less risk in the deal. Is your portfolio now under-risked?

There is no checklist or "right" way to evaluate your performance. There are a lot of metrics, and you don't have to examine each one or in any particular order. Instead, focus on the three objectives of the tracker: measuring your performance against your goals, comparing your deals against one another, and looking for future opportunities.

Portfolio analysis is a skill, and one that you will get better at with practice. So don't expect to find every single insight your first time around. But trust me, if you track your portfolio diligently, you will learn to make well-informed and high-probability decisions about the future of your portfolio.

Once you've completed your Portfolio Tracker, make sure to write out the key findings in your *PREP*. First, write down the financial metrics: Total Equity, Total Cash Flow, Portfolio ROE. Then write out how your portfolio is doing in terms of risk and resources: average risk, time invested, and your remaining investable assets. Last, note down any key insights you've gained from your initial analysis. Did you find any opportunities you want to act on? Write them down! These metrics and insights will be pivotal in developing your Investment Thesis and Action Plan later in Part 4.

Tracking your portfolio is an important first step in deciding what future opportunities to pursue. But before you can make those critical decisions, you need more information from outside your own portfolio. You need to examine the macroeconomic and market conditions going on around you. While you can't control these external forces, you can (and should) adapt your tactics based on broad market trends. In the next chapter, you'll learn the importance of the business cycle, how to identify what part of the cycle you're in, and how to gauge the market conditions in the location where you invest

Chapter 26
MACROECONOMICS AND THE BUSINESS CYCLE

For most of this book, we've focused on the details of your personal situation and your personal portfolio—and for good reason. As investors, we wish everything about our portfolios was under our control. Unfortunately, that's not the case. There are considerations outside of your personal sphere of influence that will impact your portfolio, and they need to be understood. The most important external considerations are macroeconomics and market conditions. Though they are outside your control, if you understand how these variables impact your portfolio, you can optimize your current portfolio, design deals based on present opportunities, and mitigate risk.

In the coming two chapters, we'll discuss how broad trends in the economy and the housing market can impact the performance of your portfolio, and how to adjust your tactics accordingly to take advantage of what's going on around you. These two chapters combined will correspond with the Market Conditions & Benchmarks section of the PREP. We'll start with macroeconomics and the business cycle in this chapter, which involves broad, national-level trends. In the next chapter, we'll discuss local economic and housing market conditions.

Macroeconomics is the study of broad, economy-level behaviors like inflation, prices, economic growth, employment, and monetary policy (as opposed to microeconomics, which is more akin to personal financial behavior). There are two primary elements of macroeconomics: long-term economic growth and the business cycle.

Long-term economic growth is the study of increasing the aggregate production of an economy in order to support development, prosperity, and a rising standard of living. Economic growth is typically measured with metrics like gross domestic product (GDP), employment rates, income and savings rates, consumer spending, inflation, and more. This is as "big picture" as it gets in terms of economics.

If you dive into long-term economic growth trends, you see that economic activity fluctuates over time. While most economies, like that of the United States, trend upward over time, there are short-term variances in growth. Some periods see great growth, while others see slow or even negative growth.

The periodic cycles that an economy goes through are known as the "business cycle." The business cycle has four distinct phases: expansions, peaks, recessions, and troughs . Although we all wish that the economy could just expand indefinitely with no setbacks, that isn't how market economies work. It can be frustrating, but to date, these cycles have proven unavoidable. That said, every business cycle is unique; no two recessions are identical, and neither are any two expansions. Although there is variance between cycles, it is still very helpful to understand the general patterns of the business cycle, as they are roughly correlated with different real estate investing tactics.

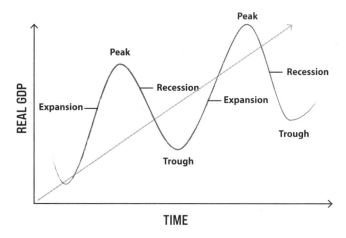

For the purposes of this book, we're going to leave the study of long-term economic growth aside. If you're like me, you'll find it a fascinating topic, but it's too broad to cover in this book. When it comes to Portfolio Management, the main thing to focus on is the business cycle. Over the course of the business cycle, critical changes occur that impact your portfolio. Interest rates rise and fall, the yield on risk-free assets changes, and the relative level of risk is in constant flux. Tactics and Deal Designs that work well in one phase of the business cycle may not work well in another. An accurate assessment of which phase of the business cycle you're in will inform the best tactical approach you should take.

THE BUSINESS CYCLE

The business cycle is driven by many broad economic factors. Each cycle is different and the variables that influence a given cycle will be different than those of the previous and subsequent cycles. That said, there are some consistent patterns in supply and demand, economic sentiment, inflation, and monetary policy that occur between business cycles that can inform our Portfolio Management decisions.

Expansion Phase

The expansion phase of the business cycle is when the economy is performing as most of us would like it to. People feel confident and are willing to spend money, which drives up demand for goods and services and fuels GDP growth. As demand increases throughout the economy, businesses ramp up hiring, which drives down unemployment and gives people even more confidence and money to spend. This economic optimism and increased demand are felt in the housing market as well. Rent prices tend to go up as vacancies fall, and property prices increase from homebuyer demand.

During an expansion, growing demand tends to outpace supply, which causes a bit of healthy inflation. Remember, inflation is roughly defined as "too much money chasing too few goods," and we start to see this in an expansion. When consumers feel good about the economy, they want to buy more than the economy has to offer. A bit of inflation isn't a bad thing, because it stimulates economic activity (people want to buy now before prices go up). The Federal Reserve currently targets about 2 percent annual inflation.

Expansions, at least in my opinion, are the easiest phase of the business cycle to identify because they are the economy performing at its best.

Expansion Phase Signals to Watch For:
- Economic optimism is growing.
- GDP is rising.

- Unemployment is declining.
- Deals get harder to find, while financing is easier to find.
- Inflation may tick up but remains close to the target range.

Expansions are the best times for the economy as a whole, which makes them good times to explore a variety of tactics as a real estate investor. Most tactics work well during an expansion. This is beneficial for investors, but it does come with some trade-offs. When times are good, everyone wants to get in on the action, creating competition for deals.

Expansion Phase Portfolio Considerations:
- There is growth in most asset classes, across property classes, and in many locations.
- Rental properties, commercial properties, and all long-term strategies work well if you can land strong deals (the better deals are in the recession and trough phases).
- Flipping can be very profitable, as can development.
- Commercial deals work across most asset classes.
- The value-add operating plan works particularly well.
- Lending can work well, but interest rates tend to be lower.

Peak Phase

Expansions don't last forever, and eventually they reach a peak stage where the economy is overheated but hasn't yet started to contract. This is where GDP tops out for the given business cycle. At this point, low unemployment, strong spending, and high confidence lead to an excess of demand that is unsustainable. Inflation rises above a healthy level, and asset bubbles can form. During the peak phase, the Federal Reserve often steps in to raise the Federal Funds Rate, which is their (rather blunt) tool for cooling off the economy and controlling inflation. Due to high prices, demand for housing and rent flatten out, as do rental occupancy rates.

Peak Phase Signals to Watch For:
- Many new and inexperienced investors enter the market.
- Debt is cheap and lending standards are declining
- Profitable real estate deals are difficult to come by.
- Unemployment levels off.
- Inflation is above the target range.
- Interest rates are rising.

The peak phase is a time for caution, especially for investors. After an expansion, there can be irrational exuberance in the markets, and people are prone to overpay for everything from luxury goods to stocks to real estate. The peak phase is a time for caution and conservative tactics for a real estate investor—even if your risk tolerance is high. There just aren't many tactics that work well in the peak phase. That doesn't mean you have to stop investing altogether, but you should focus on a narrower set of options. Pausing altogether may also be a good move. Luckily, the peak phase doesn't tend to last long.

Peak Phase Portfolio Considerations:
- Focus on Deal Designs that generate cash flow and amortization (because they don't rely on property values to drive returns).
- Owner-occupied business plans work well due to inherently low risk.
- Rental properties, and any long-term strategy, can work in theory, but profitable deals will be difficult to find.
- Lending can work well.
- Some commercial deals can make sense, while others are very risky—it all depends on the asset class.
- Flipping is risky, especially toward the end when housing prices are likely to flatten or start to fall.
- The peak phase is the riskiest time for development.

Recession Phase
As the high prices of the peak phase combine with inflation and rising interest rates, affordability and sentiment deteriorate throughout the economy. Demand for goods and services declines, dragging down consumer spending, business spending, and GDP. With less demand, employers need fewer employees, and layoffs drive unemployment higher. For real estate investors, the higher unemployment and economic uncertainty of a recession can lead to higher vacancy and a slowdown in home sales. The decline in sales volume does often lead to higher inventory, meaning deals may be more readily findable (although this isn't happening in the current cycle as of this writing). It's important to note that rent and home prices don't always fall during recessions (sometimes they grow!), but there tends to be downward pressure on pricing due to lower demand.

The most commonly accepted definition of a recession is two consecutive quarters of GDP decline, but the official designation of a recession falls to the National Bureau of Economic Research (NBER). And NBER looks at factors other than just GDP to determine *retrospectively* when recessions start and begin—meaning we don't know that we've been in an "official" recession until well after it begins, or perhaps even after the recession has ended! This is unfortunate, but just like with every other phase of the business cycle, there are clues we can look at ourselves to identify if the economy is in a recession.

Recession Phase Signals to Watch For:
- Interest rates are rising, reducing monetary supply.
- Unemployment ticks up on a national level, and across multiple industries.
- Real (inflation-adjusted) GDP growth is negative.
- Credit defaults are going up, and not necessarily in the housing sector—it could also happen in auto loans, student loans, credit cards, etc.
- Investors move to cash, bonds, and gold.
- There are more motivated sellers in the housing market.

Recessions are times of economic uncertainty and fear, but if you can take the emotion out of it, they often present investing opportunities. Similar to the peak phase, recessions are a time for conservative tactics and careful analysis. There are more motivated sellers and generally less competition during a recession, which can make deals more abundant than during an expansion or peak phase. If the prices of assets fall, it can be an opportunity to "buy low."

Recession Phase Portfolio Considerations:
- Take advantage of decreased competition for deals and negotiate with sellers to "buy deep" (buying under the property's current market value to protect yourself against the potential for future price declines).
- Motivated sellers and ill-prepared investors present opportunities.
- Focus on assets that will perform well over a long time period, and ideally buy them at a discount.
- Owner occupied and other conservative strategies work well.
- Look for creative financing options as interest rates on traditional loans increase.
- It is a risky time for flipping and development.

Trough Phase

Once the low demand, high unemployment, and high interest rates that characterize the recession phase ripple through the economy, things start to stabilize. Sometimes this happens on its own. Other times, the trough will come through intervention from the government. If the economy has been sufficiently cooled to reduce the risk of inflation, the Federal Reserve will often lower interest rates to increase monetary supply (and spending), or Congress can use fiscal policy to stimulate spending. With inflation and interest rates falling, affordability improves across the economy, demand starts to pick up, and the stage becomes set for future growth. For real estate investors, home sales and price growth are typically still low but have stabilized, and confidence starts to creep back into the marketplace.

Like every phase, it's nearly impossible to time the exact moment the economy has bottomed, but there are some signs the economy is near the trough.

Trough Phase Signals to Watch For:
- GDP and unemployment stop falling and start to level off.
- Inflation is falling or has leveled off below the target range.
- Economic sentiment is stable and perhaps even rising modestly.
- Government intervention occurs (lowering interest rates or fiscal stimulus).

The trough is an excellent time to invest. While still filled with uncertainty and relatively low sentiment, this phase is the final step before the next expansion. It's a great time to deploy your resources across a variety of tactics.

Trough Phase Portfolio Considerations:
- It's a good time to buy rentals, short-term rentals, or any other long-hold-period deals.
- Properties ripe for value-add tend to be cheap during the trough, making flipping and development very attractive.
- Even if prices haven't dropped, falling interest rates increase affordability.
- While you never want to bank on market appreciation, the potential upside of market appreciation is highest when you buy during the trough stage.

PREP WORK
MAKING YOUR ASSESSMENT

STRATEGIC ACTIVITY: Determine what stage of the business cycle we're in currently, to the best of your ability. Once you've made your assessment, write it down in your PREP, and take time to consider if your current tactics are appropriate given the macroeconomic environment. For further instruction on how to make your macroeconomic assessment, see below.

Now that you understand the basics of the business cycle, you can apply this information to your Portfolio Management plan. The first step in doing this is to take some time to identify where we are in the business cycle. As mentioned above, you can never know for sure where we are, but you can look at important clues like inflation, interest rates, GDP, and unemployment rates (just to name a few).

If you're unfamiliar with this type of analysis, there are a few solid free resources for this data.

- The Federal Reserve Bank of St. Louis maintains a website known as the FRED (Federal Reserve Economic Data). It's free and easy to use, and it aggregates a ton of macroeconomic data.
- Websites like Trading Economics, Statista, and YCharts all aggregate economic information, and most of them have free options for viewing data.
- Most quality newspapers report on this information regularly, and their websites often have places where you can track economic data.
- My podcast, *On the Market,* covers economic data through the lens of real estate investing twice a week.
- I personally review economic news and data and help investors make sense of it on my Instagram account, @thedatadeli.

In addition to reviewing data, there are a few questions I encourage you to think about as you consider the economic environment.

- What phase of the business cycle do you think we're in? How confident do you feel in your assessment?
- Are you currently using tactics that are appropriate given the phase of the business cycle we're in?
- What is the best way to deploy your resources given the macroeconomic climate?
- What is your personal assessment of the current market risk?
- How have the risk levels of your existing portfolio and your planned tactics changed? Have the prices of risk-free assets like bonds and money market accounts changed since your last assessment? If so, are your risk premiums still appropriate?

- What impact is the business cycle having on the non–real estate elements of your portfolio? Is your job or transactional income at risk due to a potential recession? What about your family—could any of them lose their job? Conversely, are times improving and can you expect a raise?

Finally, I'll note that while the business cycle tends to be driven by consistent variables, there is always the chance that an unpredictable event will disrupt everything. These are events like 9/11, the COVID-19 pandemic, or the Russian invasion of Ukraine, all of which were global events that changed the economy in unexpected ways. These events are often known as "black swan" events and are inherently unknowable. No amount of planning can predict these things; the best thing you can do is to build a portfolio that is resilient in the face of changing conditions.

While there is huge value in assessing the macroeconomic climate, you'll never get it entirely right, and that's okay. You don't need to be an expert macroeconomic forecaster to manage your portfolio. You just need to be able to read the environment reasonably well to make high-probability decisions about your portfolio. Focus on the high-level trends.

Once you have made your assessment of the current business cycle, write it down in your *PREP* under the Market Conditions & Benchmarks section. If you're using the Portfolio Tracker tool that comes with this book, enter the appropriate value in the Business Cycle section there as well. For now, that is all you need to do. But as we move through the remainder of Part 4, keep in mind the tactical considerations of the business cycle. That will be a central part of developing your Investment Thesis and creating your Buy Box in the coming chapters.

Chapter 27
LOCAL MARKET CONDITIONS

Macroeconomics influences almost everything in the economy, but it doesn't tell the whole story. Every region in the country has its own economy and its own housing market. Investors need to study what is happening in their local market to make informed Portfolio Management decisions.

Every housing market is different and will behave differently—even within the same market cycle. The Las Vegas market may respond differently to a recession than the Indianapolis market. San Diego may be more sensitive to interest rate hikes than Little Rock. Further, the behavior of each individual market changes over time. The conditions in St. Louis may have supported flipping two years ago, but what about today? Investors need to drill down beyond macroeconomics and understand the conditions in any market they currently invest in (or are considering investing in). These conditions are crucial to your Portfolio Management plan, as they dictate which markets to invest in, which Deal Design works best given the current environment, how to allocate resources, and how you should bid on prospective deals.

In this chapter we'll discuss how to interpret key housing market conditions, and how you should adjust your tactics accordingly. We'll also discuss how to conduct the crucial exercise of "benchmarking," which will help you determine what deals to pursue and if you should be selling or refinancing any deals in your current portfolio.

LOCAL ECONOMIC CONDITIONS

The first step in understanding the economy in a specific market is to examine the economic indicators we discussed in Chapter 22. As a reminder, some of the metrics to track are economic growth and diversity, population growth, household formation, wage growth, and the regulatory environment.

Like with macroeconomics, you don't need to have a perfect understanding of every variable here. Instead, I recommend just getting a feel for the trends in your area. Even if you've been investing in the same market for a while, you should keep tabs on these metrics and how they change over time. Simply knowing a few metrics, like if the population of an area is going up or down, is hugely beneficial! The more you look at these metrics, the more you'll learn—so just pick a place to start and don't worry about knowing everything. All the sources I cited earlier, like the FRED website, have localized data you can look at.

REAL ESTATE MARKET CONDITIONS

Beyond macroeconomic trends, each local market will have unique housing market dynamics: price growth, inventory levels, sales volume, and much more. By studying a few key housing market data points, you can select tactics to use, opportunities to pursue, and how to construct strong offers. Through these metrics, we can understand if the local area is in a "buyer's market" or a "seller's market" and uncover some important lead indicators that inform future performance. These metrics are like vital signs for a patient—they help diagnose what is going on and what actions should be taken next. Below are guidelines on key conditions to monitor (revisit Chapter 22 if you need a refresher on definitions).

- **Sales Price:** Look at the median sales price for your investing market and examine how it has changed over time. Ideally, break down the sales price information by asset class, number of bedrooms, and price per square foot. Use this information to update the equity values of your current holdings and to determine if the price point is attractive to you for a future investment.
- **Rent Price:** Rent prices are a key indicator for cash flow potential, so make sure to know what the median rent is in your area. Breaking down rents by the number of bedrooms (e.g., the median rent for a one-bedroom apartment versus a three-bedroom apartment) will give you even more of an edge. Use rent data to ensure that

your current portfolio is keeping up with market rents, as well as to assess if the market is appealing for another investment.

- **Rent-to-Price Ratio:** The rent-to-price ratio (RTP) is a simple proxy to estimate cash flow. RTP is a very rough proxy, but it can be useful for comparing the cash flow potential of two locations against one another, and to understand cash flow potential over time. If RTP in your area is trending upward over time, cash flow is improving. If it's declining, so are cash flow prospects.
- **Taxes/Insurance:** Tax and insurance changes can sneak up on you! Especially in the last few years, as property values have risen, these expenses have increased significantly. This can hamper cash flow and impact the performance of your portfolio. Taxes and insurance vary by market, so make sure you're monitoring them to keep your current expenses up to date and to evaluate cash flow potential for any future investment.
- **Active Inventory:** Active inventory measures the total amount of properties for sale in a market at a given time. By measuring the number of listings on the market, you can see how quickly properties are selling (demand). Inventory is an incredibly useful metric because it measures the balance of supply and demand.
- **Days on Market (DOM):** Like active inventory, DOM gives you a good sense of supply and demand. DOM is calculated by taking the average number of days that all properties in the market are listed for sale before going under contract.

Active inventory and DOM are great metrics to monitor because they help us understand if the market in question is in a buyer's market or a seller's market. When inventory and days on market are low, it's typically because there is more demand for properties than there are properties for sale. When a property gets listed, there is lots of interest, and potentially even bidding wars. This is known as a "seller's market" because the seller has all the power in negotiation. When a seller gets to choose from multiple buyers, they can dictate terms and often get the price they want. Prices typically trend upward in a seller's market.

When DOM and inventory are high, it's known as a "buyer's market" because buyers have the power. Buyer's markets occur when there are more properties for sale in the market than there are buyers. This gives buyers leverage to dictate terms and provide an opportunity to buy under list price. In a buyer's market, prices tend to stay flat or even decline, depending on the severity of the market.

Determining whether you're in a buyer's market or a seller's market is a key part of Portfolio Management. It informs when it's a good time to buy and when it's a good time to sell. It also informs how you make offers on a property. If you're purchasing in a buyer's market, you can be patient, offer under asking price, and dictate the terms you want. However, in a seller's market, you'll have to be much more aggressive in your offers, as you'll likely be competing against many other potential buyers.

BENCHMARKING

Understanding broad trends is very important, but you also need to get specific and consider what deals are available in your markets right now. Even if you're not planning to buy in the near future, you should understand what deals are available to you. You need to know how your current portfolio stacks up against alternative deals you could pursue in current market conditions.

Keeping tabs on what deals you *could* be doing is a process I call "benchmarking." The goal is to understand what rates of return are possible in your target market(s), given current market conditions. What cash-on-cash return could you earn if you bought a new deal right now? How are flips performing in today's market? Once you know this information, you can see how your own deals compare.

Returning to our example of Justin, we can see how this works in practice. Justin invests in rental properties in Charlotte, North Carolina, and owns a short-term rental in Joshua Tree, California. By researching local market conditions and benchmarking, he can learn what current deals exist in those areas. Through this exercise he learns that he could confidently invest in a new rental in Charlotte at a 7 percent ROE, and a new STR in Joshua Tree at a 6.5 percent ROE. This is very useful in helping Justin determine how to allocate his resources in the future. It's also helpful in managing his current portfolio. From his Portfolio Tracker, Justin knows Deal 1 earns a 7.5 percent ROE, while Deal 2 earns a 4.5 percent ROE. Both of these deals are in Charlotte, which has a benchmark of 7 percent—giving Justin valuable information. He now knows that Deal 1 is outperforming most deals he could get with current conditions, while Deal 2 is underperforming compared to what else is out there. Benchmarking is very helpful in deciding how to allocate resources, which we'll talk about more in the following chapter.

There are two methods for benchmarking I recommend.
1. **Analyze deals.** If you're investing in real estate, you need to learn to analyze deals. That process is beyond the scope of this book, but there are plenty of great resources that teach you how to do it, including my book on the subject, *Real Estate by the Numbers*. Once you know how, analyze deals. Lots of them, all the time. When you get good at analyzing deals, it shouldn't take you too long to run the numbers on a new rental property, short-term rental, or flip. Even if you're not looking to buy a deal in the near future, you should still be analyzing deals for the purposes of benchmarking. If you run the numbers on ten deals a month, you'll always know the average returns in your area and what a "good" deal is for you to pursue.
2. **Talk to other investors.** If you have a network of real estate investors you can talk to, ask them what types of returns they're seeing on their recent deals. If you don't yet have a network, that should be a priority for you in Chapter 30, when you develop your Action Plan. Having a network of other investors is a great advantage!

When you benchmark, remember that you should do this for each market, or submarket, you're targeting. Every market is different and will have different benchmarks. Try to be as specific as possible when you're establishing your benchmarks. For Justin, he needed to benchmark rental properties in Charlotte and STRs in Joshua Tree.

Benchmarking for rates of return is relatively easy, but you should also try to benchmark for risk and resource allocation. For example, could you get a similar return on a deal with less risk? Or could you find a deal that has slightly lower returns but would require almost none of your time? The idea here is to always have a sense of what options are available to you.

Note that in this example, I am using return on equity to benchmark—which is a versatile metric that can evaluate cash flow and flips well. I am going to keep using ROE for illustrative purposes, but you can absolutely use other metrics in lieu of ROE, or in addition to it. I like to use a combination of ROE and internal rate of return (IRR). IRR is beyond the scope of this book, but is a great way to capture the benefits of all profit drivers into a single metric.

Over the course of your investing career, you should be continuously benchmarking and keeping an eye on what deals are possible for you. I look at deals all the time, even if I'm not planning to buy. For the purposes of your PREP, and your Portfolio Tracker, you need to calculate the average ROE in your target markets—whether that's for a rental, STR, flip, or other deal type. Run a bunch of deals, talk to investors, and once you have a good sense of the ROE you could earn with current-day deals, enter that into your Portfolio Tracker.

PREP WORK
LOCAL MARKET CONDITIONS
AND BENCHMARKING

STRATEGIC ACTIVITY: Research local market conditions and develop benchmarks. Focus on getting a sense of how the economy and housing market are trending in any market you currently invest in, or are considering investing in. Then, analyze deals and talk to local investors to learn what deals are currently available in your markets, and establish benchmarks. Once you're done, write down your benchmarks and any key insights on your PREP . For additional guidance on how to research local market conditions and create benchmarks, see below.

Keeping tabs on local market conditions is a continuous and critical element of your Portfolio Management. If you haven't already, take some time to complete the following exercises before moving on.

1. Look at local real estate market conditions for every market you currently invest in or are considering. You should be able to find this information on free public websites like Zillow, Redfin, or Realtor.com.

2. Determine whether your target market(s) are in a buyer's or seller's market and write it into your Portfolio Tracker and PREP.

3. Conduct benchmarking exercises for the markets and Deal Designs you are currently investing in or are considering. If you invest in multiple markets, find a benchmark for each market. If you use or are considering multiple deal types, create benchmarks for each. As an example, if you flip and buy rentals in both Charleston, South Carolina, and San Antonio, Texas, you'll need four benchmarks: flips in Charleston, rentals in Charleston, flips in San Antonio, and rentals in San Antonio.

After you have completed the above exercise, write down your benchmarks and local market conditions on your PREP. Before moving on, take some time to reflect on the implications of your work.

- What do the economic conditions in your areas mean to you and your portfolio? How are unemployment, wage growth, and population trending?
- Are the conditions in your target markets attractive for new investments? Are the price points and rental incomes desirable, or would an alternative market be better?

- Who has the leverage in your markets? If sellers have an advantage, should you consider selling? As a buyer, how should you adjust your Deal Design to account for your current negotiating leverage?
- Of all your Deal Design options, which do you think will work best in current conditions?

With these exercises completed, your Portfolio Management plan is now well underway. We've documented your current portfolio and how it's performing. We've examined the business cycle and local market conditions to understand what trends may impact your portfolio, and what deals are available to you. Next, you need to determine the optimal allocation of your resources given current conditions. You know how your portfolio is performing and what other deals are available—so where should you be directing your resources? Is your portfolio good as is? Or should you be buying, selling, or refinancing to better optimize your results? Let's talk resource allocation.

Chapter 28
RESOURCE ALLOCATION

With a clear picture of your portfolio's current performance and an understanding of market conditions, it's time to think about how your resources are deployed. Are you using your resources as effectively as possible or could you improve your allocation? The process of assigning your resources to their highest and best use is called Resource Allocation.

We've talked about the role and importance of resources a lot throughout this book. You need capital, time, and skill for every deal and every portfolio. Through your Resource Audit and your Portfolio Tracker, you should have a clear understanding of your current resource levels and where they are allocated. But Resource Allocation is not a static decision. How you use your resources can, and will, change as your portfolio grows. Even the resource levels in a particular deal will change. For example, refinancing a property will change how much capital you have allocated to that deal. Completing a rehab will reduce the amount of time needed for a deal. What was once a great use of resources may become inefficient due to shifting economic and market conditions. Good Portfolio Management requires continuously monitoring and reallocating resources to their most efficient use.

In this chapter we're going to discuss how to think about Resource Allocation and reallocation. We'll walk through three simple steps.

1. Current Resource Use
2. Alternative Options
3. Reallocation

Learning these tactics will help you scale efficiently, manage liquidity, determine hold periods, and ensure alignment with your Vision.

CURRENT RESOURCE USE

To allocate resources well, you must know where your resources are deployed currently, and how efficiently they're being used. In other words, how well are your capital, time, and skill being used to grow your portfolio? To start, look at what resources you've committed to each of your deals. If you're brand new to real estate investing, this will be easy—because they're not being used. For active investors, most of the information needed will come from your Portfolio Tracker tool. Let's return to Justin to walk through the Resource Allocation process.

CURRENT RESOURCE INPUTS	DEAL 1	DEAL 2	DEAL 3
Estimated Equity Value	$85,115	$92,798	$79,290
Monthly Time Invested (Hours)	5	9	3
Skills	Tenant management, repairs, operations	Tenant management, repairs, operations	Portfolio Management, Partner Management

When looking at Justin's current use of resources, we can see how much capital he has deployed into each of his deals (this is equal to the value of each deal), how much time he's investing, and what skills he's putting to use. From this snapshot, we can see Justin has spread his capital and skill resources relatively evenly between his deals, while the time required for each deal varies considerably.

Next, he examines how his resources are benefitting him by looking at his returns—all of which can be found in his Portfolio Tracker.

PERFORMANCE METRICS	DEAL 1	DEAL 2	DEAL 3
Property Value CAGR	1.5%	6.5%	2.4%
Equity CAGR	5.3%	12.0%	8.0%
Cash Flow CAGR	5.6%	4.1%	14.1%
Return on Equity	7.5%	4.5%	8.5%
Simple ROI If Sold Today	111%	69%	55%
Annualized ROI If Sold Today	21%	18%	16%

Here we can see that each of his deals is performing well, all having estimated annualized ROIs above 15 percent if he were to sell the property today. But notice there are key differences between the deals. As one example, Justin has similar amounts of capital in each of these deals but Deal 1 is earning the best annualized ROI. We can also see that despite Deal 2 taking the most of Justin's time, it's the least efficient earner of cash flow (as measured by ROE). There are no right answers here—just a broad analysis of how your resources are being put to use.

When examining returns, make sure to consider return trends over time—not just what's happening today. For example, are market conditions shifting and reducing your market appreciation? Has rent growth picked up recently and your cash flow growth is accelerating? It's a common mistake (one I've certainly made) to just look at your returns at a point in time and not consider whether your deals are getting better or worse over time. This is why it's important to revisit your Portfolio Tracker at least quarterly—so you can compare this quarter's performance to the previous quarter's performance.

Declining deal performance is actually quite common. After a value-add project for a rental, for example, equity growth typically slows. That's not a bad thing: You built a lot of equity in a short time, which is a win! But it means your resource efficiency has peaked and is now declining—a sign that reallocation may be beneficial. On the other hand, if you can add more value in the future, or market appreciation is improving your deal's performance, you probably won't want to reallocate your capital.

Declining performance can happen with cash flow as well. As you build equity in a deal (again, a good thing!), the efficiency with which you generate returns can go down. Consider this simple example of Justin's first deal, held over ten years.

HOLD PERIOD (YEARS)	PROPERTY VALUE	EQUITY VALUE	CASH FLOW	ROE
1	$250,000	$64,810	$5,000	7.7%
2	$255,000	$72,466	$5,100	7.0%
3	$260,100	$80,372	$5,202	6.5%
4	$265,302	$88,538	$5,306	6.0%
5	$270,608	$96,976	$5,412	5.6%
6	$276,020	$102,387	$5,520	5.4%
7	$281,541	$107,906	$5,631	5.2%
8	$287,171	$113,536	$5,743	5.1%
9	$292,915	$119,278	$5,858	4.9%
10	$298,773	$125,136	$5,975	4.8%

The deal is doing well as property values and cash flow increase. But because his equity value is growing faster than his cash flow, the rate at which he is generating cash flow is declining. This isn't necessarily a reason to reallocate capital away from this deal, but it's something to consider as part of your Portfolio Management, especially if you're focused on earning cash flow immediately.

> *The example above demonstrates why, for Portfolio Management purposes, I strongly recommend you use the return on equity metric (ROE) rather than cash-on-cash return (CoCR). CoCR is a good metric at the time of purchase, but since it uses principal as the denominator (which is static), it's not good for measuring the ongoing performance of your portfolio. Instead, use ROE, which shows how well your equity is earning cash flow.*

Before moving on to the next step, look at how your resources are allocated in terms of Deal Design, profit drivers, and risk profile. Are all of your resources dedicated to similar deals? Or are your resources providing you with a diversified portfolio?

DEAL DESIGN	DEAL 1	DEAL 2	DEAL 3
Deal Type	Rental Property	Rental Property	Short-Term Rental
Financing	Conventional	Conventional	Conventional
Ownership	Sole Owner	Partnership	Partnership
Business Plan(s)	House Hacking	Value-Add	Buy and Hold
Management Plan	Active Management	Active Management	Hybrid
Asset Class	Duplex	Triplex	DSFR
Location	Charlotte, NC	Charlotte, NC	Joshua Tree, CA
Property Class	B	B	A

Justin's portfolio is reasonably diversified. His capital and skills are spread between deals with varying designs, while his time is primarily dedicated to Deal 2. Justin's resource allocation is aligned with his Vision, but is, of course, not something you should mimic. You just need to make sure *your* allocation is aligned with *your* Vision. If not, you may want to consider reallocating.

ALTERNATIVE OPTIONS

Once you've studied your current Resource Allocation, you need to consider what to do next. Would a different allocation of resources yield better returns? What about better diversification or risk mitigation? Of course, everyone wants to see better performance, but the key here is determining if a higher-performing allocation is feasible.

This is where your benchmarks come in. Compare your current allocations to your benchmarks and see if there are any opportunities for improvement.

Justin operates in two different markets: Charlotte, North Carolina, where he owns two rentals; and Joshua Tree, California, where he operates an STR. After doing some benchmarking, he determines that he could average about a 7 percent ROE on a new deal in Charlotte, but estimates only modest market appreciation. When he compares this to his current portfolio, Justin sees an interesting opportunity. Deal 2 is earning only a 4.5 percent ROE—well below his benchmark. This deal has seen great equity growth, but he has already completed the value-add, meaning his equity growth rate will decline, and he won't be using his valuable construction and rehab skills. Perhaps Justin should consider reallocating resources away from Deal 2 and into something that could put his skills to better use and earn cash flow and equity more efficiently.

Comparing current deals to alternative options is mostly a subjective analysis, but there are some metrics you can use. If you know the market ROE from benchmarking, you can compare how your cash flow will be impacted by a potential reallocation (this calculation is built into the Portfolio Tracker).

PORTFOLIO ALIGNMENT	DEAL 1	DEAL 2	DEAL 3
Estimated Annual Cash Flow Benefit (if traded for benchmark)	$(1,298)	$1,559	$(2,052)

As suspected, if Justin were to trade out Deal 2 for the average deal in his market, his cash flow would improve by $1,559 per year. That's not a huge amount and may not be worth the effort, but it's an important data point for Justin to consider. Meanwhile, Justin's cash flow would be negatively impacted if he were to trade out Deal 1 or Deal 3 for a market-rate deal.

Another thing to consider is the impact on any additional resources added to your portfolio. If you have capital, time, or skills you could add to your current deals, would their performance improve or are you better off allocating those resources to a new deal? This is going to be an important consideration as you build your portfolio. Should you use new capital to get a new deal or invest it into an existing deal to improve performance? Should you commit more time to a deal to increase profit or are you better off using that time to develop a new skill? Resource Allocation is a continuous exercise of optimization. You should always be asking yourself how you can best use the resources at your disposal.

For Justin, he is not yet close to his portfolio goals and wants to keep growing. He has $45,000 in investable assets and three hours of time per month to spare, but he decides he wants to use that to pursue his first commercial property—even though it will take him a year or so to build up the skill and investable assets to pull that off. In the meantime, he decides that Deal 2 is a weak spot in his portfolio and he could do better with the average deal in his market. He needs to reallocate resources away from Deal 2 and into a new deal.

REALLOCATION

If your Resource Allocation analyses reveal that a reallocation is beneficial, then you need to figure out how to do it. The tactics, cost, and complexity of a reallocation will depend largely on what resource(s) you need to reallocate.

If you're reallocating time or skill, the process is fairly simple. You just need to decide if that time or skill is still needed, and if so, who is going to provide it going forward. Sometimes, in a real estate deal, the resource requirements simply change. The most common example of this is a value-add project. If you buy an STR that needs a rehab, it will be time and skill intensive at first. Then, once the value-add is finished, the ongoing time requirements will decrease, and the construction and capital improvements skill will no longer be necessary. In these cases, reallocation is simple. You can devote your time and skills to a new deal or to other deals in your portfolio, or you can just keep them dormant for a while.

If you want to reallocate time and skill away from a deal, but the resources are still required, you have to hire someone to do them. Continuing the STR example from above, even if you wanted to stop doing guest management, it needs to be done, and you need to hire a property manager. This will, of course, impact your returns, but it will allow you to reallocate your time and skills as you need.

When it comes to reallocating capital, things get a bit trickier. The only way to take capital from one deal and put it into another is a liquidity event. Recall from Chapter 8 that a liquidity event is either selling a property or completing a cash-out refinance.

Reallocating capital from deals that produce transactional income (like flips or development) is relatively straightforward. The short hold periods these deals are designed for provide regular opportunities to reallocate capital into the best available deal. Think of it as recycling. With short-term deals, you get to continuously choose how your resources are used and can frequently optimize your capital allocation. In just a few months, you get your resources back in hand and can decide again how to best allocate your capital.

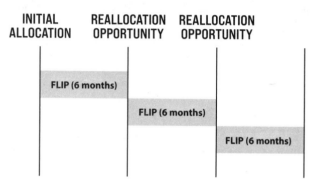

When it comes to longer-term deal types like rentals or commercial properties, you will have to be more deliberate about creating a liquidity event. These deals can be held indefinitely, so you need to decide for yourself if and when to reallocate capital. Liquidity events take time and cost money, so you need to make sure the capital reallocation is worth the expense. And if it is, which liquidity option is better: selling or a cash-out refinance?

Deciding whether you should hold on to your existing property, sell, or complete a cash-out refinance is personal. You can use some metrics like comparing the ROE of your existing deals to your benchmarks, but there is no one single metric that tells you whether selling, refinancing, or holding is the best decision. It all depends on your current performance, your resource levels, and your Vision.

For Justin, he decides that he wants to focus on getting his first commercial deal in the next eighteen months. As such, he wants to free up some of his time to network and learn new skills. With these priorities in mind, he decides to sell Deal 2 rather than refinance. If he were to refinance, he could grow his unit count, but it would take up too much of his resources and would slow down his progress toward his goal of a commercial deal. Instead, he decides to sell Deal 2, which was a value-add operational plan, and swap it for a buy and hold property. Justin is likely giving up equity growth with this approach. However, he is improving his cash flow and recovering a lot of time, which he can use to network and learn the skills needed to pursue his first commercial deal. He is thinking long-term, and allocating his resources in service of his Vision.

PREP WORK
RESOURCE ALLOCATION

STRATEGIC ACTIVITY: Determine if your current Resource Allocation is appropriate or if you should reallocate resources. Do this by following the three steps outlined above: look at your current resource usage, consider alternative options, then decide on reallocation. Write any decisions about reallocation in your PREP. For more assistance to guide your allocation decisions, see below.

By tracking your existing portfolio and regularly benchmarking the other deals available to you, you can make an analytical assessment of how to best deploy your resources. But there is also a mindset approach to Resource Allocation. You need a mindset of optimization. You should always be thinking about the resources you have at your disposal, and if they are being used as effectively as possible. Following the three steps outlined in this chapter—current resource use, alternative options, and reallocation—is a great way to ensure you're always continuously optimizing. As you go through this process, consider some of the following questions.

- Are your current resources generating the types of returns you're looking for? Are your returns coming from the best profit drivers?
- Do any of your deals require an outsized number of resources? Are any of your deals particularly efficient at using resources?
- How diversified is your Resource Allocation? Are all of your resources invested into similar Deal Designs or are you diversified?
- How many resources do you have to pursue additional deals? Do you have the capital, time, and skill to take on a new investment? Or do you need to reallocate away from a current deal to pursue the next one?
- Would adding new resources to current deals improve performance or diversification? Or are new resources best used on a new deal?
- If you are going to reallocate resources, is the benefit of reallocation greater than the cost and hassle of reallocation?
- When reallocating capital, will you pursue a refinance or a sale?

Once you have considered the above questions, think about any specific actions you intend to take. Do you want to reallocate your time toward learning a new skill, refinancing, or selling a deal? Write out any conclusions you reach about your resources on your *PREP*.

After considering your portfolio's Resource Allocation, it's time to talk about putting your resources to use by buying deals! In the coming chapter, I'll discuss some typical scaling paths that investors can take to build a well-balanced portfolio and how to think about what deals to pursue.

Chapter 29
SCALING PATHS

When considering how you allocate resources and what deals to buy next, you need to make sure you're moving closer to your goals in a systematic way. It's not all about financial performance and resource allocation (although that is obviously important). You need to scale in a deliberate way that moves you ever closer to your goals. You need to be intentional about what you buy, where, and when. This is where scaling paths come in. Scaling paths help you determine what deals to buy, think a few moves ahead, and allocate your resources. If you have an idea of what you want your ideal portfolio composition to look like a few years from now, it will be easier to make solid Portfolio Management decisions today.

If you're brand new to real estate investing, you're probably just focused on getting that first deal, and rightfully so! Getting your first deal is a huge milestone. That said, before you create your Buy Box (a specific Deal Design for your next deal) in the next chapter, it can be beneficial to your growth to think through your longer-term plan for acquiring new properties—even if you're just starting out.

Although every investor's portfolio and journey to financial independence are unique, there are some common paths investors take as they scale. That isn't to say there is a "right" way to scale a portfolio—just some well-tested approaches that help investors grow in an efficient way. We've touched on a few of these paths already throughout the book, like the tendency for investors to move from more active to more passive investments as they grow. Or that many investors look for a balanced return between equity growth and cash flow early in their investing career, and then increasingly prioritize cash flow as they approach their time horizon.

None of the scaling paths discussed in this chapter are rigid plans you need to closely adhere to. Scaling paths are also not mutually exclusive. You don't need to select one potential scaling path versus another. Many of these paths complement each other or involve very different aspects of your portfolio. Scaling paths can (and should!) overlap or even be combined with one another to maximize their efficacy. The scaling paths outlined below are not comprehensive, nor are they listed in any particular order. There are plenty of other routes and derivates of these paths that exist. These are just some of the most common.

SCALING QUANTITY

The most common way to scale a portfolio is by increasing the quantity of deals it contains. This is likely self-evident, but it will be very difficult to achieve your financial goals with just a single deal (unless that deal is very large or your goals are relatively modest). Most investors will look to increase the quantity of deals in their portfolio over time.

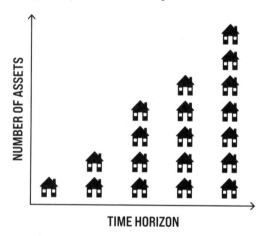

How quickly you scale quantity is up to you and will largely depend on your available resources. If you have a ton of capital and time, you can likely scale quantity quickly. If, like most people, you have to save money between acquisitions, you will likely scale quantity a bit slower, and that's okay! Just because you're looking to increase your deal count doesn't mean you necessarily have to increase the rate at which you buy property. For example, depending on your goals, you can buy one deal every two years indefinitely. You don't necessarily need to start buying deals faster and faster as you scale. In fact, scaling quantity too quickly is one of the pitfalls to avoid when growing your portfolio.

As you increase the number of deals in your portfolio, it's important to make sure you have the proper teams and system in place, as well as the necessary skills to maintain a growing portfolio. As a simple example, going from two to nine rental properties probably means more money coming in, but it also means more time commitment and more management requirements. Make sure you adjust your tactics accordingly as you scale up the number of deals in your portfolio.

SCALING SIZE

Size-based scaling is when you grow your portfolio by acquiring larger assets. As discussed in Part 3, every asset class has its pros and cons, but in terms of total cash flow and equity growth (as opposed to the rate of return), large assets tend to be best. You will get more total cash flow on a ten-unit building than a duplex, even if the duplex has a higher rate of return. Efficiencies of scale often make buying large properties a more effective use of resources.

TIME HORIZON

As such, many investors choose to scale their portfolio by buying larger and larger properties. For example, you might start your investing career with a single-family residence, then buy a small multifamily, and then go on to purchase commercial deals with large unit counts. Or you can start by flipping single-family homes, and then move on to flipping multifamily properties. Taking on larger assets is a great way to increase the total cash flow and equity value of your portfolio.

Of course, buying large assets comes with trade-offs and risks, as discussed in Part 3. Large assets require sophisticated property and asset management, and the time commitment is greater. They also come with many of the commercial property risks mentioned earlier in Chapter 21.

Scaling through size does not have to be linear. Just because you started with small multifamily and recently bought a twelve-unit property doesn't mean you can no longer buy small properties. The idea of scaling through size means that you build up the skills and capacity to consider larger and larger deals should they arise—not that each deal has to be bigger than the last.

VERTICAL SCALING

As you scale, you'll have the option of specializing in one market or diversifying across several. "Vertical scaling" is a term to describe using a broad variety of deal tactics within a single market. For example, vertically scaling could mean you focus your investing efforts entirely in a single metro area, like Kansas City. This gives you deep knowledge of the market conditions and corresponding tactics that work in the area.

PORTFOLIO

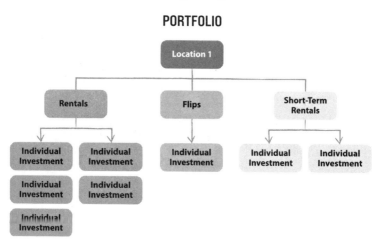

If you become an expert in your local market, you can easily diversify into new Deal Designs—like different deal types, asset classes, or business plans—more easily than you can expand into a new market. Local expertise lets you know what deal tactics are working best in the current market conditions, and how to identify the best deals. It also allows you to focus on building out one very strong set of systems: a strong team, client base, labor pool, suppliers, etc. For example, it's easier to go from buying duplexes to multifamily if you stick to Kansas City. It would be harder and riskier to go from buying duplexes in Kansas City to buying multifamily in an entirely new location, like Eugene, Oregon.

The downside of vertical scaling is its reliance on that single market. If the market you invest in experiences an economic downturn or volatility in the housing market, your entire portfolio could be negatively impacted. Additionally, not all markets offer the same types of returns and deal types. For example, there are some markets where short-term rentals simply won't work. If you're going to scale vertically, make sure the market works with the types of deal tactics you intend to use.

HORIZONTAL SCALING

Horizontal scaling is a path in which an investor holds consistent deal types, but scales across markets. For example, you can focus entirely on short-term rentals, but do it in a variety of markets across the country. This allows you to leverage your expertise in the STR deal type while diversifying across geographies.

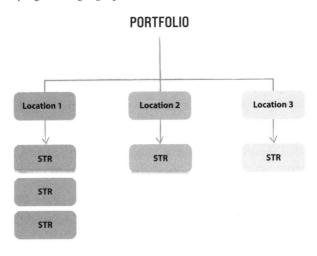

Expanding to new markets can be daunting. But if you are confident in your ability to execute on certain deal types and business plans, it doesn't have to be. If you have been managing STRs in Kansas City for years, you'll know what deal characteristics to look for and what types of team members you should seek out. Horizontal scaling allows you to diversify your portfolio across markets and take advantage of new opportunities from coast to coast.

Horizontal scaling is best suited to investors who have time to commit to learning new markets and building great teams. It's crucial to have a strong team in each market, and it takes time and skill to build up a great team of operators you can rely on.

At this point you may be thinking, "Why can't I scale across tactics *and* markets?" You certainly can, but I recommend you do it in stages. If you want to try new deal types, do it in a market you already know pretty well. If you want to test out a new market, do it with deal types you're familiar with.

As an example, if I were a buy and hold investor in Memphis, Tennessee, my next move wouldn't be flipping houses in Los Angeles. I would either learn to flip in Memphis because I know the area, or I would buy rentals in Los Angeles because I know the deal type. I like to reuse at least some of my Deal Design from deal to deal, not use an entirely new Deal Design. If you really want to take on a new deal type in a new market, I highly recommend partnering with someone who has expertise in your new market or new tactic (or ideally both!).

LIQUIDITY-BALANCED SCALING

A liquidity-balanced scaling plan is one where the investor staggers hold periods to ensure regular liquidity events. Put into simple terms, it's a plan where you sell or refinance deals in your portfolio frequently. This approach gives the investor the opportunity to regularly reallocate capital into other real estate deals, or out of their portfolio and into something else.

Liquidity balance can be achieved many ways, but two common approaches are staggering hold periods and mixing deal types. If you invest primarily in deals with long hold periods, you can design your operational plans so the target sale dates of your deals are well spaced out. For example, instead of doing three value-add projects that need refinancing at the same time, you can stagger the value-add projects so they are finished six months apart, giving you more regular liquidity and reallocation opportunities.

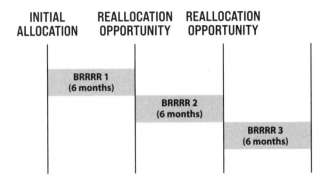

The other option for regular liquidity is to balance your portfolio between short- and long-term hold periods. For example, you can buy rental properties and short-term rentals for long-term cash flow while also occasionally flipping houses to build equity in a relatively liquid way. Because deals with short hold periods are riskier than long-hold deals, this approach to liquidity balance is a bit riskier, but it can also be very lucrative! When done correctly, balancing long- and short-term investments is an excellent way to earn returns.

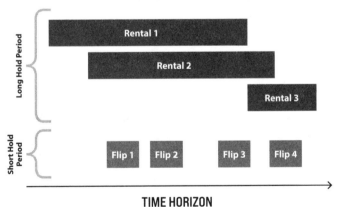

Creating opportunities for liquidity is a good idea for almost every investor. Taking this approach doesn't mean you have to sell or refinance all the time; it's about having frequent options to gain liquidity and reallocate capital. This helps manage risk and optimize performance.

DOLLAR COST AVERAGING SCALING

Commonly used in the stock market, dollar cost averaging (DCA) is a scaling path that also works well for real estate investors. The basic premise of DCA is to invest relatively similar amounts of money into the market at regular intervals, regardless of price, over time. For example, a real estate investor using a DCA scaling path could choose to invest $50,000 into rental properties in Dayton, Ohio, every two years for the next twenty years.

DCA is a popular approach because it helps investors spread out the risk of market volatility by buying over time. If you buy at regular intervals regardless of price, you may sometimes buy under market value and sometimes buy above market value. But over time, your purchases should equal out to the average growth rate of property values in your area. Remember, on average, the price of real estate in the U.S. grows slightly above the rate of inflation—so achieving around-average growth is good!

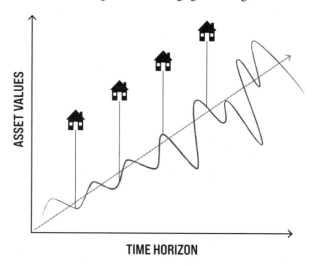

TIME HORIZON

I like DCA because I find it helps many investors get over the temptation to try to time the market, and it alleviates some anxiety about asset values. If you use a DCA scaling plan, you don't even need to think about timing the market, or what happens to asset values in the short-term. You just stick to your schedule. Subscribing to the DCA mindset is basically admitting that you don't know when market fluctuations will occur (because no one does), and that is okay, because you're going to keep buying and let the volatility in your purchase prices smooth out over time. However, if you're the type of person who wants to try to time the market or will be very worried about buying into differing market conditions, DCA may not be right for you.

EQUITY TO CASH FLOW SCALING

There is an eternal debate among real estate investors about which is more important—equity or cash flow. To me, this debate is very silly; both are important. That said, I believe that which one you prioritize depends mostly on your time horizon. If you are many years from your time horizon, cash flow doesn't have to be so critical to you because you're not relying on it to live. As you approach your time horizon, cash flow becomes increasingly important.

One approach (that I personally subscribe to) is to focus on equity growth early in your career and then shift the balance of your portfolio toward cash flow later. The idea here is not to completely ignore cash flow, but rather to seek deals for their potential for equity gains, even if that means a modest cash-on-cash return.

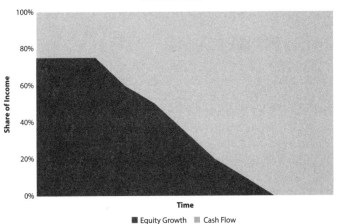

RETURN FOCUS

Due to the combined forces of value-add, market appreciation, amortization, and leverage, seeking deals that build equity can generate large amounts of capital with which you can reinvest. If you spend the early days of your portfolio amassing equity, getting cash flow later in your career is relatively easy—you can do it through rebalancing or deleveraging.

Rebalancing is reallocating resources from properties that offer good potential for equity gains to ones with a strong cash-on-cash return. For example, you could sell a property that builds equity at 7 percent per year with a cash-on-cash return of 5 percent and exchange it for a property that builds equity at just 3 percent per year but has a cash-on-cash return of 10 percent.

Deleveraging is removing some or all of your debt from a deal. Remember that although debt has many benefits, one of the drawbacks is that it reduces your cash flow. The money you pay the bank each month in principal and interest is money that otherwise would be going into your pocket as cash flow. If you bought a property for $400,000 with 25 percent down at a 6 percent interest rate and rented it for $3,200 per month, you would earn about $3,600 per year in cash flow (3.5 percent CoCR). If you deleveraged this property and instead put 50 percent down, you would increase your cash flow to $11,050 per year (5.3 percent CoCR). This approach certainly requires more principal (you're using more equity and less debt), but if you have built a lot of equity early in your career, that shouldn't be too big of an issue. Deleveraging de-risks your portfolio and provides more cash flow as you approach your time horizon, which is a double win.

ACTIVE TO PASSIVE SCALING

Most investors start with an active management plan. It is less capital intensive than passive or hybrid management, and it's an excellent way to learn the business of real estate investing. However, over time, active management faces limitations. First, many investors reach a point of scale where they cannot actively manage all of their properties. Time is a finite resource, and at a certain point you will likely have to hire out some pieces of your management or hire an "in-house" team (more on that below). There are practical limits to how big your portfolio can get using active management alone.

Second, many investors just don't want to deal with active management as they scale! One of the most common reasons people get into real estate investing is to work less and to spend more time on their passions. If that describes you, you may want to consider hybrid or passive management plans, as they let you scale up your portfolio without necessarily scaling up the amount of time you put into it. This scaling plan is possible for everyone but is particularly useful for investors who are currently, or plan to become, accredited. Accredited investors will have access to an abundance of passive investing options that nonaccredited investors unfortunately cannot participate in.

MANAGEMENT PLANS OVER TIME

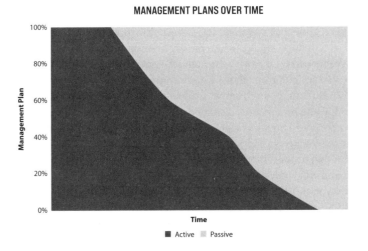

Passive investments do come with trade-offs. When you invest passively, you give up some upside in your deals to your partners, and you lose some or all control of the day-to-day operations of your deals. For these reasons, you want to only invest passively with the highest-quality operators.

IN-HOUSE SCALING

If your ambition is to build a robust portfolio and operate a complex business, you can consider building a team in-house. Rather than working with external businesses for services like lead generation, lending, contracting, or anything else, you hire real estate professionals directly.

This is an attractive option for some investors because it allows for efficiency and cost savings. For example, if you employ your own property management team, you'll have direct oversight over their operations, and your ability to scale will increase. Or, if you hire your salespeople directly, you can train them to target the exact type of leads you're looking for. This approach means you can hire people with the exact skills you need to build your portfolio, and it allows you to focus on the skills in which you are personally strongest.

On the cost side, an in-house team can produce significant savings (if you have a big enough portfolio to justify the hiring). When you hire a third party to provide services, you're paying for the service *and* the business's profit. If you hire in-house, you still have to pay people fairly for their time, but you don't have to pay the third party's margin. This can lead to huge savings when managed properly.

The benefits you realize through efficiency and savings will, however, cost you time. Rather than just scheduling and coordinating with an external team, you will now need to have regular meetings, provide training and professional development, keep your team motivated, track their tasks and hours, and conduct the countless other operational tasks that come with managing a team. And you cannot cut corners on this. If you don't properly train, compensate, and manage your team, all the cost and efficiency benefits will go out the door! If you're going to hire a team, you need to commit yourself to being a great manager of people in addition to a great investor.

Typically, bringing a team in-house doesn't really make sense unless you're looking for massive scale. If you're buying properties opportunistically and mostly on the MLS, you probably don't need to bring a team in-house. If you're trying to flip several houses per year, build a massive portfolio of rentals, or sponsor commercial real estate syndications, then it might make sense to build in-house.

MAINTENANCE MODE

This may seem like the opposite of a scaling path, but one path is just to maintain your current portfolio. You don't always need to be growing your portfolio actively. It's perfectly okay and normal to pause or stop altogether if you're happy where you are. You may not hear this path being touted on social media, but that doesn't mean it's not a perfectly legitimate—and often wise—approach. If you're retired or nearing retirement, for instance, you may not need to grow. You can just relax! Or maybe, due to life circumstances, you choose to allocate resources away from real estate investing. I've done this several times in my career, and most investors do as well.

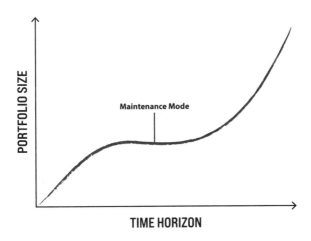

Growing very quickly can be exciting and can lead to great results, but it comes with risk, even if you have the resources to support it. Sometimes, it can be beneficial to just take a step back and evaluate if you're content with the status quo before making your next moves. This doesn't mean you do nothing—you can still work on operational efficiency and look for value-add projects in your existing portfolio. You can network and build up your skill set. Maintaining just means you're not actively looking to inject new capital or make any major reallocations for a period.

PREP WORK
SCALING PATHS

STRATEGIC ACTIVITY: Think about which scaling paths are attractive to you and aligned with your broader strategy. Remember that scaling paths are not mutually exclusive, and you can employ several different paths. Once you identify scaling paths that you intend to use, write them on your PREP. For more direction on picking scaling paths, read below.

The diverse scaling paths listed above are common approaches that have worked for thousands of investors, and they could help you over the course of your investing career. Just remember, these are very rough guidelines and are just meant to stimulate some thinking on your part. No two investors will implement a scaling path in the same way, and no portfolio will combine scaling paths in the unique way that yours will.

As an example, I scale both vertically and horizontally at the same time. I scale vertically in Colorado by owning a few properties that are either sole ownership or partnerships, which I still manage in a hybrid way. Everything I own directly is in Colorado (as of this writing) because I know the market very well, and I have a strong team in place. This suits me well while living in Europe. At the same time, I am scaling horizontally through passive investments in syndications and funds. I focus on multifamily passive investments but am willing to look at deals in almost any location in the U.S., provided that the operator is high quality and the specifics of the deal make sense. By scaling both horizontally and vertically, I'm using scaling paths creatively to suit my current needs.

Before we move on to the next section, take some time to consider what scaling paths make sense to use over the next several years. You don't need to pick every scaling plan you're going to use for the lifetime of your portfolio—just the next three years will do. Even if you're a new investor who hasn't yet bought a deal, you should think through what scaling paths you're interested in .

Once you've selected the scaling paths you intend to use in the coming three years, write them down on your PREP. Here are some questions to guide your thinking.

- What scaling path best aligns with your skill set? What path aligns with your time resource?
- How big are your goals? If you want to get big quickly, you'll need to pursue more aggressive (and higher-risk) scaling plans. Those who want to grow steadily can pursue less risky options.
- What operations do you want to take on? Are you interested in managing a full-time in-house team? Or would you prefer to work with third-party contractors?
- Do you want to specialize in one market or are you willing to build out a team and operations across multiple markets?
- How close are you to your time horizon? If you're far from your time horizon, you can pursue equity growth and higher-risk investments. If you're close to your horizon, you may want to consider de-risking, deleveraging, and moving toward cash flow.

Once you have thought through the scaling plans you want to use, write them down in your *PREP* under the Scaling Plans section. Remember you can choose more than one, and you're only looking for scaling plans you intend to use in the next three years. As you formulate an Action Plan in the coming chapter, your desired scaling plans will be a central focus point. They will play a big role in selecting what deals you should do next and how you should allocate resources.

Chapter 30
YOUR ACTION PLAN

Throughout this book you've learned a lot about the many decisions and trade-offs in real estate that make up a Portfolio Strategy. I'm sure you can now see that the challenge in growing your portfolio is not a shortage of options. The real challenge is prioritizing what options are best for you. Of the millions of potential properties to invest in, the countless Deal Designs you can use, and the Portfolio Management moves you can make, which are you going to choose to pursue next? In this chapter you will determine the specific actions you're going to take to move your portfolio forward. This is the final step in Portfolio Management: creating an Action Plan and executing it.

The goal of the exercises in this chapter is not to create a plan for your entire time horizon—that is impossible. Instead, it's to combine your Vision, Deal Design, and Property Management insights to create a multiyear plan with a high probability of success. As things change, so can your plan. If you learn a new skill, market conditions change, or you just want to shake things up, that is all part of Portfolio Management. Creating an Action Plan is not meant to lock you into tactics indefinitely. The idea is to narrow down your list of options temporarily so you can reasonably execute on your Portfolio Management initiatives. You need to commit to tactics long enough to enact them, reassess if they are working, and change your plans as needed.

The contents of this chapter are all one big prioritization exercise but will translate into several distinct sections on your PREP: your Investment Thesis, your Tactical Plan, and your Buy Box. It may sound like a lot of work, but it's not. All of these elements are by-products of one decision-making and prioritization exercise. You start with an Investment Thesis, which summarizes the guidelines you'll use to grow your portfolio in the coming years. Then you'll break down your Investment Thesis into your Tactical Plan, which is a list of specific actions you'll take to grow your portfolio. Last, you'll develop a Buy Box, which is a further narrowing of your Deal Designs to only those that will best serve you at this moment in time. Combined, these sections of your PREP will guide the actions you will take first to put your strategy into action.

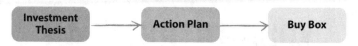

At the end of this chapter, you will have an Investment Thesis to guide your investing decisions, a Tactical Plan to pursue your Vision, and a Buy Box that details what deals (if any) you should buy next. This is where you put your Personal Real Estate Portfolio to work!

INVESTMENT THESIS

Your Investment Thesis is a concise articulation of the guidelines and preferences you will use to make Portfolio Management decisions in the coming years. It consolidates the many ideas and insights you likely have about your strategy into one unifying set of beliefs. Through your Investment Thesis, you can find focus and gain confidence in your decision-making.

You may have heard the term "investment thesis" in other parts of the investing world, most often from sophisticated institutional investors. Often, stock analysts or investors will write out an investment thesis that helps them decide which stocks belong in their portfolio. A private equity firm, similarly, may maintain an investment thesis that guides which businesses they will add, hold, or sell from their portfolio. It's the same idea with real estate investing! We need an Investment Thesis too. The reasons sophisticated investors spend time crafting an investment thesis are the same reasons you should: It helps you avoid distraction, make decisions, and implement your strategy.

I can imagine that the word "thesis" is bringing back memories of writing essays in school, but don't worry—you don't have to write any long-form content here, and I certainly won't be grading your efforts. Your Investment Thesis can just be a short bullet-pointed list; the format is not as important as the contents. The contents must be carefully considered to include the most important guiding policies about your portfolio, and nothing else. It needs to be concise, clear, and confident. A few examples of good Investment Thesis contents are:

- Focus on building equity and maximizing return while maintaining modest cash flow.
- De-risk tactics in the next six months to offset risk of potential recession.
- Employ a vertical scaling plan to capitalize on advantageous local market conditions.

These are clear guidelines that will help an investor with their portfolio-building in the coming years. While your Investment Thesis is supposed to be forward-looking, it's not intended to span the lifetime of your portfolio. Notice that my examples above talk about market conditions and reflect current preferences. As you know, market conditions and deal preferences change—so your thesis should simply reflect your current beliefs and preferences.

I like to think of my Investment Thesis in three-year periods. Three years is a short enough time that I can envision the steps I need to take, but long enough to provide ample time to act on my thesis. Even though I think of my thesis in three-year periods, I still recalibrate my thesis every few months. I think it's important to have an idea of where you want to be in three years, even if you know you're going to change your plan. Looking at just the next few months is too shortsighted and can hamper your ability to build toward bigger things. But looking at just your Vision and long-term time horizon is too long; it's not practical to plan out your portfolio for twenty years. You need to plan on an intermediate time frame, and I believe three years is the sweet spot.

To help you think through your thesis, let's return to our fictional investor friend, Justin, from earlier in Part 4. As a reminder, Justin's PREP looks like this so far:

PERSONAL REAL ESTATE PORTFOLIO

 ## VISION

Personal Values

What do you value most in life? What can you not live without?

1. Accountability
2. Competence
3. Freedom
4. Learning
5. Balance

Resource Audit

Money:
- Net Worth: $165,000
- Personal Cash Flow: $1,300/month
- Investable Assets: $45,000
- Cash Reserves

Time: 20 hours

Current Skills: Tenant management, deal analysis, partner

Risk Profile

Time Horizon: 20 years

Risk Tolerance: 3

Risk Capacity: 3

Current Risk Profile: 3

Transactional Income Plan

Stay at current job. Fulfilling + resources.

Financial Goals

Reinvestment Rate: 100%

Residual Income Goal: $200,000

Portfolio Value Goal: $2,500,000

 ## DEAL DESIGN

Deal Type

Rentals

STR

Commercial

Ownership Structure

Sole Owner

Partnership/JV

Syndication

Financing

Equity

Conventional

Commercial

Operational Plan

Owner Occupied

Value-Add

Buy & Hold

BRRRR

Management Plan

Hybrid

Passive

Asset Class

SFR

Small Multifamily

Large Multifamily

Location

Charlotte, NC

Joshua Tree, CA

Property Class

A

B

C

PORTFOLIO MANAGEMENT

Portfolio Performance	Market Conditions and Benchmarks
Total Equity: $257,202	• Recession
Total Cash Flow: $17,300	• Seller's markets in my markets
Average ROE: 6.7%	• Value-add offering best opportunities
Average Risk: 2.3	• Charlotte Benchmark 7% ROE
Monthly Time Committed: 17 hours	• Joshua Tree Benchmark 8% ROE

Scaling Plans	Resource Allocation
• Vertical scaling	• Sell Deal 2
• Active to passive	• Keep Deals 1 & 3 unchanged
• Quantity	• Devote 5 hours per month to learning commercial skills

Based on Justin's Vision, Deal Design, and Portfolio Management preferences, his Investment Thesis looks as follows:

Investment Thesis

- Continue working W-2 job while focusing portfolio on tax-advantaged equity growth. Cash flow is required for all deals but is not a priority.
- Favor conservative tactics due to uncertain economic conditions.
- Trade out any current deals that aren't meeting benchmarks.
- Despite uncertain macroeconomic conditions, local market conditions are stable. Focus on scaling vertically in Charlotte, North Carolina.
- Favor hybrid management plans to maintain twenty-hour time commitment while allowing for future scale.
- Look for opportunities for commercial real estate deal within twenty-four months.

This is a great Investment Thesis. It contains a manageable number (five to seven) of beliefs and preferences, is forward-looking, and provides clear guidance on how Justin is going to manage his portfolio over the coming few years. Notice that none of the bullet points are specific tasks or actions. The thesis should only contain high-level thinking. It sets the guardrails Justin will operate within when making his Tactical Plan.

TACTICAL PLAN

An Investment Thesis helps guide portfolio direction, but it lacks the specificity needed to start acting. This is where the Tactical Plan comes in. As a reminder, the definition of "tactic" is "a plan for achieving a particular goal." In the context of Portfolio Strategy, your Tactical Plan is a list of efforts you'll undertake to put your Investment Thesis into action. While some tactics are big and exciting projects, like buying a new deal, others focus on background work that helps investors grow, like networking and education.

Unlike an Investment Thesis, your list of tactics should be as specific as possible and written in a SMART format. As a reminder, SMART stands for Specific, Measurable, Achievable, Relevant, and Time-bound. Each tactic should have these components to increase your chances of success. Each one should also reflect your Vision, Deal Designs, and Investment Thesis. In other words, given your beliefs and the resources at your disposal, what are the exact things you intend to do in the coming years? This could pertain to Resource Allocation, risk management, buying new deals, transactional income, networking, education, and much more. The idea is to list out all major tactics in SMART format. Some examples of good tactics would be:

- Lend out $50,000 as a hard money lender within the next three months.
- Save up $25,000 to invest in my first house hack by April.
- Network with five local flippers in the next six months.

I recommend listing only seven to ten tactics. Any more will be overwhelming, and you could lose focus. Any fewer and you're likely not taking as much action as possible. If you wind up getting through all of your tactics quickly, great—make new ones!

Once a list of tactics is complete, I recommend prioritizing them in order of importance. Put the most important action you can take at the top and the least important at the bottom.

The one thing that should be omitted from your tactics is noting the specific Deal Designs for your next investments. This will come soon when we develop your Buy Box. Your list can include tactics like "Invest in a commercial multifamily property within nine months," but it shouldn't say, "Invest in an eight-to-twelve-unit multifamily property in Cleveland, Class C property, using a hybrid management plan." That level of specificity is important, but it comes in your Buy Box, not your Tactical Plan.

Returning to our example of Justin, when he breaks down his Investment Thesis into tactics, he gets the following list.

- List Deal 2 for sale within three months.
- Purchase a buy and hold rental property using a 1031 exchange from Deal 2 proceeds within ninety days of sale.
- Grow investable assets to $75,000 for use in first commercial property within eighteen months.
- Network with at least ten commercial real estate investors in the next year, and identify potential partners.
- Read *The Multifamily Millionaire, Volumes 1 & 2* and *The Hands-Off Investor* within six months.
- Develop Buy Box for commercial purchase once networking and education goals are completed.

Notice a few things about Justin's list here. The first two tactics on his list were made possible by the portfolio tracking and benchmarking work he did earlier in his PREP work. During his portfolio tracking in Chapter 25, he discovered that Deal 2 was earning the lowest returns in his portfolio. When Justin completed his benchmarking exercises, he saw Deal 2 was also performing worse than what he could get currently in his market. During his Resource Allocation exercise, he determined he should trade out Deal 2. These two tactics also align with the "Trade out any current deals that aren't meeting benchmarks" piece of his Investment Thesis.

Second, Justin has a good balance of tactics. Some he can prioritize and work on today (selling Deal 2), while also working toward the future (building up his skills and network to execute on a commercial deal in the coming years). They also represent a good mix of deal decisions, education goals, networking goals, and lifestyle goals. The initiatives aren't just big moneymaking goals. They also include foundational work to set Justin up for future growth.

Third, Justin has a manageable list of tactics, all of which are contained within his Deal Design, and are aligned with his Vision and his Investment Thesis.

With his Tactical Plan in place, Justin knows exactly what he needs to do to grow his portfolio! He has tactics to work on today to ensure he keeps moving forward, while also allowing him to see a few moves ahead and plan accordingly. For investors who are saving up money or are in maintenance mode, this is all the work that needs to be done! But if part of your Investment Thesis and Tactical Plan includes purchasing a new deal (as I hope many of yours do!), there is one more step you need to take—crafting a Buy Box.

THE BUY BOX

A Buy Box is an articulation of the Deal Design(s) you'll pursue in the near future. In the Deal Design section of your PREP, you listed out all of the Deal Design options that support your Vision—but that likely contains a varied list that isn't yet optimized for your current resource levels and market conditions. Your Buy Box narrows your Deal Design options down to only those that support your current Investment Thesis and Action Plan. Building a Buy Box will help you save time, avoid analysis paralysis, and execute on great deals.

A Buy Box really has nothing to do with a box—it's just a Deal Design target. For each deal element, you list your intentions. For example, for your next deal, do you want to buy a short-term rental or a rental property? Are you open to either? What about management plans—which ones are you willing to consider? We narrowed down your list of choices during Part 3 on Deal Design, but your Buy Box is where you get really specific: exact markets, price points, deal types, and so on.

The scope of your Buy Box will likely depend on your experience level. For some investors (mainly beginners), their Buy Box may only include a single option for each deal element. Keeping a narrow Buy Box can help new investors avoid analysis paralysis and stick to the type of low-cost, low-risk, high-learning deals that tend to work well for newbies. Over time, investors tend to open up their Buy Box a bit as their skills and resources grow. As such, experienced investors may consider multiple deal types, with a variety of operating plans, across a variety of markets. But please recognize that it takes time to build up to that level of competence.

For Justin, we know that he wants to trade out Deal 2 and use a 1031 exchange for his next deal. Given his Investment Thesis, Vision, and Deal Design choices, Justin's Buy Box could look as follows.

Buy Box

- **Deal Type:** Rental property
- **Management Plan:** Hybrid
- **Business Plan:** Buy and hold
- **Financing:** Conventional, portfolio loans
- **Asset Class:** 1–4 units residential
- **Ownership Structure:** Sole ownership/partnership

- **Property Class:** B
- **Location:** Charlotte, North Carolina
- **Purchase Price:** $250,000–$450,000
- **Rehab Costs:** < $5,000
- **Risk Target:** 2 or 3
- **ROE Target:** 7%+

Notice that this process of building out a Buy Box is really just a further refinement of Justin's Deal Design. He had previously determined what Deal Designs were aligned with his Vision. When making his Buy Box, Justin factors in his current portfolio's performance, market conditions, and his available resources to select the specific design options of his next deal.

As indicated in Justin's Investment Thesis, he is looking to target a rental property in his next deal, specifically one that uses a buy and hold operating plan. Because Justin wants to reallocate time toward learning new skills, he is going to use a hybrid management plan. Justin wants to do a buy and hold, so he will target Class B deals, because that is what his price range allows. When it comes to financing, asset class, and ownership structure, Justin is being deliberately flexible. He is not open to *every* financing option, or *every* asset class, but he lists out everything he is willing to consider. Last, because his Investment Thesis states he is going to scale vertically in Charlotte, that market is written on his Buy Box.

Justin has also listed out a few key purchase criteria he will follow. His budget allows him to target any deals with a purchase price between $250,000 and $400,000, with a subjective risk profile of either a 2 or 3.

Finally, and critically, he also outlines the performance he is looking for. For Justin's 1031 to make sense, he needs to get a 7 percent ROE or higher.

With these specific criteria written out, Justin can now focus on these exact Deal Designs. A Buy Box works as a type of filtering mechanism. If Justin sees a potential deal that meets these criteria, he knows he should spend the time doing a full analysis. If he identifies potential deals that do not match his criteria, he can quickly move on to other opportunities. This is a huge value! Being able to quickly decide which deals deserve your attention, and which do not, will make you a much more efficient investor. Your Buy Box will reduce unnecessary optionality and allow you to focus on the deals that work best for you.

Another benefit of a Buy Box is its shareability. Once Justin has his Buy Box, he can share it with his potential partners, his real estate agent, lenders, wholesalers, or anyone else he may work with to secure his next deal. It's a simple and effective way to communicate the types of deals you're looking for, both to yourself and to external parties.

PERSONAL REAL ESTATE PORTFOLIO

 VISION

Personal Values

What do you value most in life? What can you not live without?

1. Accountability
2. Competence
3. Freedom
4. Learning
5. Balance

Resource Audit

Money:
- Net Worth: $165,000
- Personal Cash Flow: $1,300/month
- Investable Assets: $45,000
- Cash Reserves

Time: 20 hours

Current Skills: Tenant management, deal analysis, partner

Risk Profile

Time Horizon: 20 years

Risk Tolerance: 3

Risk Capacity: 3

Current Risk Profile: 3

Transactional Income Plan

Stay at current job. Fulfilling + resources.

Financial Goals

Reinvestment Rate: 100%

Residual Income Goal: $200,000

Portfolio Value Goal. $2,500,000

DEAL DESIGN

Deal Type
Rentals
STR
Commercial

Ownership Structure
Sole Owner
Partnership/JV
Syndication

Financing
Equity
Conventional
Commercial

Operational Plan
Owner Occupied
Value-Add
Buy & Hold
BRRRR

Management Plan
Hybrid
Passive

Asset Class
SFR
Small Multifamily
Large Multifamily

Location
Charlotte, NC
Joshua Tree, CA

Property Class
A
B
C

 ## PORTFOLIO MANAGEMENT

Portfolio Performance
Total Equity: $257,202
Total Cash Flow: $17,300
Average ROE: 6.7%
Average Risk: 2.3
Monthly Time Committed: 17 hours

Market Conditions and Benchmarks
- Recession
- Seller's markets in my markets
- Value-add offering best opportunities
- Charlotte Benchmark 7% ROE
- Joshua Tree Benchmark 8% ROE

Scaling Plans
- Vertical scaling
- Active to passive
- Quantity

Resource Allocation
- Sell Deal 2
- Keep Deals 1 & 3 unchanged
- Devote 5 hours per month to learning commercial skills

Investment Thesis
- Continue working W-2 job while focusing portfolio on tax-advantaged equity growth. Cash flow is required for all deals but is not a priority.
- Despite slightly under-risked portfolio, continue to favor more conservative investments due to uncertain economic conditions.
- Trade out any current deals that aren't meeting benchmarks.
- Although the macroeconomic environment is cloudy, local market conditions are stable. Focus on scaling vertically in Charlotte, North Carolina, and becoming an expert in current location.
- Use only hybrid management plans to maintain twenty-hour time commitment per month while allowing for future scale.
- Look for opportunities for commercial real estate deal within twelve to twenty-four months.

Action Plan

- Deploy $100,000 in capital into syndication or funds.
- Complete cosmetic upgrades to Deal 2, and list for sale within 3 months.
- Purchase value-add rental property using 1031 exchange from Deal 2 proceeds within ninety days of Deal 2 sale.
- Set aside $20,000 current investable assets for wedding.
- Network with at least ten commercial real estate investors in the next year, and identify potential partners.
- Read The Multifamily Millionaire Volumes 1 & 2 within six months.
- Grow investable assets to $100,000 for use in first commercial property within eighteen months.
- Develop Buy Box for commercial purchase once networking and education goals are complete.

Buy Box

- **Deal type:** Rental property
- **Management Plan:** Hybrid
- **Business Plan:** Value-add
- **Financing:** Convention, portfolio loans
- **Asset Class:** 1-4 units residential
- **Ownership Structure:** Sole ownership/partnership
- **Property Class:** C, D
- **Location:** Charlotte, NC
- **Purchase Price:** $250,000–$400,000
- **Rehab Cost:** $20,000–$40,000
- **Risk Target:** 2 or 3
- **ROE Target:** 7%+
- **Equity Growth Target:** 40% in 18 months

After all his hard work, Justin now has a completed PREP. Take a minute to see how his decisions all tie together and build off one another. His Deal Designs are based on his Vision. His Portfolio Management choices are informed by his Deal Design. Combined, this represents his Personal Real Estate Portfolio. Each element is aligned with the next, and every decision he has made will move Justin closer to his personal goals. Justin has built out an excellent strategy for himself; now it's your turn.

PREP WORK
YOUR ACTION PLAN

STRATEGIC ACTIVITY: Write out an Investment Thesis, develop your Tactical Plan, and craft your Buy Box. Ensure these three elements of your Action Plan are aligned with one another, and when they are, write them in your PREP. Take time to make sure that all of your actions are aligned with your Vision and your Deal Design before finalizing your strategy. For more assistance with your Action Plan, see below.

Now that you understand the different elements of an Action Plan, and why each one is important, it's time to make one for yourself. Making your plans is the culmination of everything you've learned in this book so far. You have a Vision, you understand the various deal tactics available to you, and you know how to manage a portfolio. The task at hand is for you to align all the decisions you've made in your PREP into a cohesive Action Plan. To do this, think hard about all of the opportunities, trade-offs, and options in front of you, and decide which ones to pursue. You have Vision, you know what Deal Designs will get you there, and you know how to prioritize your Portfolio Management. Now put it down on paper! I highly recommend you use the accompanying workbook that corresponds with this book. You can find it at www.biggerpockets.com/strategybook.

As we've already discussed, the process of creating an Action Plan starts with your Investment Thesis, then you'll move on to your Tactical Plan, and then your Buy Box.

Write Your Investment Thesis

I find that writing an Investment Thesis is one of the most exciting and powerful things you can do as investor. This is where you consolidate everything you've learned—all the trade-offs, options, and decisions—into a unified approach to investing for the coming years.

To write your Investment Thesis, I recommend looking back over your PREP and any other Portfolio Management tools you have. As you do, here are some questions for you to consider.

- Of all the Deal Designs you selected in Part 3, which will best support your Vision in the coming years, given current market conditions?
- What is your Transactional Income Plan? Would a career change better support your Vision or lifestyle?
- Can you—and do you—want to invest in any new deals in the coming months or years? If so, will you follow a scaling plan? How will you procure the necessary resources to achieve your next deal?
- Is your current resource allocation optimal or can your resources be put to better use?

- What liquidity will you need from your portfolio in the coming months? Are there any major life events or expenses outside of real estate you need to plan for?
- What new skills do you want to learn?
- Is there anything you want to accomplish a year or two from now that you can start working toward today?

These are just some sample questions to get your wheels turning; you don't need to constrain your Investment Thesis to these specific questions. Instead, I encourage you to think as broadly as possible to nail down what you want to do with your portfolio and why. The whole point of this book is to develop a real estate portfolio that works specifically for you, so make sure your thesis is your own and reflects the exact reality you want to create in your portfolio.

Take some time now to write your Investment Thesis. Although there are many considerations to think through, I recommend keeping your Investment Thesis to five to seven items. Remember, you should feel inspired by and confident in your thesis. You will be referring to your Investment Thesis frequently, so make sure you're fully committed to what you write. When you're ready, write it down in your PREP.

If you are struggling to define your Investment Thesis, don't worry—it just means you might need to do some more research or analysis. If this is you, go back through the Portfolio Management exercises in Part 4, take time to do some more research, get the input of some experienced investors or trusted advisors, and keep thinking until you feel confident, excited, and ready to get to work.

Create Your Tactical Plan

With your Investment Thesis formalized, you're ready to get specific. It's time to write out the tactics you're going to work on in the near future. These tactics need to be SMART and closely aligned with your Visions and your Investment Thesis.

Similar to the Investment Thesis, there is no scientific process here. Think through your personal preferences and beliefs, and craft a list of high-probability steps to achieve your goals. I find it helpful to look at my Investment Thesis and start working backward by determining the tactics that support that thesis. Remember how Justin's thesis dictated he should trade out any deal not meeting benchmarks? He used that part of his thesis to define specific tactics for reallocating those resources. If you need some help, here are some questions to get you going.

- Do I plan to buy any deals in the near future?
- What Deal Designs are going to work best for me right now?
- Will I change any elements of my existing deals, like a new management or operational plan?
- How can I execute on my reallocation plans?
- Will I add any new resources to my portfolio?
- Should I deploy my resources now or plan ahead a few months?

- What tactics do I aspire to in the future, and what actions can I take today to help me get there?
- Are there any networking initiatives that would support my Vision?

As you write out your tactics, remember a few things: First, buying and selling are the most exciting, but don't write off networking, skill development, or transactional income tactics. These are essential to long-term success. Second, not every tactic needs to be very high priority; some can be small, incremental actions like reading a new book. And finally, each tactic needs to be SMART.

Take some time to write out your tactics. If you're stuck, it can often help to write out as many as you can think of and then whittle them down. You can start by listing out ten to twenty tactics, and then ranking them in order of which ones are the most achievable and have the highest potential impact for your portfolio. Then, narrow it down to just the top seven to ten. Once you're happy with your tactical list, write it down in your PREP.

Build Your Buy Box

If your Tactical Plan includes buying a new deal in the coming years, you need to take one last step (the last one in your entire PREP!): building a Buy Box. Your Buy Box details the specific Deal Designs you will target when looking for your upcoming deal(s). Given all the work you've already done, this should be easy!

The first step in building your Buy Box is to review the Deal Design section of your PREP. Look through and refamiliarize yourself with the big list of potential Deal Designs you wrote down as supporting your long-term Vision. It will probably be a big list that combines options that you're able to pursue and interested in pursuing now, and others you aspire to utilize in the future. That's the whole point of the Deal Design section of the PREP! But we need to narrow it down for your Buy Box, and we do that by aligning it with our Investment Thesis and Tactical Plan.

Next, select from the list of Deal Design options already in your PREP that support your thesis and initiatives. This is a filtering exercise where you remove any options that are not aligned with your Investment Thesis and Tactical Plan, and place the remaining options in your Buy Box. Go through each deal element in your PREP and ask yourself which ones support your Investment Thesis and Tactical Plan, and which do not. If you need some additional help thinking through which ones to include, you can consider these questions.

- Which Deal Design options support your beliefs about the current phase of the business cycle?
- What types of deals can you execute on today, given your resources? What can you afford?
- What Deal Designs do you have the skills to operate well?
- Which Deal Designs are aligned with your current risk capacity and tolerance?
- Which deals would support your desired profit drivers and return targets?

As you build your Buy Box, strive to find the right balance between specificity and flexibility. You want to be open to opportunities, but having too many options in your Buy Box defeats the purpose of narrowing your focus. When you're a new investor, it's better to have a narrow Buy Box with fewer tactics in order to avoid analysis paralysis. Pick a few low-risk Deal Designs and execute on one. Get into the game—it doesn't need to be perfect! As you scale, you can broaden your Buy Box to include a wider range of tactics and be more opportunistic.

If you're having trouble narrowing your list, remember that excluding a Deal Design option from your Buy Box doesn't mean you can never use it! Your Buy Box helps you target what's next—but your Buy Box will change. In the future it will likely look different than it does today. Just focus on the Deal Designs that work right now.

Once you've filtered out the designs that are not in line with your Investment Thesis, write down the remaining tactics in your *PREP*. Remember, what you write in your Buy Box should be a Deal Design you're ready and able to execute on as soon as possible.

You did it! You've now completed your Personal Real Estate Portfolio and have a cohesive strategy designed around you. Congratulations on all your hard work and on putting together your PREP. This is a huge accomplishment and a big step forward on your journey to financial independence.

Chapter 31
PORTFOLIO
MANAGEMENT
CONCLUSION

Portfolio Management is the art and science of building and managing your portfolio. It is where you shift from planning and high-level strategy to the tactics you'll use to pursue your goals. If your Vision is the "where" you want to go and the "why" of your Portfolio Strategy, and Deal Design is the "how," Portfolio Management is the "what" and the "when." Of all the things you could possibly do as a real estate investor, what are you actually going to do, and in what order?

Becoming a good portfolio manager takes time. It requires you to apply the concepts you've learned throughout this book, to analyze your portfolio, research market conditions, and develop an ambitious but achievable plan of action. It's a broad set of activities, so don't expect to be good at it right away. It took me years to feel confident managing my portfolio. Along the way I've made mistakes, and still do frequently. I scaled without a plan. I failed to track local market conditions. I trapped equity in a few of my first deals for way too long before I learned the importance of reallocating resources. But that's okay! I've still built a successful portfolio. You don't need to be an expert portfolio manager to get started. You need real-life experience investing in real estate to get better at Portfolio Management.

As you gain experience, learn new skills, and build up your network, your Portfolio Management abilities will improve. You should be revisiting the Portfolio Management section of your PREP several times per year, and with practice, you'll get better. And remember—there is really no such thing as a "right" Portfolio Management decision. What one investor may choose to do with a property can differ greatly from what you might choose to do with the same property. The "right" thing to do is subjective, and it is entirely dependent on your broader strategy. Recall how Justin used his Portfolio Tracker and understanding of market conditions to decide to sell Deal 2 and use a 1031 exchange to buy a less time-intensive deal. If that were you, would you have made the same decision? Chances are you would have done something different because your goals, Vision, and resources are different. I've made decisions few other investors would, and I say that proudly.

I know the lack of a "right" answer gives a lot of investors pause—especially new investors. I understand that; no one wants to make a suboptimal decision about an investment. But rather than seeking perfection, I encourage you to adapt a growth mindset. Get started and try to get better with each Portfolio Management decision you make. Trust your Vision, trust your Deal Designs, and make informed, high-probability decisions about how to grow your portfolio. If you focus on your long-term goals and keep trying to get better, you're going to do great. Get out there and put your Portfolio Strategy into action!

FINAL THOUGHTS

I've never felt like I fit in with other real estate educators. Having worked at BiggerPockets for many years, I've had ample opportunities to write blogs, host webinars, and share what I know. But for years I resisted. I avoided the public sphere because I didn't think I was successful enough. My portfolio wasn't big enough. I work full-time. I use partnerships. My Deal Designs aren't sexy. I don't have an in-house team. I was happy with my progress but didn't think I fit the conventional definition of "success" for a real estate investor.

Due to a confluence of circumstances and opportunities, I dipped my toe in. I wrote a few blogs, made a few (extremely awkward) YouTube videos, and was enjoying myself. To my genuine surprise, things started to take off. I was miraculously given the chance to coauthor a book with J Scott, be a guest host on the BiggerPockets podcast, and then even got to host my own podcast, *On the Market*. It's been an incredible but unexpected ride.

The single greatest benefit of my new public-facing career is the people I get to meet. Every week I talk to investors of all experience levels and from all walks of life. I regularly chat with some of the most successful real estate investors in the country, people who haven't yet done their first deal, and everyone in between. I have seen the full spectrum of values, experience levels, motivations, deal types, mistakes, and successes. It's amazing!

Over time, these conversations have completely changed my perspective on what it means to be successful as a real estate investor. I've seen people positively change the course of their entire lives by slowly investing in just a handful of rental properties. I've seen passions ignited by providing safe and affordable housing to a local community. I've seen financial freedom achieved. But I've also seen the other end of the spectrum. I've met investors with hundreds of units who are deeply dissatisfied. I've spoken with others who wanted to quit their jobs but have found themselves working more hours on their portfolio than they were at their 9–5 jobs. At a conference, a man told me he was embarrassed to be a "newbie" because he only had thirty-seven units (which is preposterous thinking). In my experience, people's satisfaction with their portfolio is almost entirely uncorrelated with the amount of money they're making.

I've come to realize that success in real estate has very little to do with how much money you make or how many units you have. It doesn't matter if you buy large multifamily deals, use creative finance, or flip houses. What matters is whether your real estate portfolio moves you closer to the life you want. Real estate is a means to an end. You need to decide for yourself why you're investing in real estate and then employ the tactics that will get you there. If you try to achieve someone else's standard of success, you won't ever get there—no matter how many units you acquire or the cash flow you make. Building a real estate portfolio is inherently personal. This realization has helped me go from feeling "unsuccessful" compared to other real estate educators to being proud of what I have accomplished. By my definition of success, things are going great. My Personal Real Estate Portfolio is working.

I wrote *Start with Strategy* to give you the tools to set your own definition of success and then develop a personalized strategy to pursue it. My hope is that through the concepts you've learned and exercises you've completed in this book, you will be able to make consistent and incremental progress toward your personal goals, whatever they may be. Do you want to move up your retirement date? Quit your job and flip houses? Build a massive business? You can successfully pursue any of these goals with real estate investing—just make sure they're *your* goals. Trying to succeed by someone else's standards is a waste of time.

As you reach the end of this book, you're now in an excellent place to pursue your financial goals through real estate investing. You understand the financial concepts and trade-offs that underpin portfolio growth. You have a Vision of the future you want to pursue. You know what Deal Designs can help you achieve your goals. And you have Portfolio Management skills to consistently move you forward. Combined, you have a personalized strategy that is designed to hit your specific goals. This in itself is an enormous accomplishment, and you should be proud of yourself. Many people aspire to take their financial future into their own hands, but few put in the work to do it in a systematic and sustainable way. You have, and that's a vital step on your financial journey.

Although you have completed this book, your strategy and your PREP will never truly be "done." As your goals, life circumstances, and personal preferences change, so will your strategy. As you reconsider your strategy and evolve as an investor, I encourage you to revisit this book frequently. The format of this book was chosen deliberately to help you complete your PREP for the first time, but also to serve as a reference guide when you inevitably update your strategy. This doesn't mean that you should be redoing your PREP over and over again in short intervals. That isn't helpful. The learning comes from crafting your plan, executing it, and learning from the results. Sometimes you're going to nail it. Some deals and Portfolio Management decisions are going to work out great. Other times, things won't go as planned. This is part of the process. Just try to keep getting better.

But enough about future iterations. You have a Personal Real Estate Portfolio in front of you! It's time to put your plan in motion. Start working toward the Vision of the future you want to create!

It means so much to me that you have spent your time reading this book and completing your PREP. Writing this book has been one of the most difficult but rewarding experiences of my professional career, and I'm honored to share it with you. I sincerely hope this book and these exercises help you achieve whatever goals you aspire to. My real estate investing portfolio has given me the freedom and opportunities to pursue the life I want—and if you work diligently to implement your Personal Real Estate Portfolio, I know it will do the same for you.

TEMPLATE PERSONAL REAL ESTATE PORTFOLIO

 ## VISION

Personal Values
What do you value most in life? What can you not live without?

Resource Audit
Money:

Time:

Current Skills:

Risk Profile
Time Horizon:

Risk Tolerance:

Risk Capacity:

Current Risk Profile:

Transactional Income Plan

Financial Goals
Reinvestment Rate:

Residual Income Goal:

Portfolio Value Goal:

 ## DEAL DESIGN

Deal Type

Ownership Structure

Financing

Operational Plan

Management Plan

Asset Class

Location

Property Class

✍ PORTFOLIO MANAGEMENT

Portfolio Performance

Total Equity:

Total Cash Flow:

Average ROE:

Average Risk:

Monthly Time Committed:

Market Conditions and Benchmarks

Scaling Plans

Resource Allocation

Investment Thesis

Action Plan

Buy Box

ACKNOWLEDGMENTS

Writing *Start with Strategy* has been one of the greatest challenges of my professional career. And although my name sits alone on the cover of this book, no effort this large is possible alone. There are countless people who have helped make this book possible—too many to name here, so please know how much I appreciate you. However, there are a few people in particular I do want to acknowledge:

First and foremost, I want to thank my wife, Jane, for the infinite ways she supports me. There is no way I could have written this book—at least with my mental health intact—without her. She has been my biggest supporter, proofreader, sounding board, and friend during this long and challenging process.

I also want to thank the rest of my family—my mom, Carla, my dad, Michael, and my sister, Elise—for believing in me and supporting me, no matter what I get myself into. From rebellious child to failing student and now to published author, you have helped me through it all.

To Lauran Arledge of Bold Font coaching for teaching me everything I know about Personal Values. Working with her was one of the most meaningful experiences of my life. Her coaching helped me become a much happier, more confident, and fulfilled person.

To the many countless active and aspiring investors I have met and spoken with over the years. Your questions, stories, challenges, and successes were a huge inspiration for this book. I hope in some way this book helps you achieve your financial goals.

Lastly, I want to thank everyone at BiggerPockets for making this book possible. Of course, thank you to Katie Miller, Savannah Wood, Kaylee Walterbach, Peri Eryigit, Jamie Klingensmith, Winsome Lewis, and Haley Montgomery of the publishing team. But also, thanks to Brian Carberry and Noah Bacon for being advance readers and providing feedback. And truly, I give all my appreciation to every member of the BiggerPockets team who builds and supports our wonderful community.

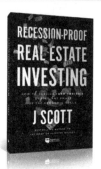
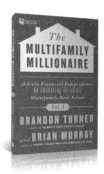

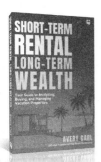

Looking for more?
Join the BiggerPockets Community

BiggerPockets brings together education, tools, and a community of more than 2+ million like-minded members—all in one place. Learn about investment strategies, analyze properties, connect with investor-friendly agents, and more.

Go to **biggerpockets.com** to learn more!

 Listen to a **BiggerPockets Podcast**

 Watch **BiggerPockets on YouTube**

 Join the **Community Forum**

 Learn more on **the Blog**

 Read more **BiggerPockets Books**

 Learn about our **Real Estate Investing Bootcamps**

 Connect with an **Investor-Friendly Real Estate Agent**

 Go Pro! Start, scale, and manage your portfolio with your **Pro Membership**

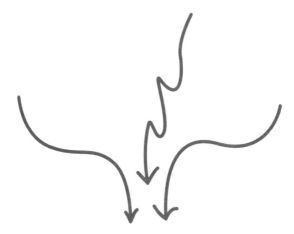

Follow us on social media!

Sign up for a Pro account
and take **20 PERCENT OFF**
with code **BOOKS20**.